exploringedenbooks.com

THE HUNTER & THE GATHERER

CATHERINE LAWSON & DAVID BRISTOW

with @WILDTRAVELSTORY

For all the restless humans who will not let us sleep and who continue to stand up, speak out and act – even when it costs them – to protect our one, amazing, blue planet. Keep talking – scream if you have to – until we all finally wake up and realise that we are all already on the slippery dip and there's no getting off. It's time to take this thing personally because clean air, plastic-free food-chain and a future for our kids are things on my wish list and yours too. Everything on this planet is on that slippery dip with us – wild spaces, endangered species, the air we breathe, the oceans that feed us – and we're all going down together. It's time to put the brakes on and do it today. So to those who still dream of a better future, who consume less and who refuse just to throw their hands in the air: this book is for you. Thanks.

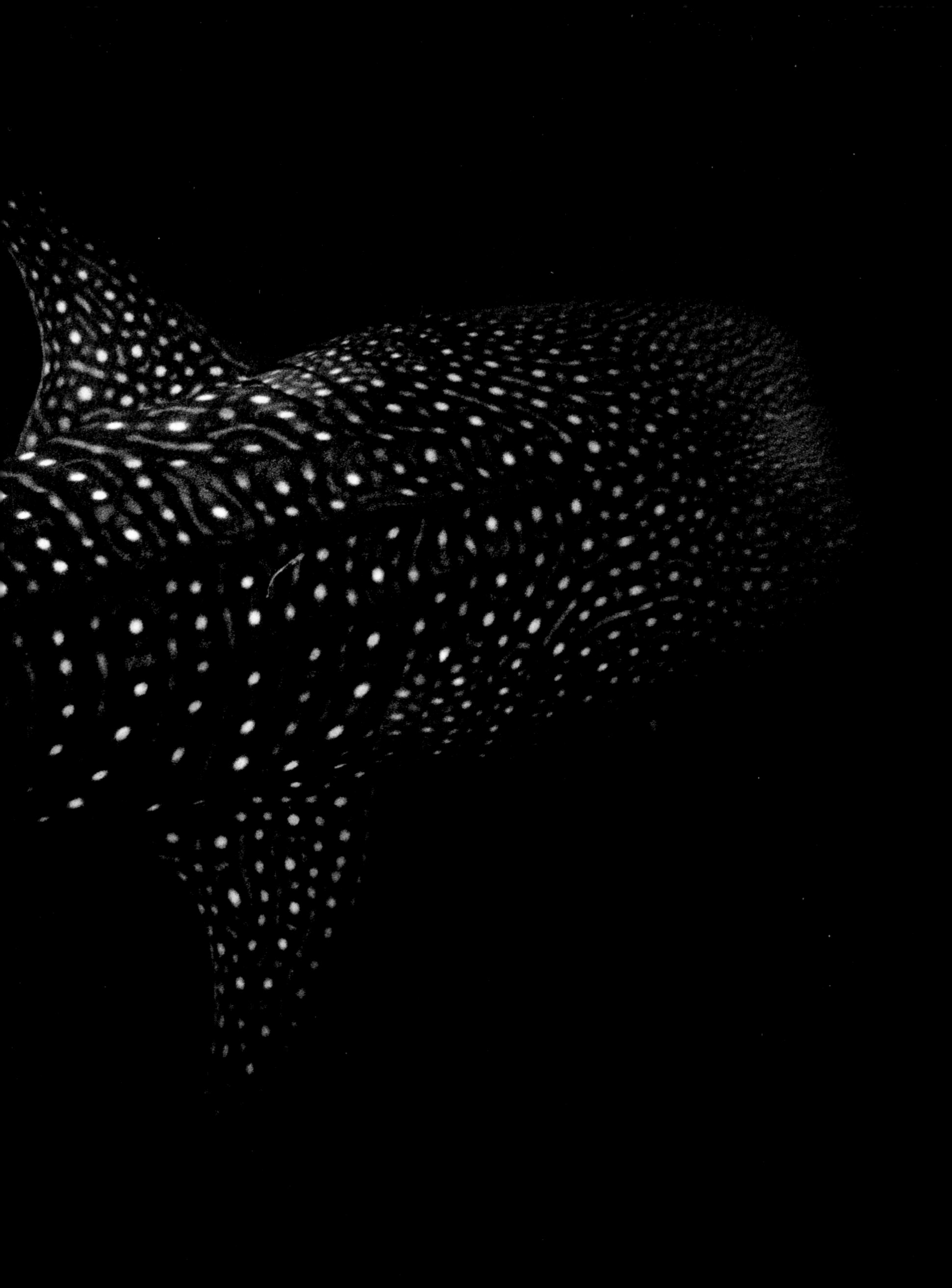

CONTENTS

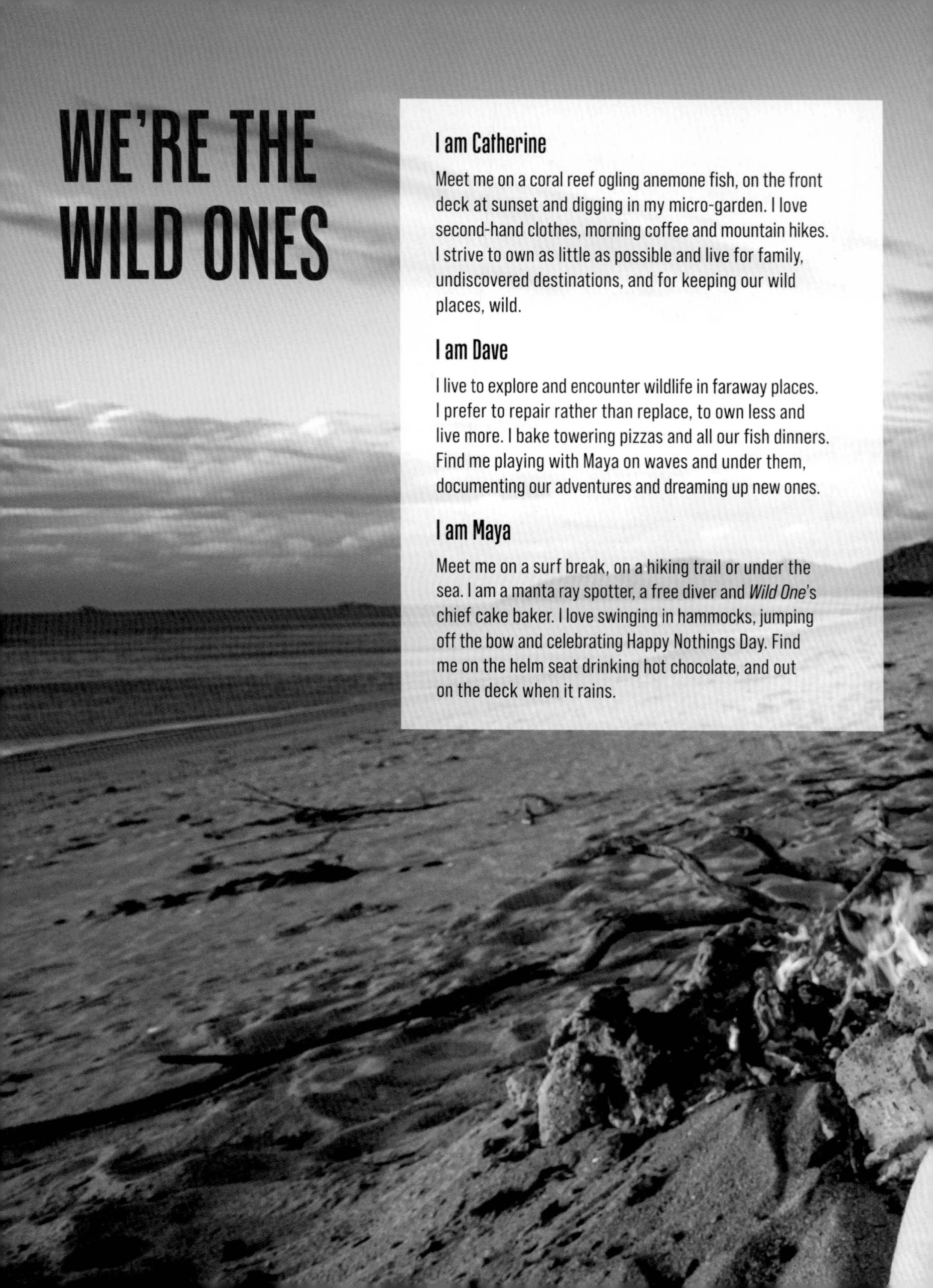

WE'RE THE WILD ONES

I am Catherine

Meet me on a coral reef ogling anemone fish, on the front deck at sunset and digging in my micro-garden. I love second-hand clothes, morning coffee and mountain hikes. I strive to own as little as possible and live for family, undiscovered destinations, and for keeping our wild places, wild.

I am Dave

I live to explore and encounter wildlife in faraway places. I prefer to repair rather than replace, to own less and live more. I bake towering pizzas and all our fish dinners. Find me playing with Maya on waves and under them, documenting our adventures and dreaming up new ones.

I am Maya

Meet me on a surf break, on a hiking trail or under the sea. I am a manta ray spotter, a free diver and *Wild One*'s chief cake baker. I love swinging in hammocks, jumping off the bow and celebrating Happy Nothings Day. Find me on the helm seat drinking hot chocolate, and out on the deck when it rains.

THE HUNTER &
THE GATHERER

Instinctively we are drawn to the sea. Lured by water, waves and sunshine, calming blue vistas and a horizon that reminds us the world is bigger than the lives that seem to define us. There's fun to be had in that cerulean strip that laps against the land: riding waves, ogling underwater life, and catching a meal that comes unwrapped and straight from the source in the freshest form possible.

To live on the sea is a dream that so many of us turn into reality. Yet even if, for now, you live happily between the two – taking time out from your lives on land to dip into the big blue and sail away – all ocean lovers are united by the watery adventures we take, the campfires we strike at sunset to cook our catches, and the feeling that life is better, simpler and richer when we live it within sight of the sea. That's how we feel after 20 years afloat.

The Hunter and the Gatherer are who we are: David, the ever-hopeful angler; Catherine, a micro-gardener and forager; plus our little fish Maya, who has spent her entire life at sea. We can't imagine a better way to live, raise a family and sate the adventurers in us.

Cruising is so much more than sailing. It's about travel, exploring empty shores, and plunging into new cultures. It's about taking time for our passions – freediving, surfing and fishing – and enduring and surviving whatever the sea sends our way. And it's about living in harmony with the watery world that buoys, sustains, and challenges us in ways we sometimes never see coming.

More than twenty years in the making, this is a book for ocean-loving foodies striving for better health, greater self-sufficiency and a tiny footprint on the sea: sailors and boaties, anglers and divers, snorkellers and surfers, and everyone whose best adventures end with feet dug into the sand, watching the sunset with good mates and great food. Our food is for tiny galleys, long passages and perfect beach sunsets, and those times when food stocks might be low, but the fish are biting.

We call these recipes faraway food and create them for people who love to eat well but love to escape more. The food we cook in this book is the food we catch. Not every day on the sea brings in a fish, but we might harvest oysters instead, find a nice, fat mud crab, or forage for coconuts to crack. Some of our vegetables are boat-grown, and others are market-bought or traded off the back of our yacht. We sprout seeds grains and pulses to produce the healthiest, most sustainable menus imaginable in the most remote and beautiful locations we can reach.

More than a recipe book, *The Hunter and The Gatherer* is a guide to creating a sustainable, healthful lifestyle on the sea with the smallest footprint possible. If you are living on the ocean or dream to one day, we'll show you how to set up a galley to feed yourself long after you leave the harbour, and how to grow, fish, forage, sprout, ferment, brew, and create your own ingredients, to inspire meals that will nurture you and your crew, wherever you sail. The recipes – all 160 of them – have been tried and tested over 20,000 sea miles, in small spaces, with limited ingredients and sometimes relentless, rocking seas. These are the meals, bites, snacks and sundowners we like most and what we hope will feed you, too, when you are far, faraway.

Every day at sea is different. A day that's blissful and fun can turn challenging in a heartbeat. There are inspiring days and daring days, times of terror and moments of such magnificence that we smile just remembering them. Yet all of this happy chaos brings an intimate connection with nature and the sea that, while not always peaceful, is deeply enriching. Nothing stops moving – not us, the sea, the boat, the fish. Even the galley moves while we are cooking. Plants are growing, bread is rising, seeds are sprouting, fish are being reeled in, and joyful kids are jumping off the bow. None of these moments are taken for granted.

Whether you are a seasoned salty or getting started on your watery journey, we hope you read this book and get excited about weighing anchor. We hope it arms you with answers and buoys you with the knowledge you need to tackle your big adventures. And we hope, in these pages, you glean what an extraordinary community of people is out there waiting, supporting each other, raising their families and being the village that seafaring people need. Most of all, we want you to be tantalised by good, fresh, sustainable food and all the amazing ways you can grow, catch, forage, harvest and cook with it.

Happy sailing,

Catherine, David and Maya

NUDE FOOD

Go Nude Too

For 25 years, I, Catherine, was a strict vegetarian (nothing with a face on my plate). But in 2019, as we set sail for Indonesia, my entire outlook on food suddenly changed. Ocean pollution and the plastics issue plagued and disheartened me daily, and I began to feel hopelessly overwhelmed. I knew I had to make it personal, and I started with my shopping trolley. All the plastic-wrapped, vegetarian convenience foods I usually bought simply had to go. I was desperate to find a less harmful way to eat, and the answer was on the end of Dave's fishing line.

Fish is what I call 'nude food': unpackaged, fresh, and caught sustainably with a single rod, hand line or speargun, with no damage to ecosystems, the seabed or other marine creatures. We buy vegetables from local markets without packaging or plastic bags, grow our own herbs and greens, and sprout seeds, nuts and beans into living food. There is always a continuous batch of fresh yoghurt on hand, sourdough bread rising on the bench, and most days, we fish and forage ashore. All of this has been a complete game-changer.

Finally, I've found the way I instinctively feel I should live, and with a bit of planning and effort, I find that it is achievable. On our boat, nude food includes the fish we spear and angle for, the oysters gathered off rocks, mud crabs trapped, and prawns gathered in cast nets. We harvest fresh coconuts for drinking, and grate and dry older coconut flesh for snacks and baking. We nurture a potted garden of salad greens, herbs and veggies, and we sprout seeds into nutrient-packed greens for salads and stir-fries. We shop at local markets selling seasonal produce and refuse plastic bags, and all of it contributes in small but significant ways to more wholesome meals and a lighter footprint on our ocean-going adventures.

Some days, when I'm fist-deep in sourdough, rinsing sprouts and grating coconut, it feels like I'm living in the 1920s. But mostly, I'm unbelievably stoked to be able to create and cultivate healthful, plastic-free food that I don't have to stand in line to buy.

I believe that lots of people feel this way and the drive towards self-sufficient living is stronger than ever, buried somewhere in our DNA. I think that more and more of us want to take control of our lives, and are hearing that primordial call to the world's richest food source, the sea. From the ocean and its verdant shores, we can gather nude food without pulling out our wallets. Plus, all of it can happen without supporting destructive commercial fishing practices.

During our years living on the water, we've learnt that being self-sufficient, stepping back just a little from supermarket-led supply chains, and living simply at sea can empower you with an immense sense of freedom.

Hunting, gathering, foraging, growing and shopping at farm gates and fresh food markets are the purest ways I know of to stay healthy, reduce our reliance on supermarket-led supply chains, and contribute far less waste to the world, especially our oceans. It's very achievable, and it truly makes a difference.

FLEXI FOOD

Recipes With Wriggle-Room

Sometimes I hate cookbooks. Invariably they call for ingredients that we just don't have on board and are rarely stocked in the remote harbour towns that we sail into. Two decades ago, when I started creating recipes for travel magazines from my tiny galley, getting my hands on the ingredients I wanted was endlessly challenging. So, I stopped trying so hard and started creating what I call flexi food – recipes with wriggle room for people afloat.

We've always had a kitchen that rocks at sea. But, even without an elaborate set-up, an excess of cookware or a vast selection of ingredients to work with, I know it's possible to eat well, savour flavoursome food and enjoy creating it too.

Most of the ingredients in this book are easy to find, fish or forage for. Heirloom tomatoes and buffalo mozzarella, as delicious as they undoubtedly can be, are not readily available when you're anchored in Australia's Kimberley or exploring some faraway tropical isle.

My recipes are mindful too of choosing the healthiest ingredients possible – the best cooking oils and sweeteners – and providing alternatives for those keen to avoid gluten, fructose, dairy or nuts. All recipes are coded to help you navigate your own personal preferences. And they list plenty of substitutes to keep them as flexible as possible so that you can swap, substitute and cook them to suit your tastes.

Cracking The Codes:

To help you find the recipe that's right for your stage of the adventure, I've highlighted those that are quick to cook or require just one pot, those you can cook on a beach campfire, and no-bake meals to cook with kids or on steamy days. Plus, there's an entire section on food that's fit for passage, so you can prep meals in advance and store them in the fridge or freezer to help give any big adventure a little kick-start.

GF = **Gluten-free**

V = **Vegan**

QC = **Quick Cook:** these are meals for when you are short on time or under sail, and the galley is no place you want to be.

CC = **Campfire Cooking:** bake these meals over hot coals with mates and brews.

OP = **One Pot:** for stovetop cooks and sailors who hate washing up.

NC = **No Cook Meals:** flame-free things to eat.

What's The Measure?

Australian cooking measurements differ slightly from the rest of the world, but making the switch is easy. In Australia, 1 teaspoon holds 5ml, 1 tablespoon equals 20ml, and 1 cup holds 250ml (a US cup holds 240ml). Don't worry, these recipes are flexible enough to allow for tiny differences in cup measurements, and where applicable, we list metric or imperial equivalents. We prefer cup measurements over weights because scales are sometimes tricky to read correctly on a rocking boat. All recipes include both Celsius and Fahrenheit temperatures.

Measuring Liquids

Cup	Metric	Imperial
1 tsp	5ml	
1 tbsp	20ml	
¼ cup	60ml	2 fl oz
⅓ cup	80ml	2.5 fl oz
½ cup	125ml	4 fl oz
⅔ cup	160ml	5 fl oz
¾ cup	180ml	6 fl oz
1 cup	250ml	8 fl oz
2 cups	500ml	16 fl oz
3 cups	750ml	24 fl oz
4 cups	1 litre	32 fl oz

Measuring Solids

Grams	Ounces
20g	½ oz
60g	2 oz
125g	4 oz
180g	6 oz
250g	8 oz
500g	16 oz (1lb)

Oven Temperatures

Celsius	Fahrenheit
100°C	210°F
150°C	300°F
180°C	350°F
200°C	390°F
220°C	430°F

What The Courgette!?

When I lived in England, I'd drive the kids in my house crazy with my weird Aussie lingo. "Put on your singlet" (vest), "Look at the size of that truck" (lorry), you get the idea. Vegetables, fruits and all kinds of baking ingredients have notoriously confusing names in different parts of the world. Here are some favourites you'll find in this book:

Bicarbonate of soda = baking soda

Capsicum = bell pepper

Caster sugar = superfine sugar

Chickpeas = garbanzo beans

Coriander = cilantro

Cornflour = cornstarch

Cos lettuce = romaine lettuce

Eggplant = aubergine

Kaffir lime = makrut or Thai lime

Papaya = pawpaw

Plain flour = all-purpose flour

Prawn = shrimp

Rocket = arugula

Self-raising flour = self-rising flour

Silverbeet = Swiss chard

Spring onion = scallion

Sweet potato = kumara or yam

Zucchini = courgette

Gathering For Your Galley

4 PERSONS

MIX

SAILING YOUR FARM

Growing A Boat Micro-Garden

Cultivating a micro-garden just makes sense when you live off the grid, and it's far easier than you might imagine. A great way to feed yourself (or at least add crunch and flavour to your salad bowl), a mini garden reconnects you to the plots of soil, you might otherwise miss when you swap a backyard for the big blue.

I'm still learning, but through trial and error over the years, I've worked out what's possible when growing food on a boat. Mine is a compact collection of hardy herbs and vegetables that thrive in shallow soil, and quick-growing greens that I can pick early in their micro stage. They grow in long, rectangular pots that fit snugly together when underway and don't easily tip over. I fill them with the best organic potting mix I can find, plant a variety of seeds, and then simply add sunshine and water.

Things I Grow

The greens I grow best when sailing in the tropics include rocket, baby spinach, cos and mesclun lettuce varieties, and kale in the cooler months. All add great crunch to salads and sandwiches and can be chopped into anything else you cook. Basil and parsley can survive a lot of punishment (including the occasional upending) and taste terrific pounded into pesto and tossed through salads. Coriander can be trickier to keep alive, so if you struggle (as I do), plant Vietnamese mint instead. It grows as a creeper and infuses spring rolls and salads with a fresh, Asian-inspired flavour. Common varieties of mint are nearly impossible to kill and can be turned into hot and iced tea, added fresh to your water bottle, and smashed into sundowners.

I used to think tomatoes (even the stunted, dwarf varieties) were impossible to grow in shallow, boat-stable planter trays. But there's one sunning itself on my back deck, positively blooming and hanging with lush, juicy fruit. It grew completely by accident, and its roots have taken over the pot, but all is forgiven now that it's filling our sandwiches! I'd like to say that anything is possible on a boat, but that's not entirely true. Shallow, sea-stable planters suit vegetables that grow above the soil and have compact root systems (unlike tubers). The height that plants grow to needs to be considered when choosing seeds and seedlings so that pots can be easily stowed when underway. Climate largely determines what will successfully grow on a boat because it's difficult to control temperature or humidity. Plant edibles that thrive in the areas and seasons you sail through, keep a stash of seeds on hand, and experiment with different crops as the seasons, and your aspirations, change.

Things Go Wrong

It's not always plain sailing. Over the years, my pots have been upended in big seas, splashed by rogue waves, and blasted by too much wind. They've been invaded by black gnats and thoroughly soaked in torrential wet season downpours when I've forgotten to rescue them from the rain. The hardiest of green things somehow survive, but as a backup, I always carry extra seeds and potting mix on board in case I need to start over.

My hardy little survivors have clocked up a lot of sea miles over the years and taught me just about all I know of gardening. The planters might occasionally get in the way, and some onboard might lament the weight of all that soil, but there's something immensely satisfying about eating what you grow, no matter how much of a garnish it might seem. Just looking at my tiny garden blooming in the thirstiest of locations gives me immense pleasure, and visiting boaties never fail to gush over our patch of green, and always leave with a few sprigs of their favourites.

FORAGING ASHORE

Many sailing grounds provide an abundance of seaweeds that can be gathered off beaches and the shallows and then dried to flavour soups, salads, and especially Japanese-inspired dishes. Virtually all seaweeds are edible (although not equally palatable), so unlike mushrooms, they are a pretty safe food to forage for. Regardless, it pays to know where, when and how to collect them. Like when foraging for shellfish, you should avoid gathering seaweed in places where towns, industry and farms intrude, and where runoff from these operations might pollute the waters, especially after heavy rains. In Australia, seaweeds tend to bloom and grow more during summer and spring, so you'll likely get the youngest fronds when harvesting in these seasons.

Popular varieties include wakame, sea lettuce and kelp, of which golden kelp is abundant and popular. It's cast ashore on the high tide, so gather it fresh soon after, just as the tide recedes. When you forage for seaweed – off the beach or from the sea – be mindful and take small amounts from different locations. This helps to preserve the habitats that seaweed provides to fish, crabs, birds and other sea creatures. Be aware, too, that some places (New South Wales and Victoria in Australia, for instance) apply rules and bag limits to gathered seaweed.

The authors of the book *Milkwood* have a great seaweed foraging guide (that's aimed at kids and East Coast foragers but has universal appeal), which you can download. Head to milkwood.net and search for seaweed.

Many seaweeds, especially robust-tasting kelp, are highly nutritious and flavoursome. Once dried, they can be powdered and pinched into soups and noodles or rehydrated and used to make delicious seaweed salads. On Indonesia's remote Kei Island, a bubbly, succulent seaweed nicknamed 'sea grapes' (*Caulerpa lentillifera*, or umibudo in Japan) is mixed with red chillies, lime juice and shaved coconut and served cold as a super-tasty salad called Lat. Look for Lat when you sail there and order it overlooking the sea.

Bush Foods

Easily harvested coconuts and tropical almonds grow abundantly on many tropical shores. In Australia, native bush foods grow wild and close to the coast right around the country. In Queensland's Wet Tropics, where rainforests meet the sea, look for native bananas, cheese fruit, sweet-tasting cluster figs that grow on the trunks of strangler figs, and deep purple-coloured Burdekin plums (visit wettropics.com for a downloadable ID chart). Other unlikely plants grow wild in anchorages across northern Australia. Some are the remnants of abandoned, faraway farms and homesteads, while others spring up thanks to the distribution efforts of flying foxes and birds. Around this coastline, I've foraged for chillies, wild limes and bush mangoes, and starchy breadfruit in bordering rainforests too. Foraging for bush tucker is easy when you know what to look for and where, so arm yourself with an identification guide. I reccomend Diego Bonetto's *Eat Weeds*, Tim Low's *Wild Food Plants of Australia* or Les Hidden's *Bush Tucker Field Guide*.

Tropical Almonds

Once, while sea kayaking up Queensland's Cassowary Coast, Dave and I spent an entire afternoon cracking tropical almonds. Also called beach, sea, or Indian almonds, they fall from tall, verdant trees found along tropical beaches from Africa to Australia, and Micronesia to the Americas, forming a dense carpet of large, green and red pods. Beneath a hard outer skin and a layer of husk, the kernel is locked deep inside. Cockatoos seem to tear them open easily, but they are simple to crack when pods are very dry.

Position the pod on either pointed end – held in a rock crevice or split piece of timber – and strike it hard with a hammer or rock. The nut will split in two (eventually) to reveal a slim and irresistible kernel. If you can stop munching on them as fast as you crack them, collect a pile, toast them and have a crack at my wickedly tasty Tropical Almond Pesto (page 214).

Tropical almonds (*Terminalia catappa*) can be eaten raw but taste best when toasted. They are most nutritious when eaten with vitamin C-rich foods to maximise mineral absorption. Although more closely related to Australia's Kakadu Plum (the world's most potent vitamin C-rich plant), the tropical almond has a similar nutritional makeup to regular almonds. It's rich in protein (from 20-25 per cent), high in vitamin E, iron, riboflavin and magnesium, and supplies good amounts of calcium, niacin, manganese and phosphorous.

HARVESTING COCONUTS

It's the most naturally widespread fruit in the world, sustaining coastal communities from Africa to the Americas across the Indian and Pacific Oceans. A single coconut palm can produce up to 100 nuts a year, which take 12 months to slowly transform from heavy, green drinking coconuts to dry mature nuts coveted for their oil-rich meat. Every single part of the coconut palm [*Cocos nucifera*] serves a very useful purpose. The great bonus for tropical sailors is that this readily available food source is highly nutritious and can be eaten at every stage of its development.

The green nut's electrolyte-rich water is an extremely hydrating drink, while the meat of older nuts can be grated and dried for shredded coconut and flour, or pressed to make oil, milk and cream. Dried outer husks are traditionally spun into salt-resistant coir ropes and can be used as kindling to get any beach campfire started. Palm fronds are skillfully woven into baskets and mats, and the sap from coconut flower buds produces coconut sugar and syrup. The tree's timber has a surprisingly attractive grain. It is sought-after for building furniture and as a sustainable hardwood substitute for housing construction too. The grain has a beautiful spotted pattern that is striking when varnished, and we used it to build a shelf on our old boat, *Storyteller*.

The coconut is known as a dry drupe because it is simultaneously a fruit, a nut and a seed. While there are dozens of varieties, all can be divided into two main types: the impossibly tall palms that few sailors dare to climb, and the very convenient dwarf palms whose young nuts can be more yellow than green. One stems from the Indian Ocean, the other from the Pacific, but both have floated across oceans and found their way aboard seafaring ships to reach almost all tropical shores in the world.

Green Coconuts

Few drinks are more refreshing than the juice from a sweet, young coconut, which is why these immature fruits are called *drinking* coconuts. Technically it's coconut water, and you'll find it inside those firm, bright green nuts that cling in clusters at the top of palms, a precarious climb away. Indonesians call them kelapa muda and frequently offer them to sailors as a welcoming gift or to trade for fishing gear or clothes. Heavy with water that sloshes around when shaken, young coconuts are ready for harvesting at about six to seven months old and contain only a slim layer of gelatinous flesh that is so soft you can scoop it out and eat it with a spoon.

I freeze young flesh to protect its rich oils from oxidation and add it to our mango and banana breakfast smoothies. To make a wickedly indulgent coconut slice, blend young coconut flesh with a splash of coconut oil and sweeten with rice malt syrup until smooth. Sandwich the mixture between your favourite biscuit or muesli base and a drizzle of dark chocolate.

Green coconuts are easily opened with the swing of a sharp machete, which we carry with us on every trip ashore for when we get thirsty. Coconut water is mostly water (around 90 per cent), and at this stage of its development, the water contains almost no fat. Slowly, the balance inside the nut changes as the coconut transitions from green to yellow and then brown. Much of the coconut's water transforms to add an oil-rich layer of flesh and create an entirely new food source for gatherers like you and I.

Somewhere between green and brown, when a coconut is around eight to 10 months old, it contains a perfect balance of sweet juice and firm flesh. This is the sweet spot for me because I get the best of both worlds, and the meat is firm enough to grate and process for cooking and baking without being too dry.

Brown Coconuts

By the time a coconut is 11 to 12 months old, it's turned brown, fallen from the tree and is easily gathered. Brown coconuts still retain some water at this age, but it's for their thick, firm layer of oil-rich flesh that you'll spend time dehusking, opening and processing them. To save you some angst, look for local tools at market stalls wherever machetes are sold, and use these spikes and coconut scrapers to swiftly open nuts and remove the flesh.

When gathering brown coconuts, choose heavier nuts that still slosh a bit when shaken. Dry nuts are sometimes rancid or already on their way to germinating (even if you can't see a sprout), which is an entirely different kind of snack. Once grated, you can dry the flesh on trays in the sun and add it to some of my favourite sweet treats. Try Blissful Balls (page 233), 5-ingredient Coconut Cake (page 245) or No-bake Fruit & Nut Bars (page 235). Use a vegetable peeler to make Kei Island Coconut Chips (page 236) for a go-to snack when you are holding the helm. Grated, dried coconut can be mixed with breadcrumbs to coat fish and prawns before frying or stirred through cooked grains.

Because coconut water loses its sugar content as the nut ages, feeding that layer of oil-rich meat, brown coconuts are nutritionally very different from their younger selves. The meat is primarily fat, but it's a special kind of fat that continues to baffle scientists and nutritionists still grappling to fully comprehend the coconut.

Coconut oil consists mainly of MCTs (or medium-chain triglycerides), the same fat found in human breast milk and many infant formulas. What scientists can agree on is that MCTs are metabolised very differently from other fats. Instead of being stored, they shoot straight for your small intestine, which prioritises this rich energy source and rapidly uses it to power you up. At its most oil-rich stage, coconut meat is high in manganese (for bone health), copper, iron, the cell-protecting antioxidant selenium, and small amounts of the B group vitamins (1, 2 and 3).

Sprouted Coconuts

After its first birthday, providing no one has come to claim it, a coconut begins to use all its nutritional goodness to create a new palm tree. When it germinates, it sends up a bright green shoot, and the water inside sustains the nut until roots grow and the tree can flourish. The inside of a sprouted coconut at this stage is quite amazing. Growing in the space where coconut water was previously found, you'll discover a large, spongy, white ball (or cotyledon) that takes just a few months to fill the entire cavity. It's covered in rich oil and has a crunchy texture, with a taste that's slightly fermented and more sour than sweet.

Despite its lack of world renown and unusual taste, this living plant embryo holds its own in tropical cuisines. It's called coconut apple in Belize and queen's bread in Hawaii. But it's pongu or seembu in different parts of Southern India, where it might be ground with soaked rice and turned into delicious Indian dosas (or pancakes). Sprouted coconut forms the foundation of many thick custardy desserts and is fried, baked and simmered into coconut-rich curries. It's also eaten raw as a crunchy, fresh snack, but the flavour of these coconut pearls takes time to appreciate. What astonishes me most about the coconut and the people who embrace its many guises is that no part of this life-sustaining tree is ever wasted.

GETTING INTO SPROUTS

Why Sprout?

You can do it in the tiniest of spaces, in any climate and on any budget, and it's the easiest way to grow your own food on board. The simple act of sprouting transforms the dormant seeds we all bury deep in our stores into more digestible, healthful, living foods. Just add water and watch them grow. Using nothing more than glass jars, you can turn a tiny handful of seeds into a voluminous batch of sprouts to create salads, protein-packed smoothies, soups and stir-fries. Add them to breads, muffins, frittatas and pies, and stir them through stews, chillies, curries and pasta sauces. Even without sprouting them, just soaking seeds makes them more healthful and digestible and cuts their cooking time too. More than this, sprouting solves the potential issue of a plant's so-called 'anti-nutrients'.

Nixing The Problem Of Anti-Nutrients

Found in vastly varying degrees in all plants and their seeds, anti-nutrients are natural compounds. Plants often use them to make themselves less palatable to the bacteria, animals and humans that might otherwise attack or eat them. Some anti-nutrients (phytic acid, lectin and saponins, for example) have been blamed for digestive and inflammation issues and for blocking the body's absorption of nutrients. Lectin plays its part in a plant's natural defence mechanism, while phytic acid (or phytate) can inhibit the availability of minerals such as calcium, zinc and iron to your body. But the simple act of soaking and sprouting inactivates these anti-nutrients, converting starches into simple sugars and unlocking nutrients that would otherwise remain out of reach.

What Can You Sprout?

Nuts and grains, beans, peas and pulses are all candidates for sprouting. We mostly sail in the tropics and have the greatest success with sunflower seeds, lentils and mung beans. I regularly sprout chia and cress seeds in my garden pots, sprinkled over the soil and left for four to five days to shoot up before I snip them for salads. Others I activate by soaking them overnight: kidney beans (for chilli) and whole red lentils (for Red Lentil Bolognese on page 170). I haven't given up on alfalfa seeds, but they don't love the humidity, so I'm moving through my stash of seeds to find new sprouts I like.

It's possible to sprout just about any legume, seed, nut or grain, from chickpeas, lima beans, flax and peanuts, to quinoa, pumpkin seeds and micro herbs (try rocket, spinach, lettuce, fennel and kale). Sprout whatever seeds you can get your hands on, and you'll soon find favourites that work in the recipes you enjoy.

How Do You Do It?

I started out with a sprouting kit, which is basically a stack of four to five trays with draining points. They allow you to sprout a variety of seeds at different stages and continuously harvest your sprouts. Mine didn't drain well enough for the hot and humid tropics, so I now use glass jars (375-500ml/12.5-17fl oz) and haven't looked back. I add a few tablespoons of seeds and soak them overnight. Then I drain and rinse the seeds and cover the jars with squares of muslin cloth or mosquito net, secured with an elastic band. Upturned in my dish drainer at a slight angle to drain, the jars remind me to rinse them morning and night.

There are lots of other ways to sprout, including in a sieve, set over a pot or pan and covered with a lid, and you can learn more by reading Isabell Shipard's *How Can I Grow and Use Sprouts as Living Food?*. After an initial soaking, seeds and pulses need to be rinsed two to three times a day until their sprouts grow to size (anywhere from 2cm to 5cm over two to five days). When you are happy with your sprouts, rinse and dry them well (just tip them onto a clean tea towel and leave them for an hour). Seal them in an airtight container lined with paper towel, and refrigerate them for up to five days. It only takes a few tablespoons of seed to sprout and fill your jars, so you don't need much to feed yourself for days.

How Do You Make Them Taste Good?

The Thais have been doing it for centuries, adding mung bean sprouts into delicious, fried Pad Thai noodles that kids can't refuse. I toss them to all kinds of dishes (whatever is on the stove, really), but sprouts really shine in these fresh, Asian-style meals:

Fresh Spring Rolls with tamarind dipping sauce (page 185)

Sung Choi Bao (page 95)

10-minute Tom Yum Kung (page 100)

Tom Yum in a Jar (page 143)

Coconut & Kaffir Lime Noodles (page 153)

or add to Laab Norhai (page 134)

What About Nuts?

Raw nuts are similar to legumes and seeds in that they contain toxins that can inhibit easy digestion. Nutritionally speaking, the best way to deal with nuts is to soak them for six to 12 hours (depending on the nut), then activate them by very slowly drying them in your oven. But very few sailors wish to leave their oven lit for between 12 and 24 hours. Gas is far too precious, and my wonky boat oven won't even cook that gently, let alone stay lit for an entire day! Plus, a lot of popular sailing grounds are just far too hot to have the oven on that long, no matter how gently.

Instead I soak, rinse and sprout my nuts for just a day or two, although they seldom reveal any actual green sprout. Almonds are our favourite, and we use them a lot, turning them into a whole bunch of helm snacks. Just soak your almonds overnight in a jar, and rinse twice daily for one to two days before you toast them, bake with them, or blitz them into almond milk. You can do the same with peanuts (they're actually a legume), but leave them to sprout for up to five days before snacking or gently roasting to blitz into butter or crush for fresh spring rolls.

Mung Beans
For the initial soak, to help seeds swell and germinate evenly, cover mung beans with hot water (around 40-50°C/100-120°F) and soak overnight. Continue to rinse twice daily with room temperature water for up to five days.

Pumpkin Seeds
Reserve the seeds from freshly cut pumpkins and soak them for 6-12 hours in a jar, sprouter or sieve. Rinse twice a day and use after about two days, even though no shoot will be visible. Gently toasted, these make a tasty snack.

Sunflower Seeds
Both hulled or unhulled seeds need to be intact (i.e. not damaged by mechanical hulling). Unhulled seeds are best grown in soil, but hulled seeds, soaked overnight and rinsed twice daily, will sprout 1-2cm (0.5-1in) after a day or two.

Quinoa
Highly nutritious quinoa should be rinsed well before cooking to reduce the bitterness from its natural coating of saponin. Alternatively, soak quinoa in a jar or sprouter for two hours, then rinse three or more times daily, and watch it sprout after about two days. Sprouts will grow a few centimetres long if you leave them for four days, which is perfect for adding to salads.

Brown Or Red Lentils
Soak overnight with room temperature water and rinse twice daily for two to four days.

Cress
I shake the seeds directly on top of the soil in my garden pots, and sprouts start to appear within 24 hours. Harvest as you please.

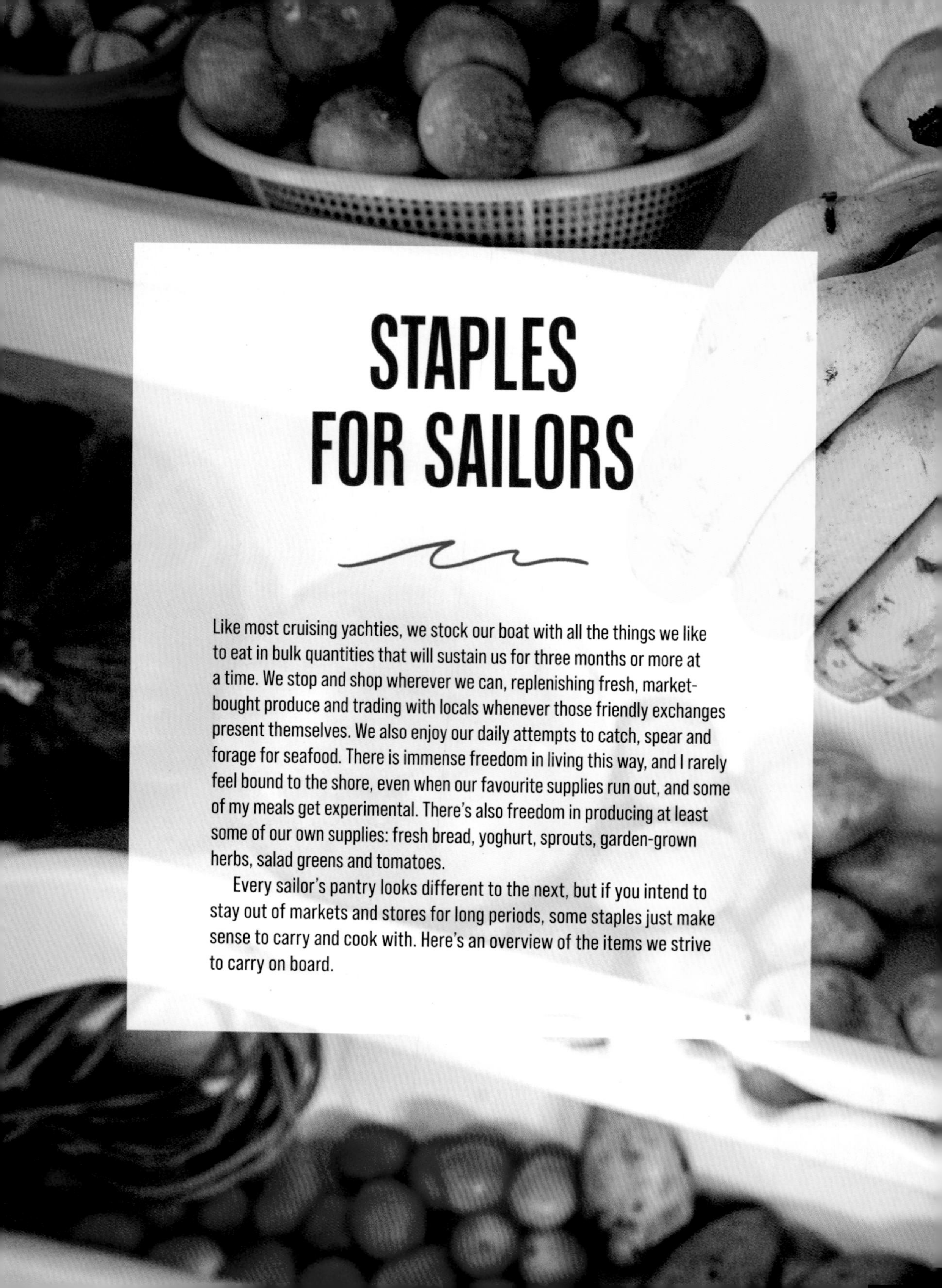

STAPLES FOR SAILORS

Like most cruising yachties, we stock our boat with all the things we like to eat in bulk quantities that will sustain us for three months or more at a time. We stop and shop wherever we can, replenishing fresh, market-bought produce and trading with locals whenever those friendly exchanges present themselves. We also enjoy our daily attempts to catch, spear and forage for seafood. There is immense freedom in living this way, and I rarely feel bound to the shore, even when our favourite supplies run out, and some of my meals get experimental. There's also freedom in producing at least some of our own supplies: fresh bread, yoghurt, sprouts, garden-grown herbs, salad greens and tomatoes.

Every sailor's pantry looks different to the next, but if you intend to stay out of markets and stores for long periods, some staples just make sense to carry and cook with. Here's an overview of the items we strive to carry on board.

Carbohydrates & Grains

Whole grains and processed grain-based foods form the backbone of any sailor's stores. Mine includes pasta, rice (basmati, brown and sushi), quinoa, rice noodles, tortilla chips, couscous and long-life flatbreads for quick-cook pizzas and lunchtime wraps. I carry rice paper sheets (for fresh rolls), crackers, frozen pastry and plenty of flour for baking sourdough bread, which I turn into croutons and breadcrumbs too. We basically store a little bit of everything and restock regularly with whatever is locally available in the towns we sail into.

Many grain-based foods generate an excess of plastic waste, especially the convenient ones. Choose carefully when you shop, and when you can, buy from bulk supply stores and markets that allow you to refill your own bags and containers with rice, flour, nuts, legumes and more.

Vegetarian Proteins

We don't eat 'meat with feet' but catch fish whenever we can. If the fish aren't biting or crocodiles keep us out of the sea, we cook up vegetarian proteins instead. These include dried red and brown lentils (for pasta sauces and sprouting), tinned chickpeas (for speedy hummus), and tinned and dried kidney beans for Mexican chillies. There are always eggs, tempeh and tofu on board (for Asian-style satays and curries), plus TVP (textured vegetable protein) and falafel mix.

Although many sailors adore theirs, I don't own a pressure cooker, so I favour smaller legumes that are quick to soften. Nutritious and cheap, red lentils are my favourite for their smooth, nutty flavour. It's not essential to soak them before cooking, but it does make them more nutritious. They are a rich source of iron, zinc, and B-group vitamins, and they transform my Red Lentil Bolognese into something truly magical. Soaking and sprouting dried chickpeas and kidney beans makes them far more nutritious, lessens their cooking times and makes them much easier to digest. Adding three to four bay leaves to the pot when cooking beans helps reduce their digestive sting, too.

Freezing Cheese

When we left Australia to sail to Eastern Indonesia recently, our freezer was chock-full of three things we knew we'd never find along our route: frozen berries, butter and cheese. I've been freezing cheese for decades and now know this: the higher the fat content, the better it survives the thawing process. That means that brie, and camembert all perform well. Cheddar and feta can be crumbly when defrosted, but your home-baked pizzas will still taste amazing. Instead of freezing feta, try preserving it in olive oil (page 213).

Nuts & Seeds

Before long stints at sea, I stock the boat with plenty of nuts and seeds, choosing whatever's available and affordable in the town I set out from. My stash might include protein-packed chia seeds (for baking and breakfasts) and sunflower, sesame and pepita seeds for snacking, sprouting and adding flavour to my sourdough loaves. Our nut stash never lasts long – almonds, cashews, walnuts and more – that add crunch to salads and stir-fries, baked slices and cakes, and to make our helm snack of choice, Nut Fix (page 237). Versatile peanuts (actually a legume, not a nut) are cheap and widely available for blitzing into nut butter or creating delicious peanut satay sauce. If you have the room, store your nuts and seeds in the freezer (or fridge) to extend their shelf life.

Preserving Eggs

Eggs are popular on our boat, and preserving them for two months or more is pretty simple. Start by getting your hands on the freshest, unwashed eggs you can find. Young eggs have opaque, bumpy shells with a uniform colour. Unwashed is important because the protective bloom that coats the egg when it is laid is still in place. It seals out oxygen and bacteria, which can penetrate the shell and spoil the egg. The cooler the conditions and the lower the humidity, the longer you can expect your eggs to last. Unwashed fresh eggs outlast supermarket eggs every time, and coating and refrigerating eggs can double their lifespan.

You can coat your eggs with butter, ghee, Vaseline or mineral oil, and even hot wax; sink them in a tray of wood ash; or waterglass them in a sodium silicate solution. All these options have drawbacks because what coats the egg eventually flavours the egg, too, so my absolute pick is organic coconut oil. A safe, natural sealant, coconut oil won't eventually go rancid (as butter does) or taint the taste of your eggs over time. To apply, simply rub the oil evenly over each egg with your hands, and return the eggs to their carton, pointy tips down. If your coconut oil is cold and solidified, simply warm it in your palms before generously coating the eggs. Store them in a cool, dark place or in the fridge for maximum longevity (especially in the tropics), and turn the cartons over every week or so.

I've coated just-laid eggs and had them last two months out of the fridge over the cooler, winter months. How long yours stay fresh depends entirely on ambient temperature and their condition when you coated them. Some say oil-coated eggs lose their 'oomph' over time and don't beat as beautifully as just-laid ones. It's a small thing to accept after long weeks at sea, but I always float them first (fresh eggs sink, bad ones float). Supermarket eggs that have been refrigerated should ideally stay refrigerated on your boat too, but a coating of coconut oil can seal their porous shells and sustain them for longer.

Fruit & Veggies

Almost nothing lands on my dining table without an excess of fresh produce chopped into it, so my fridge is always overflowing. It takes considerable effort to eat well and prepare a steady stream of nutritious meals, especially when you can't easily nip in and out of stores daily. The challenge of storing food so that it stays fresh for as long as possible comes down to some careful post-shopping day prep. No one wants to open the fridge three days later to find everything wilting and largely inedible. Sometimes it's a pain, but taking the time to wash, dry and store your supplies with care, contributes to less waste and saves you money too. Here's how I get things organised:

Into my freezer goes the produce with the shortest lifespan, lightly processed to make life easier later in the trip. I might bag up a pan of freshly sautéed spinach, roast a tray of ripe tomatoes for blitzing into passata, and peel and freeze any excess ripe fruit to blend into breakfast smoothies and Nice Cream (page 226).

I rinse, dry and wrap soft greens like lettuce and spinach in paper towel and seal them in snap-lock bags in the fridge. Carrots, cucumbers and eggplants keep well stored this way too, and I can rinse and reuse the snap-lock bags week after week. In very cool climes, you can keep cos and iceberg lettuce out of the fridge, wrapped in a damp tea towel with the outer leaves intact to retain moisture. Put them somewhere cool and check on them daily, removing only the leaves you need and rewrapping them with any wrinkled outer leaves and a damp tea towel. Cabbage likes a cool spot, too, wrapped in newspaper or placed inside a cotton bag (or old pillow case). My mushrooms go into paper bags and into the crisper.

Hardier fruits and vegetables – potatoes, pumpkins, oranges, sweet potatoes, onions, shallots and garlic – can last for months in a cool, dark cupboard. However, tomatoes, avocadoes, papayas, stone fruit, melons and pears continue to ripen once picked, so I try to buy them green and firm. The bulk of these go into a cupboard, stored in a single layer to avoid bruising. When we are ready to eat them, I'll shift a handful to the galley benchtop, refrigerating them only if they ripen too quickly, or to chill them off before eating. Big bunches of green bananas hang outside on a rope to be snapped off when they turn yellow and delicious. When you have lots of fresh veggies on board, it's crucial to keep an eye on everything and be prepared to cook up and eat whatever's ready to go or starting to look a bit tired.

In my early sailing years, when I didn't even have a fridge on board, we used to dehydrate lots of fruit and veggies. Dave and I would buy up whatever was plentiful and cheap at the local markets and raid my mum's herb garden. The hum of the dehydrator would be our background noise for days. Solanaceous (or nightshade) vegetables dehydrate really well – tomatoes, eggplants and capsicums – along with mushrooms, zucchinis, mangoes, apples and bananas. Just slice everything thinly and uniformly, drying your trays in the sun first if you want to decrease your overall power usage.

On *Wild One*, we process lots of coconut meat. The firm, drier meat of orange and brown coconuts is grated or shaved (using a vegetable peeler), placed on trays and dried in the sun. Some is bagged and frozen to bake with, and some gets a low, slow toasting in the pan, seasoned afterwards with a pinch of salt or powdered vegetable stock for snacking. We also scoop the flesh out of green coconuts when we've finished drinking the water, and freeze this softer, gelatinous flesh to add to smoothies and Nice Cream.

Tinned foods are freedom foods because they feed us when we are far off the beaten track. My stash includes lots of emergency veggies: tomatoes, corn, mushrooms, and beetroot (cos I'm an Aussie, and beets belong in burgers). If my stash starts to dwindle and I can't easily top it up again, I start preserving from scratch, loading up at local fresh markets and blanching, roasting and blitzing vegetables to create freezer foods to use down the track.

Pickles & Preserves

My father-in-law once gifted me a jar of homemade pickled green tomatoes, and I've been inspired to follow his lead ever since. I make pickles and preserves whenever I find fresh, seasonal produce that's impossibly cheap and ready to go: Chilli Peach Jam (made with mangoes and strawberries, too, see page 211), Pickled Beetroot (page 214), and crunchy, vinegary Spiced Pickled Vegetables (page 140) using cucumbers, carrots and red onion that you can munch on long after the fresh food has been eaten. We set out with a decent supply of Kalamata olives and crunchy jalapeños, and Dave keeps us smiling with a steady supply of his heavenly Coconut Sambal (page 209) which ramps up the flavour of any seafood, soup, rice or noodle dish it touches.

Milk & Yoghurt

When supermarkets are within easy reach, we drink all kinds of fresh milk and its alternatives, and keep a backup of UHT milk on board. But because David and I lived aboard for 10 years before we got around to installing a fridge, we have a serious powdered milk habit. We know the weird taste is not everyone's cup of tea, but we are fairly well immune to it now. We could have used UHT milk all those years, but it is heavy and a space hog, and doesn't separate to make tasty ricotta cheese and paneer. Full-cream powdered milk works for these cheeses and makes excellent yoghurt to cream up your curries and smoothies or as a makeshift sour cream with a squeeze of lime stirred through. We blend lots of yoghurt with frozen fruit for yummy Nice Cream (page 226).

When reconstituting milk powder, always add it to water first, stirring it well before pouring it into your mug of tea, coffee or hot chocolate. If you use lots of milk, make up a batch in a jug or sealed container and keep it in the fridge. The usual milk powder-to-water ratio is 1:4, but I make it a little creamier by simply using less water (1:3 works well for creamy coffees). Pour half

of the water in, add a cup of milk powder, stir or shake well, then top it with water and stir it again.

Dried Fruit

Because we prefer to make our own slices, biscuits and cakes on *Wild One*, an assortment of dried fruits is essential. I like to keep stocks of dates, sultanas, cranberries, apricots, and sometimes dried mango and pineapple. There is always ginger and home-dried coconut in our galley too.

Sugar & Spice

When I have the time, I prefer to season my dishes from the ground up, utilising as many fresh ingredients as possible. But ready-made pastes, sauces and spreads provide a reliable backup, and I've shared the recipes to some of my favourites on page 208. My cupboards always contain essential flavourings such as soy sauce, kecap manis (sweet soy sauce), fish sauce, tamarind, miso paste and whole-egg mayonnaise.

I keep vinegars (balsamic, apple cider, rice wine), mustard and wasabi, and a huge range of dried spices and herbs. When you stock up, buy smaller quantities of spices that you can use before their six-month shelf life is up, and plant your favourite herbs in your micro-garden, which you can solar or oven-dry to store for later.

In a perfect world where every ingredient is available to me, I'd choose fructose-free rice malt syrup over sugar any day. But hey, if ordinary sugar is all that's on offer, I'll put it in my trolley, too, because special days must be celebrated, and celebrations deserve cakes. I also keep honey for marinades, pancakes and baking.

As for drinks, we carry lots of leaf tea (herbal blends and black tea) because our beautiful old teapot has survived thousands of sea miles and is simply a joy to use. We also stock coffee, cocoa and cacao, ginger cordial (for queasy days and delicious homemade popsicles), and all the ingredients to make home-brewed ginger beer (page 206)

Oils Ain't Oils

Confusion abounds about which are the best oils to cook with. I've dug deep into this one and now stick to oils containing monounsaturated and saturated fats that remain stable at higher temperatures: olive, coconut and peanut oils. I avoid all polyunsaturated vegetable and seed oils. These include canola (or rapeseed), sunflower, soybean and vegetable (which is simply a blend of any cheap oils a manufacturer might choose to bottle up). All are highly refined, chemically processed oils with questionable nutritional value. They contain high levels of polyunsaturated fats, making them unstable and susceptible to oxidation both on the supermarket shelf, and in your body too. The fragile fatty acids that make up these oils are easily degraded, and oxidation (when oil is exposed to oxygen and begins to break down) occurs at a cellular level once fats are incorporated into your body's cell membranes. Avoid these oils wherever you can.

Sunflower, soybean and rice bran oils are also high in omega-6 fatty acids, which we need in the body, but not in the amounts we generally consume. On average, we eat up to 20 times more inflammatory omega-6 fats than anti-inflammatory omega-3s, when the nutritional sweet spot is a balance of 1:1. This imbalance is an underlying factor in the onset of heart disease, cancer, arthritis, diabetes, bowel disease and more. Resetting this balance means shifting our choice of oil back to those rich in saturated fats (coconut oil and butter) and monounsaturated fat (olive oil). Here's what I cook with in this book:

Extra virgin olive oil (cold-pressed and organic) for dressings, marinades, baking bread and focaccias, and shallow frying too. Extra virgin olive oil can withstand deep-fry temperatures up to 190°C (370°F), a fact that challenges the need for other cheap, high smoke point oils.

Coconut oil for baking and frying. Its high lauric acid content (40-50 per cent) makes it resistant to oxidation and stable at high heat. Rare in most oils, lauric acid boosts the immune system, protects against heart disease, promotes good blood cholesterol and gives coconut oil its antimicrobial and antifungal properties. The oil's medium-chain fatty acids are easily digested and stimulate the body's metabolism.

Peanut oil is another high-heat stable oil (up to 230°C/440°F). It contains a healthier balance of mono- and polyunsaturated fats and a range of important phytosterols that help block cholesterol absorption and protect against colon, prostate and breast cancers. I mostly use it in Asian-style stir-fries.

In Praise Of Olive Oil

It's the high levels of vitamin E that keep olive oil stable when cooking, so it can tolerate higher cooking heats – even deep frying temperatures – without breaking down and becoming potentially carcinogenic (as many other oils do). Along with boosting the oil's oxidative stability, Vitamin E also extends its shelf life. Olive oil is made up of monounsaturated fats, which help reduce levels of bad cholesterol and increase good cholesterol in the blood, protecting the heart from disease. And because olive oil is packed with free radical-fighting antioxidants like vitamin E, consuming raw extra virgin olive oil can help to prevent a range of cancers and diseases, and fight the effects of aging.

Confusingly, there are three main grades of olive oil – extra virgin, virgin and pure olive oil – differentiated by the level to which they have been processed and, therefore, the amounts of free fatty acid (particularly oleic acid) in the oil. Less acid is preferable and healthier, so the lower the acid levels, the better quality the olive oil, and the more you can expect to pay.

Cold-pressed extra virgin olive oil is nutritionally potent, produced from the first pressing of olives without any chemical or heat refining. It contains less than one per cent of oleic acid and retains a robust, fruity flavour. I use it lavishly, not just for marinades and salad dressings, but for baking, roasting and frying too. One grade down is virgin olive oil with around two per cent oleic acid. Pure olive oil is more heavily refined by heat and chemical means, which wipes out the oil's flavour and goodness. As a result, a little virgin or extra virgin olive oil is added back to restore taste and colour before bottling. All grades of olive oil – even extra virgin olive oil – remain stable when heated to temperatures hot enough for deep frying (175-190°C/345-370°F), so buy the best you can find and afford, and don't just save it for salads.

The Problem With Palm Oil

I specifically avoid palm oil, that controversial culprit behind the deforestation of some of our planet's greatest, most biodiverse forests. The proliferation of palm oil into around half the products sold in your average supermarket is testament to its profitability as a fast-growing, easy-to-harvest source of oil. But in the rush to make way for palm oil plantations, the virgin forest habitats of orangutans, Sumatran rhinos and Borneo's pygmy elephants continue to be destroyed. The habitats in Indonesia and Malaysia, which supply 85 per cent of the world market, are finite. They will never be restored, and these three endangered species, and their diverse ecosystems, teeter on the brink of extinction. Palm oil is not just used for cooking. If you start reading labels, you'll spot palm oil in everything from cheap chocolate, frozen pizzas, to toothpaste and pet food.

Storing Supplies

Constantly unending your storage areas to search for some urgently needed item is one thing that drives people mad on a boat. To save my sanity, I keep a running inventory of all the food stashed around the boat: what's in each locker and in what quantities. When I take something out, I cross it off the list, and when it gets bought again, I add it back on. That way, I know what I need to shop for and don't spend ages looking in vain for something we've already eaten.

Bug-proof Your Supplies

I once shared a few beers on the front deck of a friend's boat while she patiently sifted through five kilos of weevil-infested rice. Bug invasions happen to all cruisers at one time or another, but the bugs that infested my mung beans taught me how to store things properly. All grain products, seeds, nuts and pulses (including rice, flour, pasta, beans, oats and spices) can be protected from spoiling, but it takes just a little effort.

The Freezing Method

A minimum of four days in the freezer is needed to kill adult bugs, which I happily sifted out of my mung beans before drying and returning them to the pantry. But weeks later, they were again crawling with bugs, thanks to the eggs that had survived the freezer and returned me to square one. It's difficult to gauge the breeding cycle of different bugs and time things precisely so that you kill the adults, allow ample time for eggs to hatch, and then return your grains to the freezer before the next generation of bugs begins to breed. Some recommend four days in the freezer, followed by a few days on the bench at room temperature, and another stint in the freezer, but it's all a bit hit and miss. Fortunately, there is another way that doesn't require hog freezer space.

Oxygen-free Jars

Bugs can't live in an oxygen-free environment, and glass jars come to the rescue, providing a simple, non-permeable barrier to oxygen and moisture. You can re-purpose any glass jars or mason jars for storing grains, as long as they are sterile, dry, have snug fitting lids, and provided you add an oxygen absorber to each. These small sachets contain iron powder and are found in many grain-based products you buy from the supermarket. They work because iron oxidises, using up any available oxygen in a chemical reaction we know as rust. Unlike silica gel absorbents, which can contaminate food if they break open, oxygen absorbers are considered safe to use with your dried stores and are easily sourced online. Place one in the bottom of each jar before you fill it with store grains, seeds, nuts, rice, pasta or flour. Seal well, and replace the absorbers once they harden. Seal well and replace when they feel hard, bumpy or cool to the touch. Oxygen absorbers (or oxygen scavengers) start working immediately and are effective after around 48 hours.

The Party Box

Every day can be an occasion for celebration, and this is especially true when you are cruising. There is always a birthday, anniversary or festival to celebrate, an equator to cross, or a tricky passage to survive, so we carry a party box full of paper streamers, hats, candles and banners, sparklers and a stash of treats. I might have blocks of dark chocolate, caramelised nuts, puddings and long-life cream, or a special bag of coffee and bottles of good red wine. I've got lollies for kids, marshmallows for campfires, and lots of sprinkles for Maya and her friends to decorate their cakes with. Whatever excites your crew, stash a little of it in your party box for special celebrations.

Cinta
3

RESUPPLYING IN NEW PLACES

Food runs (like fuel runs) can be exciting and exhausting. Without access to your usual wheels, you might be travelling by bus, bemo or on foot, hauling backpacks, testing new language skills and shopping in a new currency too. Ticking off your shopping list can be even more of a challenge when the things you've come to rely upon are absent in new destinations. Instead, you might find unfamiliar vegetables and fruits, and packets with labels in a language you don't understand. No matter how out of your depth you may initially feel, my best tip is to try to relax and treat shopping as you would any fascinating, new cultural adventure. Resupplying takes time, so allow plenty of it to navigate markets and stores on foreign shores, and have all available crew on hand to help with the haul.

When you don't speak the local language and must shop in markets and stores, the most important tools you need are a smile and an understanding of prices and numbers. Learn to say, 'what does it cost (per kilo)?' and understand the price when given. A few friendly phrases – 'good morning' and 'thank you' – bring on smiles and help make the task of shopping infinitely more pleasant.

The first person I met when I sailed into Indonesia many years ago gave me a great piece of advice that I still use today. If you see something you like, buy as much of it as you can because you may not find it again when you reach your next port. Maintaining good supplies gives you immense freedom as a cruiser, to stay out of towns when you want to, and avoid unnecessary detours or backtracking just for food.

THE PLASTIC PROBLEM

Cruisers know better than most just how much garbage we accumulate. When you can't wheel it out to the kerb or send it back for recycling, reducing the packaging of the items we buy becomes pivotal in dealing with our own galley waste.

On *Wild One*, we stick to a few simple practices. We take our own stash of fine mesh bags to the markets to fill with fruit and vegetables, and the phrase "no plastic please" is one of the first things we learn in any new language. Markets and stores the world over often sell bulk stores of dry goods – rice, flour, lentils, coffee beans, nuts, spices and pasta – which are scooped directly into your own bags or containers. Shop this way when you can, and don't worry too much about the risk of weevils. You are just as likely to find them inside plastic-wrapped alternatives too.

When filling supermarket lists, I choose products sold in glass over hard plastic, then reuse the jars and bottles for pickling, sprouting, sourdough starter and bug-free pantry storage. I choose cardboard or paper packets where possible, and tins without a plastic lining. This takes a bit of trial and error to get right, but when I open a tin that's plastic-free, I take a photo with my phone so that I can look for it again on the next supply run.

When sailors start cruising, it's often a shock to see just how many places in the world are literally swimming in plastic. Where rubbish collection is non-existent (let alone recycling programs), you'll be forced to take care of your own waste. It's never ideal, but when locals turn their waste into the sea, burning yours on a very hot campfire is sometimes the only way to go. It's important, under such circumstances, to avoid buying hard plastics, batteries, and aerosols, and choose grocery items sold in soft plastics, refillable pouches or reusable glass jars and bottles instead.

EQUIPMENT I USE

Essentials, & Things I Just Really Like

The equipment I use is really just a condensed version of what you'd find in any home. One big omission, due to limited galley space and consciousness of power usage, is a lack of electrical gadgets. For the first time in 20 years, and only because my latest boat came with them, I have a microwave oven and a toaster on board. But there is no coffee machine, food processor or bread maker (yet). I have a little bit of everything, based entirely upon the way I like to cook and what was already on my boat. Adapt this list to include the gear you need to make the dishes you and your family love.

Stovetop, Oven, Griller: mine is LPG-powered, with two stovetop burners, and like most boat ovens, is small and temperamental (although we've learnt to work together). Despite loving my oven, my first four boats had no such luxury, yet I still managed to bake bread on my stovetop.

Microwave: this is a first for me, and I find it handy, especially since it runs off the sun (via an inverter) and reduces our gas usage. It's far from essential, but it is super handy on long, rough passages to reheat meals and minimise my time 'downstairs'.

Barbecue: our back deck barbecue is a Weber that runs on LPG and is used when we are cooking for a crowd, grilling big fish, and for baking sourdough to perfection in my camp oven. It's nice because using it keeps the heat outside, but it's not essential.

Fridge & Freezer: whatever the capacity you have, you manage with.

Stick Blender: for smoothies, sauces and pastes.

Heavy-based Frypan: for cooking stovetop bread and pizzas and for sweating onions, garlic and vegetables, low and slow.

Wok or High-sided, Non-stick Frypan: for stir-fries and fried rice.

Saucepans: I've got four sizes, one with a steamer and one big enough to boil a mud crab or cook up pasta for a crowd.

Cast Iron Camp Oven: for baking bread and campfire cooking.

Chopping Boards: plastic for seafood, wooden for everything else.

Large Colander: not just for draining pasta, but making cheese and resting fresh fish fillets overnight, too.

Sharp Knives: fish filleting knives, a bread knife, all-purpose chopping knives, paring knives, a shucking knife for oysters, and, because there's nothing worse than a blunt knife, a sharpening block too.

Utensils: whisk, egg flips, tongs (one short, one long for campfire cooking), graters (including a micro), wooden spatulas, stackable measuring cups and spoons, a sushi mat, bamboo skewers for seafood barbecues, vegetable peelers and more.

Mixing Bowls: multiple sizes.

Scales: helpful for bread and beer making, although they're not very accurate when the boat's rocking.

Yoghurt Thermos: with internal containers.

Baking Trays, & Bread & Cake Tins: different sizes and shapes.

Glass Jars: for sprouting and muslin squares for covers.

A Note On Thermal Cookers: a magazine that I write for once sent me a thermal cooker so that I could create a series of new recipes. Lots of sailors and travellers swear by them, and perhaps I gave up too soon. I could never inject the depth of flavour I was after or get the right textures from ingredients that were thrown together and 'cooked' simultaneously over the course of the day. My thermal cooker took up too much valuable galley space, and I never wanted to start thinking about dinner as I was cleaning up the breakfast dishes. If you love the idea and are a forward-thinking kind of cook, add one to your list.

On The Water

PASSAGE PLANNING

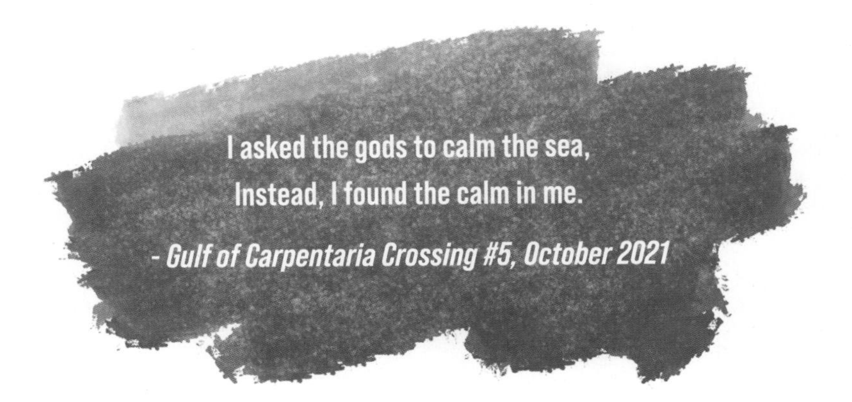

The thing about sailing that keeps me on my toes is the unavoidable truth that the sea decides. Despite all the best planning, weather watching and systems checks, you can never really be sure what will happen on passage or what conditions and challenges you will face. Sometimes it's dull, sometimes you're whispering to the heavens, and sometimes the boat hits its sweet spot and just hums along. This, of course, affects what we eat, but since no one ever complained that they were too prepared for a passage, here are a few tips to help you get your next one right. When planning for passages, even those that last just a few nights, it helps to consider these three things:

1. The number of people you are feeding and the meals and snacks each crew member favours when the sea gets sloppy and appetites wane. This also includes babies and children who need specific snacks, drinks and mini-meals.

2. Tally up the number of meals your crew will eat before you reach your endpoint, and then add plenty of extras in case of weather delays or a lack of wind. Think about snacks and drinks, too, especially for those on overnight helm shifts.

3. Consider the conditions and sea-states you will likely encounter and, realistically, what can be achieved in the galley in those seas. I marvel at sailors who can bake bread in a gale, but since that's not me, Dave and I plan meals that either of us can put together quickly without turning green.

Making Meals

Unless the sea is relatively calm, we try not to spend too much time in the galley on passage. Not everyone has a freezer on board, or a fridge that can handle lots of ready-to-go meals. If you do, consider preparing batches of Puttanesca Pasta sauce and Red Lentil Bolognese, some Veg-out Burger patties and jars of Coriander (or Tropical Almond) Pesto that can be defrosted later in the passage. Pumped with excitement, we rarely sleep much over the first few days, and all this awake time makes for hearty appetites. We invariably crave 'proper' food over snacks, so I ward off the munchies by prebaking things like Save-the-day Silver Beet Pastries, and Rustic Pumpkin Pie, and fry up a big batch of fish for one-handed snacking, like Easy-peasy Panko Strips.

I bake as many loaves of sourdough as the fridge and freezer can handle. These I slice for sandwiches and dunk into mugs of Roasted Garlic & Tomato Soup, which I make and freeze well in advance. Fruit is peeled, prepped and frozen, too, for icy breakfast smoothies, and I keep the fridge stocked with cheeses, boiled eggs and jars of Spiced Pickled Vegetables to snack on and to fill lunchtime wraps. If I haven't already overstocked the fridge, I'll pre-cook a pan of Easy Persian Pilau and freeze vegetable fried rice to heat up when underway, served with finely chopped greens, chilli and fried eggs.

Some sailors like to cook all their passage food at once, but most freezers won't love you if you fill them with too many lukewarm meals. Instead, in the week before any passage begins, I cook up double or triple amounts of every meal I make and freeze the leftovers in suitable portions for our upcoming passage. My freezer doesn't have to work too hard, and I get a head start on my food prep. When you freeze meals, store them in the most compact way possible, either in square or rectangular containers that you can stack close together, or in sturdy (or doubled) snap-lock bags.

One-handed Helm Snacks

If you have room in the fridge for some easy tummy-fillers, make a batch of nori rolls (maki sushi) or Fox Sushi to graze on during your first day at sea. We fill ours with avocado and cucumber, or fresh (or tinned) tuna. Served with pickled ginger and soy sauce, they are easy on the stomach and great for cutlery-free eating while sitting in the cockpit and sailing. Before every passage, Maya bakes the best one-bowl ginger and coconut cakes I've ever tasted, which stay deliciously moist for days.

We also fill a crate with snacks and keep it in the bridgedeck within easy reach of everyone on board. It's stocked with fresh fruit, ginger cookies, muesli bars, plain crackers, corn chips or pretzels, and lots of dried fruits, nuts and seeds. Into it goes our refillable water bottles, a jar of preserved ginger (to soothe tender tummies) and mints to suck on and starve off sleepiness at night.

The menthol aroma of peppermint helps to keep you awake, and it works by stimulating the hippocampus, that part of your brain that controls mental clarity and alertness. Drink a mug of peppermint tea, rub a few drops of peppermint oil on the back of your neck (steering clear of your eyes), or suck on extra strong mints: all will help you feel more awake and help maintain focus and attention.

I also stock the pantry with a range of instant snacks and meals: just-add-water soups and pasta sauces, crackers and spreads, tinned baked beans, pancake mix and a variety of two-minute noodles. All of these foods provide a comforting backup when quick meals are required. I also fill every water bottle we own and make an emergency supply of drinking water, just in case.

Emergency Stores

Seasoned cruisers always have plenty of food on board to cope with delays caused by bad weather, absent wind, breakages or distracting anchorages that are just too lovely to leave. Fridges (like anything on a boat) can falter at the most inopportune moments, and usually when they are full! When our boat buddies *@sailingexcelsior* had their fridge fail them on passage, they also lost a week's worth of precious fresh veggies. Before long passages or any journey that takes you on a remote, shop-free route, top up your supplies of hardy veggies (like pumpkins and potatoes) and other long-life, dry goods. Foods that will feed you after long weeks at sea include rice, noodles, pasta, flour, tinned vegetables, dried, frozen and freeze-dried fruits, nuts, crackers and spreads.

Last-minute Panic Buys

There is always room on a boat for one more treat: a fresh loaf of bread, some cakes and fruit, or chocolate bars to hide until you really need them! Before we set sail, I fly through the supermarket, grabbing one more of everything to ensure the galley is stuffed to its gills. I've never regretted my panic buys because supplies disappear much too soon, and eventually, you open your cupboards and only foreign labels stare back at you. That's when you know you've gotten yourself far, faraway, but there's no harm in delaying that moment by stocking up with a decent, last-minute panic shop.

SEASICKNESS & QUEASY BELLIES

Seasickness can strike at any time, and even the most stoic sailors are not immune. For many, it's worst when the sea lacks a rhythm or when you are head first in the engine bay, cooking a meal or attending to kids. And usually, just when you really want to curl up on the couch in misery, the sea calls you to attention to reef sails and make decisions (interestingly, the word *nausea* comes from the Greek word *naus*, meaning 'ship').

A fortunate few swear they are never afflicted, but I expect these sailors keep a firm fix on the horizon and stay outside in the breeze. Having your hands on the helm helps enormously, too, bringing you in tune with the boat and restoring your balance. The helm seat is my favourite place to be in a blow because with my hands on the boat (even if I'm clinging for dear life), I move in unison with it rather than resisting and reacting. Being pitched and tossed inside brings on seasickness fast, but on deck, the fresh air and a soft gaze out to sea always helps.

When it comes to remedies, I've tried more than a few, from acupressure wristbands to natural oils and various over-the-counter drugs. Everyone has their preferred elixir, but none have worked better for me than natural ginger and fresh air. I bake ginger into cakes and cookies, nibble crystallised chunks on the helm, sip ginger cordial and freeze it into icy poles. I'm rarely queasy these days because I know my limits, and for me, rough conditions mean that fussy meals, reading and schoolwork are completely off the table.

Ginger

The rhizome of the *Zingiber officinale* plant, ginger is widely regarded by sailors as a safe and effective preventative for nausea and seasickness when taken in advance. Many scientists agree, even if they are still grappling to understand just how ginger works.

An oft-cited 2002 clinical trial of 13 candidates – men and women susceptible to seasickness - found that taking 1000mg of ginger before experiencing adverse motion conditions not only reduced the severity of nausea but delayed its onset and shortened recovery times too (Lien, Sun, Chen, et al., 2003, American Journal of Physiology).

If you are a sufferer who has tried every pill, potion and gadget on the market, returning to ginger can be a breath of fresh air. All available research points to the power of ginger's volatile oils – gingerols and shogaols – that stimulate the production of digestive juices and neutralise the stomach acids that cause nausea and motion sickness. Scientists believe that eating ginger stabilises blood pressure, which lessens nausea too. This is altogether different to the way anti-nausea drugs and acupressure bands work, by interrupting or shutting down messages to your brain. Guidelines on recommended daily adult dosages range from 1000 to 1500mg, taken in small doses spread throughout the day, a dosage supported by the findings of Lien, Sun, Chen, et al.

You can buy ginger fresh, crushed, powdered, preserved, pickled or crystallised. A knob of fresh ginger keeps forever when bagged and frozen, and ginger tablets are a good standby, available from chemists. While it can work miracles, it pays to remember that ginger is a natural blood thinner and, in very high doses, may cause heartburn. If you prefer to put your trust in homeopathic remedies, naturopaths often recommend baptisia and Nux Vomica to settle seasickness, especially when nausea progresses to vomiting.

Ginger For Queasy Bellies

Ginger works best as a preventative, so mix up this quick remedy before you set sail. Combine two teaspoons of freshly grated ginger with two tablespoons of honey, which is enough for four doses. Take one dose about 45 minutes before you get moving and as needed throughout your journey. If you start to feel nauseous, you can also nibble on crystallised (or candied) ginger or scoop out some of my tummy-calming Pear and Ginger Sorbet. Ginger tea also works great. I make ours by grating 1 to 2 teaspoons of fresh ginger into a cup of hot water with a squeeze of lemon and a spoonful of honey. Leave for a few minutes, then sip slowly, breathe deeply and try to relax.

Tummy Calming Ices

Honey Melon & Ginger Ice

Feeds 4 · Prep 10 mins + Freezing · GF, V

1 honeydew melon

2 tbsp ginger cordial

250ml (8.5oz) sugar-free lemonade (lemon soda) or soda water

Cut the rind and seeds from the melon and slice it into chunks. Blitz with ginger cordial until smooth, then stir in the lemonade or soda water. Pour into a shallow metal tin, cover with foil and freeze for 3 hours or until frozen around the edges. Break up with a fork, spoon into glasses or bowls, and serve.

Pear & Ginger Sorbet

Feeds 4 · Prep 15 mins + Freezing · Cook 25 mins · GF

⅓ cup finely chopped fresh (or frozen) ginger

6 sprigs fresh mint

rind of one lemon

2 cups no-added-sugar apple juice

400g (14.oz) tinned pears in natural juice

1 free-range egg white

In a small saucepan, gently heat the finely chopped ginger, 6 roughly chopped mint sprigs, lemon rind and 1 cup of apple juice. Bring to the boil, then reduce the heat and simmer, covered for 20 minutes. Leave the mixture to cool, then strain and reserve the juice. Puree the pears and pear juice and combine them with the cooled ginger mix and the remaining apple juice. Pour into a glass or ceramic dish and freeze for 4 hours.

Remove the sorbet from the freezer and break it up with a metal spoon. Whisk the egg white until stiff peaks form, then fold it into the sorbet. Transfer to a food processor or use a hand beater to blend the sorbet into a smooth, icy mixture. Return to the freezer for 8 hours or until set.

GALLEY REMEDIES & NATURAL FIRST AID

We try to keep our boat as chemical-free as possible. For me, that means creating simple, natural products to safely clean everything from hands to benchtops and bathrooms, and which keep the boat bug- and mould-free. The following recipes contain gentle, non-toxic ingredients that are easily stored and have a hundred uses. All contain essential oils, which degrade in heat and light, so store them in a cool cupboard, safely out of reach of small children.

Since sailing adventures are imbued with more risk than most, having a well-stocked first aid kit - and knowledge of how to use it – is essential for all of us. Mine contains all the usual pills, potions and remedies, many of which are natural products well suited to the sailing life. Here are some simple, natural ways to deal with the dings and scrapes that most regularly strike sailors.

Minor Cuts & Scratches

Indigenous Australians have used tea tree oil for centuries as an antiseptic for treating skin infections and cleaning and healing minor cuts, scratches and grazes. A cut is considered minor only when it is shallow (less than 1mm deep), doesn't expose fat or muscle tissue, is not gaping, measures 1cm or less, and stops bleeding within 15 minutes of applied pressure. To treat a minor cut or scrape, wash and dry the affected area well, then apply a dab of aloe vera gel mixed with two drops each of tea tree (*Melaleuca alternifolia*) and pure lavender oils. Alternatively, mix a few drops of either oil with witch hazel or a cup of fresh, cool water and cleanse the wound by applying with cotton wool. Repeat a couple of times a day until the cut heals.

Bites & Stings

Mosquitoes: to relieve the itch, pain and swelling of mosquito bites, apply a neat dab of tea tree oil, which has analgesic (pain-relieving), anti-inflammatory, and antimicrobial properties to fight bacteria, fungus and viruses. For kids and anyone with sensitive skin, dilute a few drops of tea tree oil in a tablespoon of witch hazel or any cold-pressed edible oil (almond or olive oil) and apply to the bite. At a pinch, you can relieve pain by rubbing the area with a slice of lemon or a dab of apple cider vinegar.

Bees: Nothing brings a kid to tears quicker than a bee sting. Once you've removed the stinger by scraping sideways across the bite (a credit card works well), pour some vinegar over it, or hold a fresh slice of onion over the sting for immediate pain relief.

Bull Ants: Little kids might love the old 'pee on it' remedy, but for everyone else, gently rub the sting site with aloe vera gel to relieve the pain and reduce swelling. Aloe vera is a natural pain reliever, antiseptic and healing agent sold as a gel. Store it in the fridge to keep it nice and cool.

Jellyfish: pouring or spraying immediately with undiluted vinegar is the best first reaction to treating and relieving the pain of jellyfish stings. Some marine stingers – Irukandji and box jellyfish, for example – can be deadly. Learn to identify these and seek immediate medical assistance if encountered.

Bruising, Sprains & Swelling

Along with rest, elevation and ice, a salve containing arnica flowers (*Arnica montana*) applied up to four times daily can promote healing and reduce the bruising that comes with sprains. Arnica works by entering your skin's small capillaries to stimulate circulation and to move on the toxins that cause inflammation and swelling. Just a few drops of arnica oil is all it takes, but it should never be applied to broken skin or used on children under two years old.

Minor Burns

Any serious burn – one that is bigger than your palm, extremely painful or blistered – requires immediate and continued dousing with cold water as you make your way towards the nearest hospital. For minor burns, pour cold water over the affected area as soon as possible and continue for at least 10 minutes or until the pain subsides. To protect and soothe the burn after it has cooled, smear with pure, certified organic aloe vera gel (*Aloe barbadensis*), and cover with a loose, non-stick dressing. You can grow your own aloe vera plant on board and use it. Lucas' papaw ointment works to heal minor burns (including sunburn), as does naturally antimicrobial honey, but it needs to be therapeutic, sterile honey, and it should never be used on children or patients with a known sensitivity to bee or pollen products.

Colds

Struggling with a cold at sea can make you feel especially miserable, but this simple steam inhalation can help clear your head. Eucalyptus and tea tree are known for their potent antimicrobial properties. Add a few drops of either oil and a squeeze of fresh lemon juice to a bowl of boiling water (a crushed handful of fresh leaves works brilliantly too). Place your head over the bowl, cover it with a towel, close your eyes and breathe deeply for five to ten minutes, taking a break to breathe cool air whenever necessary.

Sore Throats

Bay leaves can help fight bacteria and viruses (which most colds are). Pour boiling water into a cup containing four bay leaves, set aside to cool slightly, then use as a mouth gargle. Or, add a cinnamon stick, a teaspoonful of honey and a squeeze of lemon juice, and sip it slowly. I make an effective saltwater gargle by dissolving one teaspoon of salt in a half-filled mug of hot water. Set aside to cool slightly, and then gargle until it's empty.

Headaches

Peppermint oil and analgesic lavender oil can both help to relieve headaches. Simply massage a few drops of either oil into your temples and around the nape of your neck, breathe deeply and relax for a few minutes. For children and those with sensitive skin, mix the lavender oil first with a little edible oil before applying it to their skin.

Available from health food stores, Rescue Remedy can help you cope with sudden stress or sleep difficulties that often lead to headaches (including stress exhibited in pets).

Aches & Pains

There are plenty of heat rubs on the market to soothe achy legs and joints, but here's a simple, natural salve you might like to try. Blend equal amounts of ginger, eucalyptus and peppermint essential oils with two teaspoons of a cold-pressed edible oil and gently massage directly into the affected area.

About Essential Oils

Essential oils are potent: never consume them, keep them out of reach of children and don't get them near eyes, mouths or genitals.

Do an allergy test first: before using essential oils or aloe vera on your skin for the first time, dab some on the inside of your elbow and wait a few minutes. If a rash appears or the skin begins to sting, wash it off and use something else.

Always dilute essential oils before using them on children by blending them with witch hazel, pure water or edible oils such as olive, coconut or almond oil.

Store essential oils in small, dark glass bottles, out of direct sunlight and in the coolest place possible to keep them stable.

WILD ONE

Mossie
Spray
Hand
Sanitiser

Bug Repellent

Mosquitoes are expert detectors of body heat and human scents, with the most pungent being carbon dioxide and sweat. You're a target in the tropics because your body is hotter, you wear fewer clothes, and you sweat more, expelling odorous lactic acid and allowing bacteria to cultivate on the skin. That is why the most effective repellent is simply taking a shower (or at least throwing yourself overboard for a rinse). Wash before dusk to lower your body temperature, use unperfumed soap and resist spraying with antiperspirants afterwards.

Some species of mosquitoes are lured by the carbon dioxide we breathe out, which is why those females buzz around your face and attack hands and feet too. The blood at your extremities is much more CO_2-rich since it's furthest from your lungs, where CO_2 is filtered and exhaled. Mossies can hit their mark because hands and feet in the tropics are often left exposed.

For all kinds of mossies, a repellent can really mask your scent, but since your skin sucks up whatever you feed it, avoiding toxic repellents is vital. If you do choose a DEET-based repellent, especially when cruising through malaria-prone countries, try spraying it on your clothes rather than on your skin. Otherwise, find a natural option and apply it early, generously and often. I've patiently tried and tested my fair share of natural repellents, and here's what works for me.

⅓ cup witch hazel

⅓ cup carrier oil (almond, jojoba, olive)

1 tsp (100 drops) of essential oils

Combine witch hazel with your choice of carrier oil and add any combination of these mossie-deterring oils: tea tree, lavender, thyme, lemongrass, peppermint or eucalyptus, and a few drops of citronella or cinnamon, or both. Make up a gentler batch for kids by adding just half the quantity of essential oils. Store in a dark glass bottle, shake well being applying and avoid the eyes and mouth. Like all natural repellents, they should be applied to clean, perfume-free skin. Spray it on early, generously and often.

Hand Sanitiser

I use a lot of hand sanitiser on the boat because it saves water usage in the bathroom and is gentler on the skin than many soaps. My homemade version lacks the high-alcohol content (minimum 60 per cent) that combats every pathogen you might encounter on trips ashore, but I find it perfectly suitable for use on board and especially in the bathroom. It's a fresh take on the age-old 'Thieves Oil', which grave robbers used during the Middle Ages to prevent catching bubonic plague from the infected bodies they touched. I stick to essential oils with known antibacterial and antimicrobial properties and regularly experiment with different combinations of these scents.

1 tbsp pure organic aloe vera gel

2 tbsp witch hazel

100ml water

15 drops of pure essential oils: choose tea tree, eucalyptus, rosemary, thyme, lavender, peppermint, lemongrass, lemon, and just 1-2 drops of either clove and cinnamon, or both.

½ tsp vitamin E oil (optional)

Pour all ingredients into a dark glass bottle, shake well, and use to fill as many spray bottles as you need.

Surface Cleaner

I use this vinegar-based cleaner to sterilise and clean all the hard surfaces on my boat: benchtops, stainless steel sinks, fridges, stoves, my dining table and all the messes in my bathroom. I add antimicrobial essential oils, favouring fresh scents like lemon and eucalyptus, but you can choose the ones you like best.

1 cup filtered water

1 cup white vinegar (at least 5% acetic acid content)

¼ tsp essential oils (about 25 drops)

Combine all ingredients in a large spray bottle, shake well, spray surfaces and wipe with a clean, damp cloth. Vinegar shouldn't be sprayed on marble or granite surfaces, but that's rarely a concern on boats.

Mould Spray

There are two ways I kill surface mould on my boat.

Pure vinegar: for mould on hard surfaces, spray generously with undiluted vinegar and wait for at least an hour (or more). Half-fill a small bucket or bowl with equal amounts of vinegar and water, add a squeeze of washing-up detergent and use a clean cloth to wipe all surfaces and remove the mould. Change your rinse water regularly if cleaning a large surface area.

Clove oil spray takes a little longer to work, but I find it more effective at slowing the return of mould. Dilute 1/4 teaspoon of pure clove oil in one litre of water, shake well and pour into a spray bottle. Spray on walls, ceilings and bathrooms and leave for 24 hours before wiping off with a clean, damp cloth. Respray all surfaces and leave them to dry. I use the same mixture to kill mould on soft fabrics, too, especially those items that are difficult to launder: pillows, doonas, kid's stuffed toys, couch cushions, backpacks and winter coats. You really need to saturate the fabric and then leave items to dry in the sun, so this method is not ideal for precious fabrics that might hold a stain. Clove oil will kill mould, but it won't remove the mould stain (you'll need to wash and bleach items for that).

COOKING WITH KIDS

Cooking is a bit like life: it doesn't always turn out the way you planned, and it often gets messy, but it is far more fun when shared. For kids, the fun in your galley makes for great playtime (all that measuring and mixing, rolling, stirring and taste-testing), and I've never met a kid that I couldn't coax to join the chaos.

I have learnt a few tricks to make the experience rewarding for everyone. I like to start by letting kids choose their own recipes to prepare, even if I steer them towards speedy ones they can create without too much adult interference. The recipes really need to be simple, because if an adult has to constantly take over, mini-chefs have a habit of quickly wandering off.

Older kids (around ten years plus) have all sorts of recipes at their disposal because using knives, the stove and the oven under your guidance are usually within their capabilities. However, if your kids are younger, you'll need fast, simple dishes that are safe to prepare and that the kids can claim to have cooked all by themselves.

Once you've chosen a recipe, set out all the ingredients, gather an assortment of measuring cups, mixing bowls and wooden spoons and wash the kids' hands. If cooking with school-age kids, get them to read through the recipe and use cup measurements to practise maths along the way.

No-bake slices, desserts and cakes are all good choices for young cooks, with plenty of measuring, stirring, yummy spoons to lick and a great 'canvas' to decorate afterwards. Healthy meal options that excite them include frittata slices, cheese and vegetable muffins, individually styled pizzas and any meal that can be eaten without cutlery. Try rolling and wrapping little packages to eat with hands: dumplings, sung choi bao in lettuce cups, pastries, sushi and fresh rice paper rolls.

Maya has been playing alongside me in the galley since she was a toddler and now smiles with satisfaction when the night's meal is completely her own. Stage a cooking session with kids when there is no rush to get food on the table and try not to fuss about the mess until all the baking is done and dusted.

Tips For Mini-Chefs

Play it safe: Choose recipes with little or no stovetop activities.

Keep kids busy: Keep those short attention spans focused by choosing recipes that require rolling, measuring, mixing, cracking of eggs and stirring.

"I made it myself": Let young cooks do as much as possible by themselves. Too much adult interference and independent kids will get frustrated and switch off.

Keep it tasty: You don't have to cook sweet treats all the time. Seek out healthy dishes with tastes and textures that your kids will enjoy eating.

Expect a mess: Cooking with kids is generally messy, so clear the bench and have extra quantities of ingredients on hand so that should something get spilt or knocked over, the experience won't end in tears.

Tried-and-true works best: Choose recipes that are foolproof and preferably that you have tried before to reduce the chances that the recipe fails and your disappointed child takes it personally.

Maya

MONINI

COOKING OVER FIRE

I love campfire cooking. It's fun, simple and smoky hot coals not only add an unbeatable aroma to food, but they demand that you sit down around them, relax and take in your surroundings while some freshly baked food sharpens your appetite. End-of-day beach campfires are a great way to interact with whoever happens to be in your anchorage without actually having them on your boat. The bonus for messy boat people like me is that you don't have to run around shoving things into random cupboards before people turn up, or play paper-scissors-rock with your crew over who gets to clean the toilet.

Striking a campfire on the shore quickly gathers people together and pulls you off the boat for a leg stretch, a swim in the shallows or beach games with kids. If you hit the sand with a pot of bread to bake, fish parcels to grill or potatoes to roast, you can salute the sunset and then head back home with dinner already done. There is one tiny downside to campfire cooking, and it's the sand that wrangles its way into foil-wrapped potatoes and destroys your carefully grilled fish when someone shakes their sarong.

To keep my meals sand-free, I like to cook in a cast iron camp oven with the lid firmly in place. Heavy, yes, but camp ovens can withstand a lot of heat, cooking food evenly without burning or sticking, just as long as they are properly oiled before use. Mine is big enough to bake a sourdough loaf or a damper or roast a pile of vegetables. With its lid firmly in place, it can be partially buried in hot coals on the edge of the fire to bake away while we stoke the fire and stare into the flames. A wire rack or grill basket placed over hot campfire coals separates the foil-wrapped fish from the sand. If we get lucky with crabs, the elevated wire rack holds our biggest saucepan, too, filled with water to boil up our catch.

When we're doing a lot of beach hopping, my assembled campfire kit includes:

our camp oven

our wire rack or grill basket

lighters

aluminium foil for wrapping up roast veggies

olive oil for coating the camp oven

pot mittens and tea towels

long tongs for turning grilled fish and potatoes

folding camp shovel (for shifting hot coals)

bucket for extinguishing our fire

a beach mat

natural bug repellent (page 57)

mugs, plates and cutlery

a bottle of port

a bag of marshmallows to enjoy as the campfire embers burn down

Just about anything you can cook on a stove, in an oven or on a barbeque, you can cook over a fire, but some things are easier than others. Here are my tips for some easy, delicious food you can cook ashore.

Baking Bread: Get a good, hot fire going, and then wait until the flames die down to a nice bed of smouldering coals. Oil your camp oven well and preheat it by placing it briefly on the hot coals while you dig a shallow hole on one side of your campfire, away from any flames. Shovel a few amber coals into the hole. Transfer your bread dough into the camp oven, secure it with a lid, place it in the hole and cover it with hot coals. Baking time will depend on the size of your loaf and the heat of your fire. Check it after 20 minutes – when baked, bread will sound hollow when tapped – and allow up to 30 minutes or until your loaf is golden.

Campfire Veggies: Cook your veggies in a second camp oven placed directly on hot coals at the fire's edge. I like to cook this way because it's waste-free, but you can also fire-roast potatoes and chunks of sweet potato by double-wrapping them in aluminium foil. Be generous with your foil to keep sand out, and spray or smear the first layer with olive oil to prevent the foil from sticking to your veggies. Buried beneath the coals, medium-sized potatoes take about 40 minutes to cook, so get them cooking before you start grilling your fish.

Paperbark Fish: Indigenous Australians traditionally bake the best barramundi, wrapping big fish in paperbark and burying it in hot sand. When you've got some time on your hands, it's a pretty foolproof (and waste-free) way to cook just about any large-size firm fish and a bit of fun too. To get started, dig a shallow pit (about 40cm deep) and let a small wood fire burn down to coals. Gut and wash your fish and wrap it tightly in several sheets of paperbark, sneaking in some fresh herbs (try lemon-scented myrtle if you can find it), a handful of roasted macadamia nuts, or some garlic and butter.

When the fire dies down, throw some green grass and fresh leaves over the coals, place your wrapped fish in the pit and cover it with hot coals. Traditionally, Indigenous Australians would have heated river stones on the fire and put them on top of the fish to help it cook. Fill the pit loosely with sand and let the fish bake for about an hour (90 minutes for a really large fish). Carefully dig it out and leave it to rest for 10 minutes before unwrapping and eating right on the beach. You can also oven-bake paperbark barramundi for an hour at 200°C (390°F) and let it stand for 15 minutes before unwrapping.

Chargrilled Bamboo Fruit: For a super easy campfire dessert, thread chunks of fresh fruit onto bamboo skewers that have been soaked in water for 20 minutes: strawberries, mango, peaches, plums, nectarines, bananas or pears. Grill the fruit sticks over campfire coals or on a solid barbecue plate, and serve drizzled with honey or melted chocolate and UHT cream, a dollop of custard or some thick Greek yoghurt.

Once you're done cooking, revelling and fire-gazing for the night, it's important to extinguish your fire with heaps of seawater rather than just covering it with sand. Fires covered in sand can smoulder well intothe following day (and the sand stays very hot) when some unsuspecting beachcomber, child or wildlife could walk across it and get burned. Just as bad, the fire can reignite and start a wilder fire.

Bebe
Girls

The Hunter

FISH

We love it when locals sidle alongside *Wild One* in dugouts laden with fresh fish, fruit and bush taros to trade. It's a chance to swap things we could both use, learn some language and laugh a little too. We always have things on board that remote-living people want: sunglasses, shirts, goggles or fins, hats and fishing lures, and school supplies for kids.

The worst trade we ever did was easily the most enjoyable. On the west Papuan coast, flying fish harvesters run out buoyed ropes slung with palm frond mats that lure flying fish to lay their eggs in a thick, bright orange mass. In return for squid jigs and reels, we were gifted an armload of flying fish eggs, which taste like sulphur and salt with a texture that's difficult to swallow. Despite the bonus bananas that were thrown in, the fish eggs were still not our finest of trades. But we practised Bahasa Indonesian and had a really good laugh, and then waited until they'd disappeared before sliding those fish eggs back into the sea. When it comes to fish, we prefer ours fully grown.

Boat-caught Pelagics

Our boat *Wild One* really pulls its weight when we sail, and it's a rare (or rough) day on the water when we don't have at least one hand line out. We regularly (fingers crossed) catch all kinds of tuna and mackerel, giant trevally, and maybe a mahi mahi (dolphinfish or dorado) or a wahoo this way. I tend to keep the lines out longer than Catherine, but as long as we wind them in before sunset, we can usually avoid snaring sharks and the delicate mission of getting them off the line without harm.

On long, leisurely sails, we'll often detour across sandy shoals or pinnacles where large pelagics (and the seabirds that give them away) tend to hunt. We use large hand lines secured to the stern rails with bungy loops to take the shock load when a large pelagic bites down. Ours are wrapped with overpowered 350-500 pound mono to prevent big fish from snapping the lines. I add a heavy-duty swivel, and trolling lures are crimped on for strength and to make the system more streamlined. I never tie knots, and we rarely lose a fish and never a lure (although they do get retired after too many bites). My favourite lures are Halco's deep diving, red-and-white 'Qantas' lures, but when big pelagics are around, I swap the standard treble hooks out for large singles. There are a few reasons I choose hand lines over boat rods. Firstly, hand lines are dirt cheap and available everywhere (we often beachcomb them off the high tide mark). They have no moving parts to break and are very quick to wind in when retrieving a catch, although you do need a bit of strength to wrangle in big fish. Being on a catamaran, we can run out two lines without them fouling each other.

But we do run them at different distances (one 25 metres, the other 40 metres) and with lures that swim at different depths.

Catching fish by boat is by no means a certainty, but it increases our chances of reaching an anchorage with protein ready to cook. I can't stress enough how important it is to kill your catch swiftly and humanely, even when underway. If the sailing conditions become too hectic to deal with a potential catch, I feel it's better to pull the lines in rather than catch a fish that I can't treat properly and respectfully.

There are lots of ways to bring large pelagics on board when underway, but here's what I do aboard *Wild One*. Once gaffed and safely on board, dispatch your catch humanely and swiftly by spiking its brain. The brain is located in the middle of the fish's head, just behind the eye, and you will know when you've hit it because your fish will spasm briefly, its fins will flare for a moment, and then the fish will then go limp. To bleed the fish, lay it flat and cut behind the gills with your knife facing towards the fish's head. Slice from top to bottom until you see blood flow, then repeat on the other side. Submerge or rinse the fish well in salt water, or if conditions permit, drag it by its tail for a minute or two to flush and clean it ready for filleting.

Slice off your fillets (don't wet the fish again if you can help it), and place them in a large colander over a bowl (covered with a beeswax wrap or similar) to drain and rest in the fridge. This resting helps drain the lactic acid that builds up in large, fighting pelagic fish. I usually drain fillets overnight, and whatever doesn't get eaten while it's fresh is bagged, labelled and frozen.

Some sailors abhor the idea of sending fresh fish to the freezer, but when we're cruising, especially in remote sailing grounds, fish provide an essential source of protein, and nothing is wasted. Those species that are prolific and sustainably caught, prepared with respect and fully utilised to reduce wastage, can help to feed you and your family when stores are a distant memory, and on all those days when the fish aren't biting.

Shore Fishing

Boat life can get busy, but when I do have some downtime, you'll find me holding the end of a rod while nursing something cold at day's end. When we jump into the dinghy to explore a new anchorage or to head ashore, I'll always run a few lines out in the hope of snaring a fish before we hit the beach. If we have to use our fuel, we may as well turn every dinghy run into a fishing expedition. When trolling in the tender along reefs, sand troughs or mangrove-fringed shorelines, I use a scaled-down version of the hand reels on board, or cast an overhead bait caster rod with smaller hard body lures or soft plastics. This rod combo is extremely accurate when trying to land a lure into a tight location, or when chasing those ever-elusive barramundi, mangrove jack, and delicious varieties of cod. These fighters demand patience and are all excellent eating, but if things don't go your way, the mangroves are also great places to gather a feed of oysters at low tide. In northern Australia, queenfish and trevally are regularly caught while dinghy trolling over sandbars, off river mouths, over inshore reefs, and sometimes by rod while standing on a beach with a beer.

Spearing Reef Fish

We spend a lot of time cruising in the tropics where coral reefs, and the trout, snapper, jobfish and trevally they nurture, are generally abundant. Anytime we can get in the water is an adventure, and while we are exploring a new reef, spearfishing provides a selective way to get dinner on board. With a long enough breath-hold and plenty of patience, spearfishing can provide us with a meal in a manner that's sustainable and respectful to the reefs. This is really what got me into spearfishing because I can consciously choose a fish that is of suitable size and abundant in the places we drop anchor without harming any other fish in the process. It's also a great skill to learn, provides an excellent workout, and is one of the most authentic ways to take a fish. I use a Rob Allen 1200 Sniper rail gun with dual bands and a 7mm carbon steel shaft. I find that the shaft stays true and is more accurate than other guns I've owned.

When You Have To Buy Fish

Sometimes the fish just aren't biting, and the reef fish are too skittish and too small to be speared. When we face a dry spell, we revert to our vegetarian ways, tucking into tempeh, beans, eggs and lentils. There's always the option of buying fish as we go, from passing fishermen who visit our anchorages or in local markets where the daily catch comes with few food miles. But bigger centres and supermarkets challenge conscious consumers who want to know just how sustainable their dinner really is. It can be difficult (and sometimes impossible) to know where and how a fish has been caught and whether a particular species is abundant in the location where it was taken.

These questions matter. Over three-quarters of the world's oceans are over-fished. Thanks to our collective, growing hunger for seafood, all ocean ecosystems, including by-catch populations, are in peril. The bulk of the guilt can be levied at large-scale fishing operations – trawlers, longliners and gillnetters. But even at local levels, the stripping of coral reefs and continuing use of dynamite (blast) fishing has a devastating, irreversible impact.

When a blast went off in eastern Indonesia's Kei Islands in late 2022, we thought our rigging had snapped and the mast was coming down. We rushed out on deck, puzzled and perplexed, only to see a boatload of fishermen working with hand nets to scoop up fish. This desperate means to a meal is short-sighted at best, and the heartbreaking destruction of the reef and its minute and complex ecosystems will haunt these island populations for decades to come.

Fish farms or 'sea ranches' don't always provide a better alternative and can be incredibly wasteful. Take, for example, Australia's southern bluefin tuna. This critically endangered species is caught from the wild and fattened in feedlots off the South Australian coast, primarily for export to foreign markets. The Australian Marine Conservation Society (AMCS) reports that it takes up to 12 kilograms of wild-caught fish to grow one kilogram of southern bluefin tuna. The maths just doesn't add up, and wild-caught fish stocks used as tuna food are jeopardised further by the release of pollution from aquaculture farms back into the sea via uneaten fishmeal, antibiotics, vaccines and concentrated fish waste.

The good news is that you can wade through the confusion by downloading the *Sustainable Seafood Guide* app or check your choices at goodfish.org.au. In the USA, download the *Seafood Watch Consumer Guide* for an list of best buys wherever you live (seafoodwatch.org).

Yakitori Grilled Fish

Makes about 15 · Prep 10 mins + Marinading time
Cook 40 mins · GF

750g (1.5lb) firm white fish (about 3 fillets)

2 garlic cloves, crushed or finely grated

peanut or coconut oil for grilling

1 bunch of broccolini (or other fresh greens)

3 spring onions (scallion), sliced green tops

2 tbsp toasted sesame seeds

⅓ cup of ready-made yakitori sauce (or DIY)

15 bamboo skewers

Yakitori Sauce

½ cup tamari (or soy sauce)

½ cup mirin

¼ cup sake

¼ cup water

2 tsp brown sugar

1 spring onion, green tops only

To make your own yakitori sauce, combine all sauce ingredients in a small saucepan and, over high heat, bring the mixture to a boil. Reduce the heat to low, and simmer uncovered until the liquid is reduced to a third of its original volume (allow 25-30 minutes). Set it aside to cool.

Meanwhile, soak 15 bamboo skewers in water, so they don't burn during grilling. Cut the fish fillets into bite-sized chunks and place them in a mixing bowl with the garlic and about half the yakitori sauce (keep the remainder for basting). Allow the fish to marinate for 30 minutes in the fridge.

When ready to eat, oil your grill, hot plate or frypan and get a medium to high heat going. Thread the fish pieces on skewers and discard the marinade. Cook the fish skewers for about 10 minutes, turning and brushing with reserved yakitori sauce. Meanwhile, trim the broccolini stems (or other greens, choy sum works well), and blanch or stir-fry until tender. Place the fish skewers on a serving plate and top with tender broccolini, fresh, sliced spring onions and toasted sesame seeds.

Cape Flattery Spanish Mackerel

with mango salad

Feeds 4 · Prep 15 mins · Cook 5-10 mins

4 Spanish mackerel fillets
(or other firm large fillets)

juice of a lime (about 2 tbsp)

3 tsp fish sauce

3 tsp rice malt syrup
(or equivalent sweetener)

1 small garlic clove, finely chopped

1 tsp dried crushed chillies

2 tsp Thai-flavoured herb paste

¾ cup plain (all-purpose) flour

salt and pepper

coconut or peanut oil for frying

¼ cup chopped roasted peanuts

fresh coriander (cilantro)
sprigs (optional)

Mango Salad

2 firm, ripe mangoes
(or 425g/14oz tin, drained well)

½ small red onion

227g (8oz) tinned water
chestnuts, drained

100g (3.5oz) salad greens

¼ cup fresh coriander sprigs

Dressing

juice of a lime (2 tbsp)

2 tsp fish sauce

3 tsp rice malt syrup
(or equivalent sweetener)

2 tsp rice vinegar

1 tbsp peanut oil

1 tsp dried crushed chillies

Good things happen when you find yourself far, faraway. When asked to shoot a cooking video after long months at sea, we found ourselves rather short on supplies. Fishing wasn't allowed in our island anchorage, so we sailed to the mainland in search of something to cook. Fringed by coconut palms and a strip of silky white sand (reputed to be amongst the purest in the world), Cape Flattery's shimmering blue bay is where big fish get airborne and sea eagles soar. You can cast a lure off the oyster-encrusted rocks for mangrove jack and barramundi or troll (as Dave did, to my enormous relief) for a huge, 122cm-long Spanish mackerel.

Teamed with a sneaky tin of mango I found hiding in the back of the cupboard and some green things from my micro garden (rocket, kale, lettuce and coriander), this dish continues to remind me that it's possible to eat well, no matter how far away you find yourself. Spanish mackerel is a strong-flavoured fish that can handle a potent marinade. If that's not what's swimming in your waters, substitute any other firm, large fillets.

To marinade the fish, whisk together the lime juice, fish sauce, rice malt syrup, chopped garlic, crushed chillies and Thai herb paste in a mixing bowl. Add the fish fillets, coat them in the marinade and refrigerate for 30 minutes.

Meanwhile, prepare the mango salad. Slice the mangoes (drained well if using tinned), and thinly slice the red onion and water chestnuts. Combine in a salad bowl and refrigerate. Pour all the dressing ingredients into a glass jar and shake well. Refrigerate until needed.

When it's time to eat, shake the flour into a shallow dish and season generously with salt and pepper. Heat 1-2 tablespoons of peanut or coconut oil in a frypan, coat the fish lightly in seasoned flour and drop straight into the pan. Cook for about 2-3 minutes a side (depending on the thickness of the fillets).

Add the salad greens and coriander sprigs to your salad bowl, pour over the dressing and toss well. Serve alongside the fish, topped with crushed roasted peanuts and coriander sprigs.

Queenfish Kokoda

Feeds 6 · Prep 10 mins · Rest 2-3 hrs · GF, NC

Love it or hate it, raw fish gets a lot of people excited. When you land a beautiful fish (and it doesn't have to be tuna), or someone gifts you a couple of fresh fillets after a day at sea, ceviche is a tasty, no-fuss way to get any meal started. This Fijian-style ceviche, known as kokoda, balances out the raw fish perfectly and packs it with flavour. To add crunch (and stretch the dish), stir through chopped tomato, cucumber and fresh capsicum before serving, and dish it up in coconut shells, clams or lettuce cups. Otherwise, savour it in its virgin state, slowly.

500g (1lb) queenfish (or any firm white fish)

2-3 limes

¼ tsp sea salt

2 finely chopped spring onions (scallion)
(or ½ red onion or 4-5 shallots)

⅓ cup finely chopped coriander (cilantro) and mint

1 fresh red chilli, finely chopped
(or 1 tsp dried crushed chilli)

⅓ cup coconut milk

cracked black pepper

extra fresh coriander sprigs to serve

Optional: add 1 roughly chopped tomato, 1 small cucumber (diced) and ½ small capsicum (bell pepper), chopped.

Trim and rinse the fish, pat dry and cut into small cubes. Place in a mixing bowl and squeeze over 1 ½ limes. Season with salt, and toss to combine. Refrigerate for 2-3 hours until the fish turns opaque. When ready to eat, drain the fish, add the spring onion, chopped herbs, chilli, coconut milk, a generous pinch of black pepper and any extra vegetables, and stir well. Serve with lime wedges and extra coriander sprigs.

24-hour Gravlax

Feeds 4 · Prep 15 mins · Rest 1 day · NC

Dill grows reliably in salty environs, so if you have it in your herb pots, use it to flavour any small catch of firm white fish that comes your way. The only other thing you need is patience, because this meal is one whole day in the making.

225g (0.5lb) queenfish (or other firm white fish)

1 lemon

2 tsp coarse sea salt

good pinch of cracked black pepper

1 ½ tbsp finely chopped fresh dill

1 tbsp extra virgin olive oil

Serve with bread toasts.

Combine the finely grated zest of half a lemon, 2 teaspoons sea salt, a crack of black pepper and 1 tablespoon of the chopped dill. Rub the mixture onto both sides of the fish fillet, sprinkle with 1 tablespoon of lemon juice, then cover and refrigerate. Save the rest of the lemon or juice.

After 24 hours, rinse and pat the fish dry with paper towel. Place the fillets on a chopping board and use a very sharp knife to cut wafer-thin, diagonal slices. Make a dressing by combining the juice of half a lemon with 1 tbsp of extra virgin olive oil and 1/2 tbsp of fresh dill. Drizzle the cured fish with the dressing and serve with bread toasts.

with blue murder

Easy-peasy Panko Strips

Makes 10 · Prep 10 mins + 30 mins Marinading Cook 10 mins · QC

A fresh catch of fish doesn't need much fussing with, so this classic crowd-pleaser has only one twist. Give your strips a 30-minute dip in a zesty, garlicky marinade before breadcrumbing and frying them to golden perfection.

400g (14oz) firm white fish

2 garlic cloves, finely chopped

½ lemon, zest and juice

salt and pepper

1 tbsp extra virgin olive oil

2 free-range eggs

1 cup panko breadcrumbs

½ cup plain (all-purpose) flour

coconut or peanut oil to fry

Serve with lemon wedges, Zesty Dill Mayo (see page 216) and Dave's Coconut Sambal (see page 209).

Slice the fish into 10 thin strips. Combine the garlic, lemon zest and juice, a pinch of salt, a generous grind of black pepper and extra virgin olive oil. Whisk together, add the fish strips and refrigerate for 30 minutes.

Whisk the eggs and place them in a bowl alongside the breadcrumbs and 1/2 cup of flour seasoned with plenty of salt and pepper. Dip the fish strips in the flour, then egg, then panko crumbs. Heat 1-2 cups of coconut or peanut oil in a wok or deep pan and fry the fish in batches over medium heat for 2-3 minutes or until golden. Serve with Zesty Dill Mayo and Dave's Coconut Sambal.

Crisp 'n' Soft Tacos with apple-slaw

Feeds 3-4 · Prep 20 mins · Cook 10 mins

On one passage to Indonesia, I nurtured pots of rocket, kale, cress and mignonette lettuce. When fruit flies attacked in the romantically named Forgotten Islands, I waged battle with garlic spray and vinegar traps until I conceded defeat. My ailing greens were snipped into one amazing Father's Day salad and the following days were distinctly salad-free. This dish is for all those times when lettuce is a delicious, distant memory, but you absolutely crave some crunch.

300g (10oz) firm white fish

⅓ cup plain (all-purpose) or rice flour

1 tsp ground cumin

salt and pepper

2 tbsp coconut or peanut oil

8 mini tortillas

lime wedges

coriander (cilantro) sprigs

Chilli Avocado Salsa

½ ripe avocado, finely chopped

½ red chilli, finely chopped

1 tsp lime juice

Apple-slaw

1 cup finely shredded green cabbage

½ green (or any) apple, julienned

1 spring onion, (scallion) finely sliced

¼ cup chopped fresh coriander leaves (excellent but optional)

1 tbsp mayonnaise

1 tsp lime juice

For the apple slaw, combine the cabbage, apple, spring onion and coriander in a mixing bowl. Mix the mayonnaise and lime juice in a small glass jar and shake well. Season with salt and pepper to taste, then pour the dressing over the apple slaw and toss well. Refrigerate until ready to eat.

Slice the fish across the fillet into pieces about 1.5cm (1/2in) thick. Combine the flour and ground cumin in a dish, season with salt and pepper and toss in the fish to coat well. Heat 2 tbsp of coconut or peanut oil in a pan over medium-high heat and fry the fish pieces for about 3-4 minutes, turning occasionally.

For the salsa, combine the avocado, chopped chilli and lime juice and set aside. Warm the tortillas in a lightly oiled pan or barbecue plate (or char over a flame), and fill with apple slaw, fried fish and a dollop of chilli avocado salsa. Serve with extra coriander sprigs, if you have them, and lime wedges.

Beach-baked Coral Trout

Feeds 2 · Prep 10 mins · Cook 30 mins · GF, CC

We finned on, ogling parrotfish crunching on lime and tangerine coral, and lagoon rays snoozing beneath us on the sand. A coral trout darted suddenly out of sight, scattering a thousand gleaming fusiliers, and the hunt began. With Maya scouting and duck-diving ahead, Dave speared a trio of trout that simply made our night.

We gathered driftwood, mixed some marinades, and coated, wrapped and baked our fresh catch over crackling hot coals as the sun went down. With Bintangs in hand, feet dug into the sand, and our boat swinging at anchor in a hidden West Papuan lagoon, no fish dinner ever tasted so good.

1 coral trout (any legal size, swap for other reef fish if necessary)

1-2 tbsp extra virgin olive oil

2 large garlic cloves (or 2 tsp minced garlic)

6 shallots (or a small brown onion)

5cm (2in) knob of fresh ginger (or 2 tsp minced ginger)

2 limes

2 red chillies (optional)

1 tbsp rice malt syrup (or honey*)

Serve with Som Tam Malako (green papaya salad, page 132).

** Using rice malt syrup instead of honey keeps this dish fructose-free.*

Get a small beach fire burning and let it die down to a bed of hot coals. Scale, clean and rinse your fish, and pat dry with paper towel. Rub with olive oil and place on a large piece of aluminium foil. Finely slice the garlic, shallots, ginger, lime and chillies, and assemble on top of the trout.

Drizzle with rice malt syrup, securely fold up the foil, and add a second layer to keep sand out. Place it on hot campfire coals (away from any flames) and bake for about 15 minutes a side. Serve with Som Tam Malako and chilled beers.

Spicy Thai Fish Burgers

with pickled chilli salad

Feeds 4 · Prep 25 mins · Cook 10 mins

¼ cup whole-egg mayonnaise

1 tsp wasabi paste

500g (1lb) firm white fish

1 tbsp soy sauce

1 tsp sesame oil

½ tsp crushed ginger

1 large egg, lightly whisked

1 cup stale breadcrumbs

2 sliced shallots

40g mixed leaves

4 hamburger buns

Pickled Chilli Salad

2 Lebanese cucumbers

½ tsp salt

2 tsp sugar

1 tbsp rice (or white) vinegar

1 small red chilli, seeded and finely sliced

1 small red onion, thinly sliced

2 tsp lemon juice

1 tbsp fresh mint, roughly chopped

1 tbsp fresh coriander, roughly chopped

To make the pickled chilli salad, slice the cucumber into long strips using a vegetable peeler. Place it in a bowl and top with the marinade ingredients: salt, sugar, vinegar, chilli, onion, lemon juice and fresh chopped herbs. Refrigerate for half an hour.

Combine the mayonnaise with the wasabi paste and refrigerate until needed.

For the fish patties, finely chop the fish and combine them with the soy sauce, sesame oil, crushed ginger, lightly whisked egg, breadcrumbs and sliced shallots. Shape the mixture into 4 patties and refrigerate until ready to eat.

Barbecue or pan-fry the burgers for about 10 minutes. Lightly toast the buns, spread them with wasabi mayonnaise, and add a handful of mixed leaves and the fish burgers. Place some pickled salad on top and serve.

Indian-Spiced Fish & Chickpea Salad

Feeds 2 · Prep 10 mins · Cook 10 mins · QC

400g (14oz) firm fish fillets

½ tsp smoked paprika

1 tsp ground cumin

1 tsp ground turmeric

1 tbsp plain (all-purpose) flour (GF if preferred)

salt and pepper

2 tbsp peanut or coconut oil

4 large pappadums

Chickpea Salad

2 ripe Roma (or other) tomatoes, diced

¼ red onion, thinly sliced

½ continental cucumber, thinly sliced

400g (14oz) tinned chickpeas, rinsed and drained

½ bunch coriander (cilantro)

½ tsp cumin seeds

1 tbsp sesame seeds

juice of 1 lime

Combine the smoked paprika, ground cumin, turmeric and flour in a mixing bowl and season well with sea salt and black pepper. Slice the fish into large chunks, toss well in the spice mix to coat and set aside.

For the chickpea salad, combine the tomato, red onion, cucumber, chickpeas and coriander leaves in a salad bowl. Gently toast the cumin and sesame seeds over low heat, remove from the pan and set aside to cool.

Pour 2 tablespoons of peanut oil into a frypan over medium heat. Fry the fish in batches for 2-3 minutes or until crisp, turning once. Transfer the fish to a wire rack. Microwave or deep-fry the pappadums. Toss the salad with a generous squeeze of lime juice, and serve topped with crispy pieces of spiced fish, a sprinkle of toasted seeds and pappadums.

Ginger Fish Wontons

in Chinese broth

Feeds 4 · Prep 15 mins · Cook 15 mins · OP

250g (0.5lb) white fish, finely chopped

2 tsp finely grated lemon zest

1 heaped tbsp finely chopped fresh coriander (cilantro)

1 spring onion (scallion), whites only, finely sliced

2 garlic cloves, finely chopped

2 tsp crushed or minced ginger

1 tsp light soy sauce

½ tsp sesame oil

20 wonton wrappers, at room temperature

Chinese Broth

6 cups vegetable stock

1 tbsp soy sauce

2 tsp finely grated (or minced) ginger

2 red chillies, finely sliced

2 garlic cloves, finely chopped

Serve with fresh coriander sprigs, ⅓ cup sliced spring onions and chopped fresh red chilli.

For the wontons, combine the fish with lemon zest, coriander, spring onion, garlic and ginger. Add the soy sauce and sesame oil and mix well. Lay the wonton wrappers on a dry flat surface. Place a heaped teaspoonful of the mixture in the centre of each wonton and, using your finger, lightly brush the edges with water.

Fold each wrapper in half diagonally to form a triangle, gently squeezing out the air as you seal with your fingertips. Fold the 2 corners over to meet each other, add a touch of water and press together to seal the wonton into a crown shape.

For the broth, combine all the ingredients in a large saucepan. Bring to a boil, reduce the heat and simmer for 10 minutes. Strain the broth and return it to the stove over medium heat. When it returns to a simmer, add your wontons and cook, uncovered, for 4 minutes. Serve topped with fresh coriander, sliced spring onions and chopped red chillies.

Fresh Spring Rolls with tamarind dipping sauce

Makes 6 · Prep 10 mins · Cook 10 mins · GF

50g (1.8oz) vermicelli rice noodles

1 medium carrot

1 Lebanese cucumber (or ½ continental)

1 cup fresh sprouts

small bunch of fresh coriander (cilantro)

1 tbsp coconut or peanut oil

2 garlic cloves, finely chopped

1 tsp finely grated fresh (or minced) ginger

1 red chilli, finely chopped (or ½ tsp dried chilli flakes)

250g (0.5lb) firm white fish fillets (or firm tofu)

1 tbsp fish sauce

2 tsp lime juice

black pepper

6 dried rice paper sheets

Tamarind Dipping Sauce

1 fresh red chilli, finely chopped (or ½ tsp dried chilli flakes)

2 garlic cloves, finely chopped

1 tbsp sugar

60g (2oz) piece of tamarind pulp

1 tbsp fish sauce

1 cup water

In Cairns, where I've spent more than a few long, hot summers, tamarind trees grow abundantly. The local kids love them because they are excellent climbing trees, but mostly because the peanut-shaped fruit pods that rain down on the seaside playground known as Muddy's are a delicious, sweet 'n' sour snack. They are packed with vitamin C (which every sailor needs), and processed tamarind pulp keeps forever in the fridge. If you love the zingy flavour of this sauce, try making up a jug of Iced Tamarind Juice, too (see page 188). If you don't have fish, use tofu or tempeh instead.

Prepare the dipping sauce by boiling all the ingredients in a small saucepan for 5 minutes. Strain to remove the tamarind seeds and set it aside to cool.

When ready to eat, soak the rice noodles in boiling water for 2 minutes (or until soft), then rinse with cold water, drain well and set aside. Finely julienne the carrots and cucumber, rinse the sprouts, and pick the leaves off the coriander.

Heat your cooking oil in a non-stick pan over medium/low heat and gently fry the garlic, ginger and chilli. Slice the fish (or firm tofu) into thick strips, add to the pan and cook for 3 minutes, turning once. Add the fish sauce, lime juice and a generous grind of black pepper, and stir gently to coat the fish (or tofu), then transfer with the sauce to a dish to cool.

Put everything on the table for your guests to assemble, or make the rolls in advance so they are ready-to-eat.

Half-fill a large frypan with cool water. Immerse 1 rice paper sheet in the water until soft, and carefully transfer it to your plate or a clean benchtop. Add some noodles, fish or tofu, carrot, cucumber, sprouts and fresh coriander sprigs. Fold 1 corner of the wrapper over the filling, fold in the 2 sides and roll up.

Serve the spring rolls while the fish is warm or chilled – your choice – with tamarind dipping sauce.

Barbecued Fish Laab

Makes 6 · Prep 10 mins · Cook 5 mins · GF, QC

After long years spent travelling through Southeast Asia, I got tired of gazing wistfully at people devouring deliciously aromatic laab. The national dish of Laos (and so good the Thais borrowed it as their own), laab headlines menus all over Southeast Asia. Each is made differently according to local flavours and styles, but often with meat served too raw and wriggling for me. I came up with this way of infusing all those perky, fresh flavours into fish sticks, which can be barbecued, grilled or pan-fried in minutes.

1 garlic clove, finely chopped

¼ red onion, finely chopped

1 tsp finely grated fresh ginger

2 tbsp finley chopped coriander (cilantro)

1 small lime, finely zested

2 pinches of salt

pinch of dried chilli flakes

400g (14oz) firm white fish (fresh or defrosted)

1-2 tbsp coconut oil

6 bamboo skewers

Serve with fresh lime and salsa of tomato, cucumber and coriander.

Soak 6 bamboo skewers in water for 20 minutes. Blend all the seasonings into a paste and mix with the finely chopped fish and 2 teaspoons of coconut oil. Use clean hands to form the mixture onto the skewers, squeezing out excess moisture if necessary (especially if the fish has been frozen).

Brush the fish with a little extra oil and barbecue, grill or panfry the sticks, turning occasionally, for 4-5 minutes. Serve with a squeeze of lime and salsa of roughly chopped tomato, cucumber and coriander leaf.

Tandoori Pan Pizzas

Makes 4 small pizzas · Prep 10 mins + Chilling time Cook 10-15 mins

It really doesn't matter how you make and bake these pizzas (use fresh dough or instant bases, oven-bake or grill them). What matters here is what's happening on top: a flavour-packed ensemble of Indian-spiced fish teamed with salty paneer, sweet mango and just a hint of fresh coriander and lemon.

1 tbsp extra virgin olive oil

500g (1lb) firm white fish, cut into 3cm (1in) cubes

⅓ cup plain Greek yoghurt

2 tbsp tandoori paste

1 tbsp lemon juice

1 quantity of pizza dough (see page 202) or 4 naan breads

⅓ cup 10-minute Mango Chutney (see page 211)

1 onion (any), cut into thin crescents

200g (7oz) paneer (to make your own, see page 204)

¼ cup unsalted roasted cashews

big handful baby rocket (arugula)

⅓ cup coriander (cilantro) sprigs

Heat 1 tablespoon of olive oil in a frypan over medium heat. Cook the fish cubes, turning gently, then set them aside to rest and cool. Combine the yoghurt, tandoori paste and lemon juice in a bowl, add the fish, toss to coat, cover and refrigerate for an hour.

Make a batch of pizza dough or use ready-made naan bread and spread the bases with mango chutney and add onion, fish, crumbled paneer and cashews. If you have an oven, bake at 220°C (425°F) for 10-15 minutes.

For stovetop and grill baking, cook your homemade bases in a heavy-based frypan over low heat for 10-12 minutes, turning once. Then, load them up and place them under a hot grill until golden. For ready-made naan breads, simply add toppings and then grill them off.

Once baked, top with baby rocket and coriander and serve.

Hot Rub Fish Tacos with quick-pickled onion

Feeds 4 • Prep 10 mins • Cook 10 mins

600g (1.2lb) Spanish mackerel fillets (or other firm white fish)

4 large tortillas (or 8 mini)

2 ripe tomatoes, diced

3-4 tbsp pickled jalapeños, chopped (optional)

1 baby cos (romaine) lettuce

handful of fresh coriander (cilantro) sprigs

⅓ cup whole egg mayonnaise

⅓ cup natural Greek yoghurt

2-3 tbsp extra virgin olive oil

Spice Rub

2 tsp hot paprika

2 tsp ground cumin

2 tsp ground coriander

2 tsp fennel seeds

1 tsp mustard seeds

2 tsp dried oregano

salt and pepper

Quick Pickled Onion

1 large red onion, thinly sliced

⅓ cup lime juice

1 tbsp apple cider vinegar

½ tsp salt

1 tsp rice malt syrup (or sugar)

½ tsp sumac

For the quick pickled onion, place the sliced onion in a clean glass jar. Add lime juice, vinegar, salt, rice malt syrup and sumac, and shake well. Refrigerate for 30 minutes before serving, and store in the fridge for up to 2 weeks.

Mix the rub spices together. Cut the fish into 1-2cm (3/4in) thick slices, coat well with the rub, and then season on both sides with salt and pepper. Warm 1-2 tablespoons of olive oil in a frypan (or use a BBQ hot plate) and cook the fish in batches over medium heat for about 3-4 minutes per side, depending on the thickness of your fish pieces. Set aside to rest.

Mix together equal amounts of mayonnaise and Greek yoghurt. Rinse and dry the lettuce leaves. Warm the tortillas and serve them filled with the fish, lettuce, diced tomato, sliced jalapeños, pickled onion, coriander leaves and a generous drizzle of yoghurt mayo.

Quick Sri Lankan Curry

Feeds 4 • Prep 5 mins • Cook 15 mins • GF, QC

- 350g (12oz) Spanish mackerel (or other firm white fish)
- ⅔ cup coconut cream
- 1 cup fish stock
- 1 cup diced tomatoes
- 1 medium onion, sliced
- 5 bay leaves
- 2 tsp dried chilli flakes
- 1 cinnamon stick
- 1 garlic clove, finely chopped
- 1 tsp grated fresh (or minced) ginger
- 1 tbsp curry powder
- salt and pepper to taste

Serve with steamed rice or crusty bread (gluten-free if required).

Cut the fish into bite-sized cubes. Combine half the coconut cream and the fish stock in a large pan over medium heat. Stir in the tomatoes, onion and all seasonings. Bring to a boil, add the fish, reduce the heat and simmer for 5 minutes. Add the remaining coconut cream to the pot, stir, and then take off the heat. Remove the bay leaves, then serve with crusty bread or steamed rice.

One-dish Fish Saganaki

Feeds 4 • Prep 5 mins • Cook 20 mins • OP

- 1 tbsp extra virgin olive oil
- 1 onion, finely sliced
- 2 garlic cloves, crushed
- 1 tsp dried oregano
- ¼ tsp dried chilli flakes
- 400g (14oz) tinned whole tomatoes
- black pepper
- 2 x 250g (0.5lb) fish fillets (anything firm and white)
- ¼ cup pitted Kalamata olives
- ½ cup (75g) crumbled feta

Serve with crusty bread and chopped fresh parsley.

Over medium heat, warm the olive oil in a heavy-based frypan and sauté the onion, garlic, oregano and chilli for 3-4 minutes, stirring. Add the tomatoes, chopping roughly, and season with a good grind of black pepper. Bring to a simmer.

Chop the fish into large pieces and add to the pan with the olives. Cover and cook for 7 minutes. Take off the heat, add the crumbled feta and place under a hot grill for about 5 minutes until the feta starts to soften and brown. Serve with crusty bread and a little chopped fresh parsley.

Momon Bay Mackerel Bites

Makes 20 · Prep 10 mins · Cook 10 mins · GF, QC

We may not have invented the barbecue, but everything about it just screams Australian: you do it outside, any fool can have a go, and it doesn't matter much if you make a mess.

What I love about barbecuing is that all kinds of seemingly unrelated titbits can be thrown onto the grill and served in unison. From wrapped fish parcels to marinaded prawns, slices of sweet potato and unhusked ears of corn, stuffed mushroom caps, halloumi cheese and pots of buttered asparagus spears and baby bok choy. For breakfast, my Dad fries up mini omelettes on the barbecue hotplate, teamed with thick wedges of toast, grilled mushrooms, and a caramelised tomato relish he stirs in a small cast iron pot on the side.

Credit for these tasty fish bites rests entirely with Dave, who not only created the recipe, but caught the fish too.

500g (1lb) Spanish mackerel (or other firm fish), fresh or frozen

2-3 garlic cloves, finely chopped

1 onion (or a handful of shallots), finely chopped

¼ tsp Chinese 5-spice

¼ tsp salt

½ tsp black cracked pepper

½ tsp dried oregano

pinch of hot smoked paprika

⅓ cup frozen spinach, thawed

3 tbsp tomato paste

1 tbsp kecap manis

4 sun-dried tomatoes, chopped

100g (3.5oz) cheddar, grated

extra virgin olive oil for frying

Roughly chop the fish and place it in a large mixing bowl. Fry the garlic and onion in a little olive oil until coloured. Add to the fish with all the spices, thawed spinach, tomato paste, kecap manis and chopped sun-dried tomatoes.

Use a stick blender to roughly blitz about half of the mixture (leave some of the fish chunky to create texture). Add the grated cheese and mix well with a spoon. Form into small balls (about a tablespoon each) and either panfry, grill or barbecue the fish bites over medium to high heat. These are too flavoursome and moist to need any kind of dipping sauce.

Simmered Mackerel Bites

in eggplant sauce

Feeds 4 · Prep 5 mins · Cook 30 mins · GF, OP

This dish takes Dave's Momon Bay Mackerel Bites to the next level, transforming them into a truly hearty meal. Cook this on the stove or over hot coals on the beach.

To turn these versatile bites Italian, leave out the Chinese 5-spice, kecap manis and cheddar cheese, and add 1 tablespoon of finely chopped fresh basil and 100g (3.5oz) of crumbled feta before rolling them into balls.

1 batch of Momon Bay Mackerel Bites (the Italian version)

1 tbsp extra virgin olive oil

1 brown onion, finely chopped

1 large garlic clove, finely chopped

1 small eggplant (aubergine), diced (about 1 cup)

2 tbsp tomato paste

2 x 400g (14oz) tinned diced tomatoes

1 cup vegetable stock

a large handful of fresh basil leaves

¼ cup Kalamata olives, halved

salt and pepper

Serve with extra basil leaves and parmesan cheese.

In a large saucepan or camp oven, heat 1 tablespoon of olive oil over medium heat and gently fry the onion, garlic and eggplant for 3-4 minutes until the onion is soft. Add the tomato paste and stir, then add the tinned tomatoes, stock and fresh basil. Cover the pot and bring it to a boil. Add the fish bites and olives, and season with salt and pepper. Reduce the heat and gently simmer the sauce for 20 minutes with the lid on. Serve topped with extra basil leaves and parmesan cheese.

PRAWNS & SQUID

Casting For Prawns

Our very first sailboat – a 20-foot, swing-keel Hood - was launched on the shores of Hinchinbrook Island. It was here that I learnt to throw a bait casting net, an unwieldy sort of tool that's perfect for catching the prawns (shrimp, to you American readers) that gather close to shore over the wet season. Gathered up in one's arms with half of it flung over your shoulder, the net is delicately cast so that it opens into a wide circle and nets a catch of unsuspecting prawns. It's harder to work than it looks, but with time and practice, people do eventually stop laughing.

Look for prawns off mangrove-fringed beaches, and wear a long-sleeved shirt when you cast to protect against possible contact with often deadly marine stingers. Their translucent tentacles are easily tangled in your net and go unnoticed until you gather it in your arms and feel the sting. If your shirt has buttons, turn it inside out. That way, when you fling your net, it won't hook up on your buttons, snare and strangle you, and grant you a staring role in your mate's next YouTube clip.

When juvenile prawns mature and make their run for the open sea, look for them in estuaries and around river mouths, especially on outgoing tides. Perfect conditions involve heavy rain and warm, dark summer nights on a waning moon.

Catching & Cleaning Squid

You need patience and finesse to snare 'all-seeing' squid, but this abundant food source is quick to prepare and even faster to cook. Attach a squid jig to a hand reel or rod, and use jerky, quick bursts to mimic the backwards motion that a prawn makes through the water.

Squid prefer clear over turbid waters and tend to emerge in plain sight on the latter part of a rising tide. They don't like strong currents and seek shelter – around reefs, in beds of seagrass and kelp, under jetties and around pylons – in depths of up to 4-5 metres (12-15 feet). Squid shelter beneath boat moorings and around anchor chains, too, making them rather convenient for yachties to catch. Except when artificial lights are around, squid are more likely to be snared in the late evening or at dawn. When you get one on your line, reel it in slowly and steadily, and kill the squid quickly (before you get inked) by giving it a solid squeeze just behind the eyes, or by spiking it between the eyes.

To prepare a squid, cut the tentacles off just below the eyes (keep them or discard them, it's up to you). Pull the head away from the tube (you might need to stick your thumb inside the tube to loosen any connective tissue), and give it a twist to separate it. Remove and discard the beak. Use your thumb to separate the skin from the flesh, working your way around the tube and peeling off the outer layer of skin and membrane (this should also remove the wings). Pull and slide out the quill, and turn the entire tube inside out to rinse well. Your tube is now ready to be stuffed, scored or sliced into rings.

Sung Choi Bao

Feeds 2 · Prep 15 mins · Cook 10 mins · GF, OP

400g (14oz) green prawns (shrimp), any size

¼ cup almonds

2 garlic cloves, crushed or minced

8 green beans, finely sliced

1 cup bean sprouts

½ cup finely chopped fresh basil

2 spring onions (scallion), finely sliced

2 tbsp lemon juice

½ tsp crushed dried chillies

2 tbsp kecap manis

1 tbsp peanut or coconut oil for frying

Serve with 8 baby cos (romaine) lettuce leaves.

Peel, devein and finely chop the prawns. Refrigerate until needed. Gently toast and finely chop (or process) the almonds. Prepare the vegetables and measure out the seasonings, ready to cook.

Heat 1 tablespoon of peanut or coconut oil in a wok or large frying pan over low heat and gently fry the garlic until fragrant. Crank up the heat to medium, add the finely chopped beans and stir-fry for 1-2 minutes. Add the almonds, bean sprouts, fresh basil, spring onion, lemon juice, chilli, kecap manis and the chopped prawns, and stir-fry for about 1 minute.

Take it off the heat and set it aside to cool slightly. Wash and dry the lettuce leaves, fill with your prawn mixture and serve.

Gremolata Prawns

Feeds 2 · Prep 10 mins · Cook 5 mins · GF, QC

There is something immensely satisfying about eating what you grow, no matter how much of a garnish it might seem. Just looking at my blooming little boat garden gives me so much joy, and it only takes a few sprigs of fresh herbs and greens to perk up a meal. Gremolata makes even the tiniest amount of parsley really shine, and partners perfectly with these garlicky, quick-cook prawns.

12 large green prawns (shrimp)

1 tbsp tomato paste

1 garlic clove, finely chopped

1 tbsp white wine

1-2 tsp extra virgin olive oil

Gremolata

2 tbsp pine nuts, toasted

1 tbsp finely chopped fresh parsley

1 tsp finely grated lemon zest

Serve with lemon wedges and cracked black pepper.

Peel and devein the prawns, leaving the tails intact. Combine the tomato paste, garlic and white wine in a small bowl and spoon over the prawns. Make your own gremolata by combining all the ingredients in a bowl, then set it aside.

When it's time to eat, heat a little olive oil in a non-stick frying pan and fry the prawns for a minute a side. Serve immediately topped with a generous dollop of gremolata, lemon wedges and some cracked black pepper.

Baked Prawn & Noodle Rolls

Makes 12 • Prep 20 mins • Cook 30 mins • GF

100g (3.5oz) rice noodles

1 tsp peanut oil

2 garlic cloves, finely chopped

1 red chilli, finely chopped

1 tsp crushed ginger

1 tbsp fish sauce

2 tsp lime juice

½ tsp black pepper

200g (7oz) cooked prawns (shrimp), peeled and chopped

½ cup roughly chopped fresh mint

2 shallots, sliced

12 rice paper sheets

Serve with Chilli & Ginger Sauce (see page 217).

Preheat the oven to 210°C (410°F). Soak the rice noodles in boiling water until soft, then drain well. Heat the peanut oil in a wok and gently fry the garlic, chilli and ginger. Add the fish sauce, lime juice, black pepper, prawns and noodles, and stir briefly. Take off the heat, set aside to cool and then stir in the fresh mint and sliced shallot.

Immerse a rice paper sheet in a large pan of cool water until it has softened, then transfer it carefully to a benchtop. Add 2-3 tablespoons of the mixture, fold in 3 sides and gently but firmly roll it up. Continue until you have 12 rolls. Bake the rolls on a tray lined with baking paper for 30 minutes. Serve with Chilli & Ginger Sauce or your favourite dipping sauce.

Korean BBQ Prawns

Feeds 2 • Prep 10 mins + Marinading Cook 10 mins • GF

250g (0.5lb) peeled raw prawns (shrimp)

1 small white onion, finely grated

3 garlic cloves, crushed

1 tbsp tamari (or soy sauce)

½ tsp sesame oil

2 tsp coconut oil

1 tsp finely grated fresh ginger

2 tsp rice malt syrup (or brown sugar)

2 pinches ground black pepper

150g (5oz) bean thread vermicelli noodle

1 baby cos (romaine) lettuce

Serve with 1 finely sliced spring onion (scallion), 1 finely sliced small red chilli and toasted sesame seeds.

Combine the grated onion, garlic, tamari (or soy sauce), sesame oil, coconut oil, ginger, and rice malt syrup (or brown sugar) in a bowl. Season with pepper and stir well. Add the peeled prawns and toss gently to coat. Refrigerate for 30 minutes.

Gently toast 2 tablespoons of sesame seeds over low heat until aromatic, then set them aside. Plunge the noodles into boiling water to soak for 3 minutes. Drain the noodles, rinse them with cold water and set them aside. Separate the lettuce leaves, rinse and pat dry.

When ready to eat, heat a wok over medium heat. Wok-toss the prawns for 1-2 minutes, turning frequently, then take them off the heat. Fill each lettuce cup with some noodles, add some prawns, and top with finely sliced spring onion, sliced chilli and toasted sesame seeds.

Salt 'n' Pepper Calamari

with Thai chilli salad

Feeds 4 · Prep 20 mins · Cook 5 mins · GF

Maya *loves* calamari, but it's easy to get it wrong. Cook it quickly – for no more than a minute – and have your crew gathered, ready to devour it straight out of the pan. You don't need a salad to enjoy this dish (a squeeze of lemon or lime will suffice), but I love the hot and sour flavour of this Thai chilli salad and the fact that you *can* prepare it long after the lettuce runs out. The salad begs for fresh coriander, but don't stress if there's none on board; it tastes great without it. If you don't have squid tubes, use fish pieces, prawns or tofu, all of which team perfectly with the zesty Thai chilli salad.

500g (1lb) squid tubes (about 4)

¾ cup rice flour

salt and pepper

1 cup coconut or peanut oil

Thai Chilli Salad

1 garlic clove, crushed

½ long red chilli, deseeded and finely chopped (or 1 tsp dried chilli flakes)

1 ½ tbsp rice malt syrup (or sugar)

1 tbsp fish sauce

1 ½ tbsp lime juice

1 bunch fresh coriander (cilantro)

10 long green or 5 snake beans, finely sliced

10 grape or cherry tomatoes

100g (3.5oz) baby spinach leaves (optional)

1 tbsp dried fried onion

For the Thai chilli salad, combine the garlic, chilli, rice malt syrup (or sugar), fish sauce and lime juice in a mixing bowl. Finely chop the coriander stalks (reserve the leaves) and slice the green beans as finely as you can. Quarter the tomatoes and toss everything together. Just before serving, toss in the coriander and spinach leaves, and garnish with fried onion.

Rinse the squid tubes and pat them dry. Cut down one side of each tube to open them up, score in a criss-cross pattern and cut them each into 6 pieces. Heat a cup of oil in a wok or frying pan. Season the rice flour with salt and pepper and coat the squid pieces well. Fry them in batches for about 1 minute and drain on a wire rack or paper towel. Serve immediately with Thai chilli salad.

Seared Squid Puttanesca

Feeds 4 · Prep 10 mins · Cook 20 mins

6 large squid tubes

½ brown onion

1 garlic clove

4 anchovies

2 tbsp extra virgin olive oil

pinch of crushed dried chillies (optional)

splash of red wine

2 cups passata

1 cup water

1 tbsp capers, rinsed and drained

⅓ cup halved Kalamata olives (about 15)

⅓ cup sliced sun-dried tomatoes

500g (1lb) pasta (any kind)

Serve topped with parmesan.

Clean the squid tubes and pat them dry. Score in a criss-cross pattern with a sharp knife and slice into bite-size squares.

Finely chop the onion, garlic and anchovies. Warm 1 tablespoon of olive oil in a large pan over medium heat and gently fry them for about 2 minutes with a good pinch of crushed dried chillies (optional). Add a splash of red wine and simmer for 3 minutes, then pour in the passata, 1 cup of water, capers, olives and sundried tomatoes. Simmer uncovered for 10 minutes.

While the sauce simmers, bring a large pot of water to the boil and cook the pasta until al dente. When the sauce is done, take it off the heat and cover it with a lid. Warm a little olive oil in a frying pan (or use an oiled barbecue hot plate) and sear the squid for about 1 minute, turning frequently.

Gently toss the squid, sauce and pasta together and serve topped with parmesan.

10-minute Tom Yum Kung

Feeds 2 • Prep 15 mins • Cook 10 mins • GF, OP

Decades ago, while backpacking through Ayutthaya, Thailand, a streetside chef taught me to make tom yum. In a kitchen barely big enough to swing a wok, Kwan taught me more about Thai cookery than I've learnt in the years since. Firstly, leave flavourings whole to impart more subtle flavours, and never strain them out before serving. They add far too much colour, excitement, and aroma as you eat.

Tom yum uses only a tiny portion of seafood, and the balance of flavours are fine-tuned. Taste as you go adding a touch more sweetness, extra saltiness (a pinch of stock powder or a splash of soy), and for some sourness, extra fish sauce or lime juice. Chilli is a personal thing, but since it's cooked quickly, even large slices impart only subtle heat here.

3 cups water

12 small prawns (shrimp), peeled

⅔ cup squid rings

1 tsp salt

1 tsp rice malt syrup (or sugar)

2 tsp vegetable stock powder

1 brown onion, sliced in crescents

10cm (4in) knob of galangal, sliced

6-8 kaffir (makrut) lime leaves

2 lemongrass stalks, sliced

4-5 small red chillies, sliced

1 tbsp fish sauce

1 tbsp chilli sauce

1 lime, squeezed

1 tomato, sliced into crescents

4 spring onions (scallion), sliced

a handful of sprouts

⅔ cup fresh coriander (cilantro), chopped

Serve with extra sliced chilli.

In a saucepan, bring 3 cups of water to the boil. While you wait, slice all your vegetables and assemble the seasonings. When the water boils, add the prawns and squid and season with salt, your sweetener of choice and powdered vegetable stock. Boil, stirring for about 3 minutes. Add the onion, sliced galangal, lime leaves, lemongrass and chillies, and stir. Season to taste with fish sauce, chilli sauce and the juice of 1 lime.

Add half the tomato and sliced spring onions, the sprouts and 1/3 cup of chopped coriander. Taste and adjust the flavours to suit your palette. Stir in the remaining tomato and coriander, and take off the heat. Pour into bowls and serve topped with the remaining spring onion and extra, sliced chillies.

Thai Pumpkin Soup

with turmeric prawns

Feeds 4 • Prep 15 mins • Cook 20 mins • GF

2 tbsp coconut (or peanut) oil

1 lemongrass stalk

4 kaffir (makrut) lime leaves

2 spring onions (scallion), whites only

3 garlic cloves, coarsely chopped

800g (2lb) pumpkin, cut into 2cm (1in) chunks

400ml (13.5 fl oz) coconut milk

½ lime, zest and juice

1 ½ tbsp rice malt syrup (or sugar)

2 tsp fish sauce

a handful of fresh coriander (cilantro) leaves (to serve)

1 red chilli, finely chopped (to serve)

1 tbsp fried onion (to serve)

Turmeric Prawns

400g (14oz) prawns (shrimp), peeled, deveined

1 tsp ground turmeric

1 tsp ground cumin

salt and pepper

extra virgin olive oil for frying

Heat 1 tablespoon of oil in a heavy-based saucepan over medium heat. Bash and bruise the trimmed and peeled lemongrass stalk and add it to the pan with the kaffir lime leaves, finely chopped spring onions, garlic cloves and the peeled, chopped pumpkin. Stir for about 3 minutes, then pour in the coconut milk and 2 cups of water.

Bring to a simmer, reduce the heat to medium-low, cover and cook for 10-15 minutes or until the pumpkin is tender. Remove the lime leaves and lemongrass. Mix the lime zest, juice, rice malt syrup (or sugar), and fish sauce and pour it into the soup. Use a stick blender to blitz the soup until smooth. Season to taste and cover to keep warm.

While the soup simmers, toss the prawns in turmeric and cumin and season well with salt and pepper. Fry them with a little olive oil for 2-3 minutes, turning occasionally. Ladle the soup into 4 bowls, garnish with fresh coriander leaves, chopped red chilli, and some fried onion, and top with a serve of crispy prawns.

***Tip:** This soup is so good you can serve it without prawns, but together, they create something extraordinarily good.*

Mangalorean-style Squid

Feeds 2-3 • Prep 10 mins • Cook 10 mins

3 squid tubes (about 300g/10oz)

½ red onion, finely sliced

1 garlic clove, finely chopped

1 tsp grated fresh ginger

1 large tomato, finely diced

1 tsp ground chilli (optional)

½ tsp salt

1 tsp sweetener
(rice malt syrup or sugar)

1 tbsp tamarind paste

¼ cup fresh coriander
(cilantro), roughly chopped

2-3 tbsp coconut oil for frying

Curry paste

1 tsp cumin seeds

1 tsp coriander seeds

1 tsp fenugreek seeds

1 tsp black mustard seeds

1 tsp ground turmeric

2 garlic cloves

1 red chilli

3 tbsp finely grated fresh coconut

Serve with coconut rice (page 160).

When is a curry not a curry? When it's Indian, for starters. We commonly associate curries with India, but no such dish traditionally exists. Ready-blended curry powders might be handy, but they would never find their way into an authentic Indian kitchen. Instead, cooks grind and blend separate combinations of spices for each dish in their vast repertoire.

The word seems to have originated with the British, who took the Tamil word 'kari', meaning sauce, to apply to all spicy Indian stews. Yet Indian spice blends may contain up to 25 different spices, always stored whole and ground just before cooking. Ginger and garlic are always fresh and fried very gently in butter or ghee, so they brown without burning.

When cooking a 'curry', stir your spices constantly, so they don't burn or overcook. Never hurry a curry – low and slow is the way to go – because simmering wet dishes for the longest possible time allows flavours to fuse and intensify and for gravies to thicken.

This South Indian dish calls for fresh coconut, which is much juicier and imparts a far more aromatic flavour than dried coconut can. If you do use dried coconut, rehydrate it first, or get yourself somewhere warmer where you can sit beside a coconut palm and jig for a catch of fresh squid too.

For the curry paste, gently warm the whole seeds in a dry pan over low heat until aromatic. When cool, grind them (use a mortar and pestle or a mini grinder), and then add turmeric, garlic and chopped chilli. Add the coconut and a couple of tablespoons of water, and blitz again until smooth. Make this paste in advance (and double the recipe if you love it) and keep it in a tiny jar in your fridge, covered with a bit of oil, ready to flavour any seafood or vegetable dish.

Clean the squid tubes and slice them into rings. Warm a little oil in a large pan (or wok) over low heat and very gently fry the red onion. Add the garlic and ginger and fry for 1 minute more before stirring in the squid rings and frying off the fresh curry paste.

Add the chopped tomato, ground chilli (optional), salt, and enough water to create a sauce. Turn up the heat and simmer until the squid is tender (2-3 minutes should suffice). As it simmers, balance the flavour by adding up to 1 teaspoon of sweetener and up to 1 teaspoon of tamarind paste, to taste. Serve it with coconut rice.

CRABS & CRAYS

Catching & Cleaning

Green Crabs Or Brown?

Two of the world's four species of mud crab inhabit Australian shores: the giant or green mud crab (*Scylla serrata*), found on the east coast and into the Northern Territory, and the brown or orange mud crab (*Scylla olivacea*) found from the Gulf of Carpentaria all the way west into WA. The giant (green) mud crab grows to approximately twice the size of the brown – up to 280mm in diameter and up to 2.5kg – but, just to confuse you, both can appear similarly coloured.

Apparently, each was so named because of the environments they were thought to dwell in, but in reality, both species may be found in bays, river and creek estuaries, on coastal flats, in mangroves and occupying muddy banks below the low tide mark. Muddies favour more saline waters, so will often move downstream after heavy rains to escape the freshwater flow. This explains why they appear more abundant at river mouths during the wet season.

Catching A Crab

Crab pots are a handy hunting tool to have on board because when you've just filleted a fish, putting the frame into a crab pot is the perfect way to turn waste into something else to eat. If you are chasing mud crabs and have just pulled into an anchorage lined with muddy banks and mangroves, drop your crab pots close to the tree roots but allow for low tide depths so that your pots, the crabs and any bycatch, are not left high and dry. Check your pots regularly and remove any crabs before setting them again. We've occasionally pulled crabs out of their burrows, but this takes either luck (us) or skill.

Spotting the differences between male bucks and female jennies is easy. Jennies have smaller claws, and if you turn your crab over, a jenny will have a broader abdominal flap, while the buck's flap is distinctly triangular. It's best practice to release all Jennies to maintain breeding stock.

Freezing & Spiking

According to the RSPCA, humanely killing any saltwater crab is a two-step process that begins with making the crab insensible or impervious to pain. To do this, you can either plunge the crab into a saltwater ice slurry (not always feasible on a boat) or put the crab in the freezer for an hour. Once it stops moving or reacting to being handled, spike the crab swiftly. Crabs have two nerve centres, so you'll need to send a knife tip through both.

Turn the crab on its back, lift the tail flap and insert a sharp pointed knife through the rear nerve centre at an 85-degree angle (look for the hole over this hind nerve centre). Next, look for the shallow depression over the front nerve centre, and insert the tip of the knife through it (ideally at a 60-degree angle). Do this quickly, as spiking should take less than 10 seconds. Never kill your crab by boiling it, and don't drop marine crustaceans into a freshwater slurry, as it can cause osmotic shock. To clean your crab, turn it over and remove the underside (tail) flap by lifting it up and twisting it off. Remove the top shell, clean out the spongy material inside and rinse it clean. Refrigerate the crab until you are ready to cook.

Rock Lobsters & Crayfish

The terms crayfish and lobster are often used interchangeably, but technically speaking, crayfish live in freshwater and lobsters in the sea. The crays we commonly catch in Australia, by setting pots and freediving offshore, are actually all rock lobsters: western rock lobsters (WA), southern rock lobsters (southern Australia), brightly coloured tropical rock lobsters (also called painted or ornate crayfish) and more. Basically, if you catch it in the sea and it has no claws, it's a rock lobster. Having claws makes it a lobster, and there are only two species worldwide – the European and the American lobster (neither of which call Australia home).

Setting pots is generally considered the easiest way to catch rock lobsters. The problem in the tropics, where we spend a lot of time sailing, is that the most abundant species – the painted or ornate rock lobster – rarely enters them. That you have to snare them by hand suits us because, as freedivers, this is how we prefer to hunt. Painted rock lobsters (known locally as painted crays) occupy habitats as beautiful as their multi-coloured carapace. Search for them at depths of three to five metres, in crevices and holes under coral bombies and rocks, on shallow onshore and offshore reefs. These rock lobsters favour caves and overhangs at deeper depths too.

When diving for painted crays, you need patience, a sizeable breath-hold and a good eye to locate the kinds of secluded holes they favour (and to find one that's home). Wear gloves, not only to protect you from the painted crays themselves, but also from any soft corals (especially burning fire corals) that you may inadvertently brush against. The most important thing to do once you find one is to act swiftly. Grab it at the back of the head or the whiskers, and pull it swiftly from its hole. Painted crays will quickly retreat once they sense your intentions, so don't hesitate if you sight one of good size.

Coastal environments worldwide, and in every state and territory in Australia, have different regulations controlling rock lobster and lobster catches, their sizes, seasons and permitted methods of catching them. School up before you hit the water, and always return any undersized lobsters or females (especially those with eggs) to the water as soon as possible.

To humanely kill a rock lobster, first render it insensible by placing it in a saltwater slurry or in the freezer for an hour. Unlike crabs, rock lobsters have multiple nerve centres, but you can sever them all by turning the lobster onto its back and swiftly 'splitting' it in half lengthways. Use a large, sharp knife to make one rapid cut through the centreline connecting the head, chest, abdomen and tail. These nerve centres are located closer to the underside of the lobster, so you don't need to slice all the way through the tough carapace to kill it. However, doing so gives you two nice-sized halves to barbecue or pan-fry for the recipe that follows (page 112).

Flowering Ginger Crab

Feeds 2-4 • Prep 10 mins • Cook 15 mins • GF, OP

This is one of my favourite ways to eat crab. Drenched in a rich, flavour-packed sauce that begs for a bed of steamed rice, one decent crab can stretch a long way. This dish is quick to prepare and uses hardly any ingredients. Cook it up when you've got more bellies to fill than crabs in your pot. Authentic Chinese recipes call for flower crabs, also known as blue swimmers. We use a mud crab because they are meatier and less fiddly, and they're what we mostly catch in northern Australia. Use any crab you can get your hands on.

1kg mud crab (green or brown) or blue swimmer crabs

⅓ cup oil (peanut or coconut)

3cm (1in) piece of ginger, finely grated (or 1 tsp crushed ginger from a jar)

2 garlic cloves, minced

3 shallots, finely sliced (or half a small brown onion)

2 tbsp fermented soya bean paste

1 cup water

2 free-range eggs, lightly beaten

Serve with steamed rice.

Kill your live crab kindly and prepare it for cooking. Remove the claws and crack them slightly with the back of a knife so that the meat absorbs plenty of flavour. Cut the mud crab into 4 pieces (or cut blue swimmers in half).

Heat the oil in a wok (or large, heavy-based saucepan) over medium heat. Gently fry the ginger, garlic and shallot (or onion) for 1-2 minutes until fragrant, but don't let it brown. Add the soya bean paste and cook for 1 minute more.

Add the crab, ladling over the sauce, and cook until the crab colours (about 4-5 minutes for muddies, less time for blue swimmers). Pour in the water, cover and steam until cooked. Take off the lid, stir in the beaten egg and keep stirring until your sauce thickens. Serve immediately.

Salt 'n' Pepper Crabs

Feeds 6 • Prep 10 mins • Cook 10-15 mins • GF, QC

This is such a simple dish it probably doesn't need a recipe. But just to remind you how delicious they are, here's one of the easiest, tastiest ways to tuck into blue swimmers.

12 blue swimmer or sand crabs

2 lemons

salt and pepper

2 cups peanut or coconut oil

Serve with Zesty Dill Mayo (see page 216).

Once your crabs have been humanely killed (see page 104), remove their shells and rinse them clean. Cut each crab in half, leaving the legs attached, and drain on paper towel. Squeeze the lemons over the top and season well with salt and pepper.

Heat 2 cups of oil in a wok or large pan and deep-fry the crabs in batches for 2-3 minutes until red. Take care because the hot oil will spit! Drain the crabs on paper towel. Serve immediately with Zesty Dill Mayo.

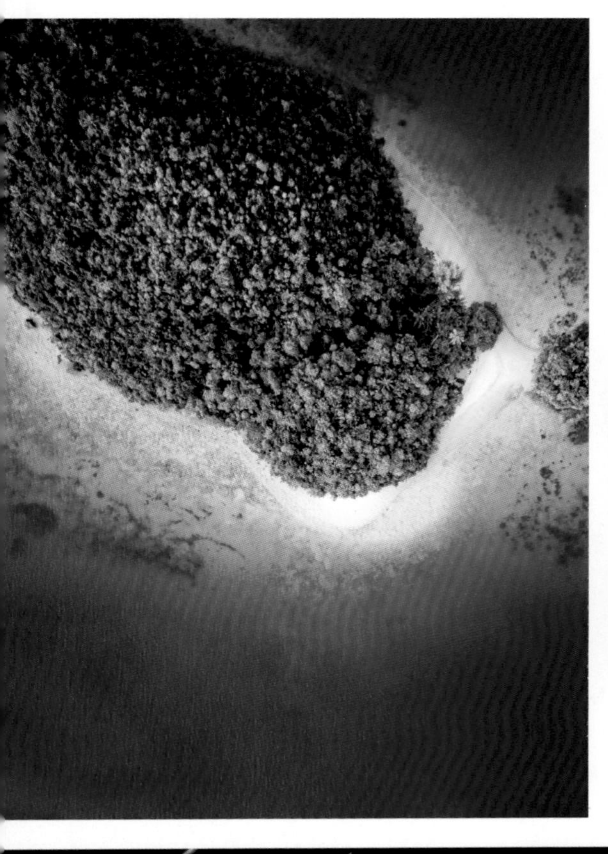

Lazy Charred Crab

with mango lime aioli

Feeds 2 • Prep 10 mins • Cook 5 mins • GF, QC

Every recipe has a story, and this one belongs to Labuan Dabu, a coral-fringed bay on Indonesia's Pulau Kai Besar. We'd anchored there to shorten the overnight run to Triton Bay for our first whale shark swimming adventure, and it was so sublime we stayed for a week. The snorkelling and spearfishing were great, but while dinghy-exploring deep into the bay, a freshwater spring led us into the mangroves where Dave wrangled a big 'ole muddy out of its hole with his bare hands. We renamed the cove Mud Crab Bay. On that lazy afternoon, we prepared it exactly as described here, charred to perfection on the back deck barbecue. All you need is a hot grill plate, a set of tongs, a lime, and some salt. Pack all the flavour into a sensational aioli, grab a beer and dig in.

1 large mud crab (green or brown)

1 lime, sliced into wedges

extra virgin olive oil

Mango Lime Aioli

1 free-range egg

½ cup extra virgin olive oil

1 ripe mango (about 100g/3.5oz), finely chopped

½ lime, juice and zest

1 small garlic clove, finely grated

salt

To make the aioli, you'll need a stick blender with a whisk, or a hand whisk and a strong arm. Crack an egg into a large jar (or a bowl for hand whisking). Gradually drizzle in 1/2 cup of extra virgin olive oil as you slowly lift the stick blender through the mixture, whisking for about 1 minute (or 3-5 minutes by hand). Add the mango, lime juice, zest, garlic, and a pinch of salt. Change attachments and blitz everything until it's smooth, then refrigerate.

Once your crab has been humanely killed and cleaned (see page 104), remove the claws and cut the crab into 4 pieces. Rub it all with olive oil and place it on a hot grill over the fire or barbecue, turning and charring it for about 10 minutes. Take the crab off the heat, crack open the claws and serve immediately, teamed with mango aioli, lime wedges and sea salt.

Lemon Chilli Crab Stacks

Makes 35-40 • Prep 10 mins • Cook 15 mins

When you can't get your hands on the real thing, this tinned crabby snack is just what you need. Serve it at sundown with something chilled (cos it's just a little bit fancy). The mini coconut pancakes transport me to some place brighter, but if you don't have it in you to fry up a batch, serve with toast, crackers or slices of fresh sourdough bread instead.

1 tbsp lemon juice

zest of 1 lemon

1 tsp (or more) finely chopped red chilli (or dried chilli flakes)

1 tsp fish sauce

2 tsp sugar

340g (12oz) tinned crab meat

1 tbsp finely chopped fresh coriander (cilantro) (optional)

coconut oil for frying

Mini Coconut Pancakes

1 cup plain (all-purpose) flour

pinch of salt

1 large free-range egg, lightly whisked

1 tbsp lemon juice

zest of ½ a lemon

1 cup coconut milk

Whisk together the lemon juice, zest, chilli, fish sauce, and sugar. Add the drained crab meat and refrigerate.

For the coconut pancakes, combine all ingredients and whisk together to form a smooth batter. Heat a large, non-stick frypan over medium heat, add enough oil to coat the pan, and fry small dollops of the batter in batches. Keep cooking until you have about 35-40 pancakes. Cool the pancakes on a wire rack.

When ready to eat, stir the chopped coriander into the crab mixture (if using) and top each pancake with a small spoonful. Serve immediately.

Chilli Mud Crab

Feeds 4-6 • Prep 10 mins • Cook 15 mins • GF, OP

I rarely cook with ready-made sauces, but making things from scratch means I spend longer in the galley. Dave can get dinner done in 10 minutes. He's a champion at quick cooking because he's not afraid to cut corners, and he's happy to use whatever's on hand to make good food taste great. This is his kind of spicy, saucy seafood. It's simple to prepare and ready in record time without compromising on flavour one bit.

2 mud crabs (green or brown)

¼ cup peanut oil

4 cloves garlic, finely chopped

2 fresh red chillies, seeded and thinly sliced*

1 tbsp grated ginger*

2 tbsp finely sliced spring onions (scallion) (optional)

Simmer Sauce

½ cup liquid vegetable stock

½ cup tomato sauce

¼ cup sweet chilli sauce

1 tbsp soy sauce

Serve with steamed rice or crusty bread.

** Swap with ready-to-go minced chilli and ginger if necessary.*

Once your crabs have been humanely killed and cleaned, remove the claws and legs and crack them with the back of a knife to open the flesh up to flavours as they cook. Cut each crab in half lengthwise and each half into 2 or 3 pieces (depending on the size of your crabs). For the simmer sauce, combine all ingredients and set aside.

Heat the oil in a wok or large saucepan on medium-high, and fry the garlic, chilli and ginger until fragrant. Add your crab pieces and cook for about a minute, turning frequently, until they turn orange. Pour in the sauce mix, toss the crab to coat each piece well, and bring the sauce to the boil. Reduce the heat to low, cover the pot and simmer for about 10 minutes. Serve with steamed rice or fresh crusty bread and a scatter of sliced spring onion (optional).

Crab Spaghetti with chilli crumbs

Feeds 2 • Prep 10 mins • Cook 20 mins

No fresh crab? This perfectly acceptable cheat gets crab lovers through those dry spells when mangroves are a distant memory. It's so easy and uses barely anything fresh, which means you can whip this up when fresh supplies are dwindling, and on passage too.

1 cup breadcrumbs (panko or homemade)

¼ cup extra virgin olive oil (plus 1 tbsp)

1 large garlic clove, finely chopped

¼ fresh red chilli, finely chopped (or a good pinch of dried chilli flakes)

250g (9oz) spaghetti

½ brown onion, finely chopped

1 punnet cherry tomatoes, halved (or any tomato, chopped)

170g (6oz) tinned crab meat

1 lemon (zest and juice)

1 tbsp chopped fresh dill (optional)

Use ready-to-go breadcrumbs or make your own from day-old bread, hand-grated or blitzed in a mini chopper. Heat 1/4 cup of extra virgin olive oil in a large frypan over medium-low heat. Add the breadcrumbs, garlic and chilli, and cook for 8 minutes or until crisp. Season with salt and pepper, and set aside.

Bring a pot of water to the boil and cook the spaghetti until al dente. While the pasta cooks, gently fry the onion in 1 tablespoon of olive oil for 2 minutes over medium heat. Stir in the cherry tomatoes and cook for 2 minutes until soft. Stir in the crab meat, lemon zest and juice, and cook for 3 minutes until everything is heated through.

Drain the pasta and toss it through the crab sauce with 1 tablespoon of chopped fresh dill (optional). Loosen with a little pasta water or olive oil, and serve topped with a generous scoop of chilli crumbs.

Coral Sea Painted Crays

Feeds 2 · Prep 10 mins · Cook 15 mins · GF

We'd been on the helm since midnight, braving big swell off the Escape River mouth and racing ahead of gale-force winds gathering quickly to the south. Stormy squalls hid the horizon, and there was no place to hide, but we hoped to be tucked around the tip of Cape York before the weather really went to hell.

The crayfishing dory came out of nowhere, tossed clean out of the sea, its propeller spinning mid-air atop one enormous cresting wave. It veered straight for us and skillfully sidled alongside while Dave battled to hold course in the heaving, four-metre swell. Over the roar of the wind and waves, we confirmed precisely two things: yes, we were all "mad bastards", and yes, we'd love some crays. These painted crays were thrown over our rails as we surfed recklessly at 13 knots, and I raced to scoop them up before the sea crashing over the stern stole them back.

The dory peeled away, returning to its mother ship rolling at anchor behind the slenderest of sand cays. With dinner in the bag, we rounded Cape York at dusk and toasted a 'Tip of Australia' sunset with these buttery, pan-fried painted crays.

- 2 painted (or other) crays
- ¼ cup butter, softened
- 3 garlic cloves, minced or crushed
- 2 tbsp (40ml) dry white wine
- ½ fresh lemon (or lime)
- salt and black
- 1 tbsp chopped fresh parsley, plus extra to serve (optional)

After humanely freezing and splitting your painted crays into two halves lengthways (see page 105), twist and break the tail pieces away from the head. Give the tails a quick rinse.

Melt the butter in a small pot over medium-low heat. Add the garlic and gently sauté for 1 minute. Pour in the white wine and simmer until slightly reduced (2-3 minutes). Squeeze in the lemon (or lime) juice, and add a pinch each of salt and pepper and 1 tablespoon of parsley (optional but nice). Whisk until the sauce is well combined. Take off the heat and pour half the sauce into a bowl.

Barbecue or panfry the crays over medium heat for 5-10 minutes (depending on the size of your crays), turning and brushing with butter sauce as they cook. Serve drizzled with some of the remaining sauce and an extra sprinkle of fresh parsley.

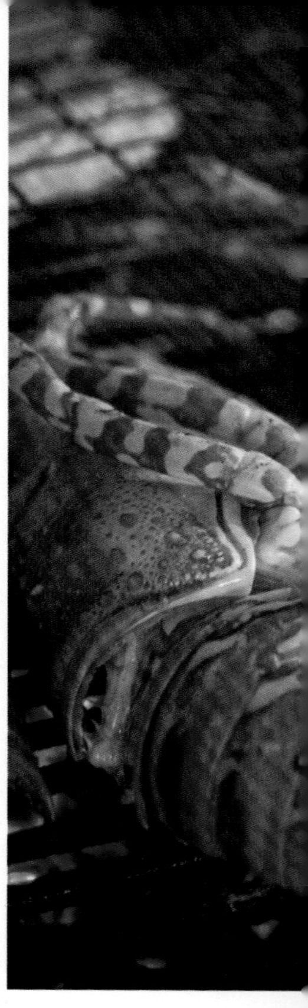

CONSERVATION SOCIETY

MUSSELS, OYSTERS & CLAMS

Collecting Oysters

It doesn't take a lot of skill to gather up a feed of oysters, but you do need to get yourself somewhere remote. In those unpopulated places where large-scale industry and big coastal towns are largely nonexistent, we feel secure collecting oysters and find that there is little competition for this food source. Harmful toxins can accumulate in shellfish over time, so it's best to avoid collecting them in any place you'd consider busy, or in calm bays and waterways that lack a thorough daily flow.

We tend to collect our oysters intact, knocked clean off the rocks with a hammer and stored in a bucket of saltwater until we are ready to shuck them. To open an oyster, pry your shucking knife into the shell's hinge and twist to break it, or tap firmly with a hammer (or rock) until the hinge falls away. You can use a screwdriver at a pinch, but you'll likely end up with a fair bit of shattered oyster shell to wash out. When you have the oyster in your (preferably gloved) hand, use your knife to gently slice through the oyster's adductor muscle, which joins it to its shell.

Smaller varieties of oysters might be eaten raw, straight off the rocks. Meatier varieties, like the large black lip oysters found across northern Australia, are tastiest (to my palette, at least) when crumbed and fried. Collect them in your bucket to take back on board for cooking.

Purging Pipis, Clams & Cockles

When I was a little kid, my entire family would line up along the shoreline, balancing fishing rods and dancing the twist in the wet sand to dig pipis out with our toes. We thought it was the most fun you could have at sunset, although at the time, I wasn't really a fan of our simmered pipi dinners.

There are lots of wild shellfish in the world, and of the bivalves, the terms clam, cockle and vongole (Italian for clam) are often used interchangeably. One of Australia's most sustainable kinds of seafood, pipis are distinctly triangular-shaped with smooth, sometimes colourful shells. Confusingly, they are also known as Coorong or Goolwa cockles in South Australia, and surf clams elsewhere. In fact, true cockles are a type of clam: sweet tasting, heart-shaped and ribbed on the shell. But they are found only in saltwater and at greater depths than other clams, which might be fresh or saltwater dwellers.

All sand-dwelling bivalves will retain some sand in the muscle, along with bacteria and other microorganisms, so you need to purge them before cooking.

Rinse your shellfish in a bucket or large bowl of seawater to remove any mud. Discard those that are open, floating or damaged. Tip out the water and refill to cover the shellfish by a couple of inches. Leave them for eight hours (overnight is best), changing the water at least once, preferably more often, to keep it oxygen-rich. Keep them in a cool spot but not in the fridge.

When it's time to cook, rinse the shellfish again. Lift them into a colander to drain, then tap or bounce the shellfish on a chopping board. Live shellfish will remain tightly shut, while dead ones will open up and should be discarded. Do this, and you'll happily prevent sandy, dead shellfish from spoiling an otherwise delicious meal.

Bangkok Oysters

Feeds 2 • Prep 10 mins • GF, NC

Our mate Robbie Risk is a national park ranger and a Larrakia man. He grew up in Darwin, where longbums are a local Indigenous delicacy, dug from the mangroves and roasted on campfire coals. When we sail into Garik Gunak Barlu National Park on the Northern Territory's Cobourg Peninsula, Robbie takes us to the water's edge. We pin our hopes on a couple of mud crabs, but the tide is wrong, and there are crocs about. Our 'smoko' of bush tucker comes down to a dozen hot, foaming longbums.

A cone-shaped crustacean, longbums are mud whelks: chewy and salty with an earthy edge that fire smoke just can't seem to temper. Despite Robbie's zeal, the longbum is a bit of a hard sell. I try one, straight off the campfire coals and sizzling, and politely nibble away at the edges. The texture is a bit challenging, but in a survival situation, Maya reminds me, this would be Bear Grylls' best day. Afterwards, we retreat with rumbling bellies to Robbie's place. When Robbie hands us a bag of fresh chillies, we use them to turn a feed of foraged oysters into the kind of 'bush tucker' I like best; chilled on ice and served at sunset with home-brewed beers and lots of laughs.

12 oysters in shell

1 tbsp lime juice

2 tsp finely chopped fresh coriander (cilantro)

1 tsp finely chopped fresh or minced red chilli

¼ tsp fish sauce

¼ tsp brown sugar

pinch of ground white pepper

To prepare the oysters, lift each from its bed with a paring knife, rinse and dry the oyster shell and replace the meat. Whisk together the lime juice, coriander, chilli, fish sauce, brown sugar and pepper. Spoon a little dressing over each oyster and eat!

Oysters Oreganata

Feeds 6 • Prep 10 mins • Cook 5 mins • QC

On our first day in Momon Bay, when the low tide exposed the reef and all the good fish were hiding from the sun, we ventured into the shallows and plucked enormous, meaty oysters from the seabed. They were a meal in themselves, so we eagerly filled our bucket and grazed on them with pals at sundown. When the fish were biting again, we ate coral trout and mackerel, but the oysters remained the star of that trip, infused with herby flavour and coated with enough crunch to get the kids tucking in too.

12-18 oysters, shucked

2 large free-range eggs

1 tbsp milk

1 cup plain (all-purpose) flour

½ tsp cracked black pepper

pinch of crushed chilli flakes

½ cup grated parmesan

½ cup panko breadcrumbs

2 tsp finely chopped fresh oregano (or ¾ tsp dried)

extra virgin olive oil for frying

extra chopped oregano or parsley to serve

Serve with lemon wedges and aioli.

Set out three bowls and fill one with flour seasoned with pepper and chilli flakes. Whisk eggs and milk together in the next, and in the last, combine the grated parmesan, panko breadcrumbs and oregano. Pour olive oil into a heavy-based frypan to a depth of about 2cm (1in), and warm it over medium-high heat.

When the oil is hot, dip each shucked oyster into the seasoned flour, then the egg mixture, and finally, the parmesan and panko crumbs. Gently slide the oysters into the hot oil and cook in batches for a minute a side. Drain on paper towel or a wire rack, and serve with lemon wedges, aioli, and a sprinkle of finely chopped oregano and parsley.

Squid Ink Linguini

with littleneck clams

Feeds 4 · Prep 10 mins · Cook 10-15 mins

I love a good fable, especially the implausible ones, like when a holy hermit goes to dinner in a nobleman's house and uses his powers to turn a meal of earth-stuffed pasta into something cheesy and delicious.

A lifelong recluse, William the Hermit was a sinner who became a saint. In between, he transformed lives (and pasta dishes). What transforms this dish is delicious littleneck clams, which need nothing more than garlic, white wine and tomatoes to bring out their sensational, salty flavour.

Dramatically coloured squid ink pasta seemed a good match for this creation, but any thick, substantial pasta would do.

375g (13oz) squid ink pasta

5 tbsp extra virgin olive oil

2 garlic cloves, crushed

2 tbsp fresh parsley, finely chopped

½ cup dry white wine

1kg (2lb) littleneck clams (fresh or frozen)

400g (14oz) tinned diced tomatoes

pinch of dried chillies

Serve with shaved parmesan.

If your clams are fresh, scrub and purge them overnight, ready for cooking (see page 115). If frozen (and precooked), rinse them in clean, warm water and drain.

Cook the pasta until al dente, drain and add a splash of olive oil. Meanwhile, heat 2 tablespoons of oil in a large pan over medium-low heat. Sauté the garlic, then stir in parsley, fresh clams (if using) and wine. Increase to medium heat, cover and steam for 2 minutes.

Add tomatoes, dried chillies and 3 tablespoons of olive oil. Cover and cook for 5 minutes or until the clams open. If using frozen clams, cook the tomatoes, chilli and olive oil for 3-4 minutes, then add the clams to warm them through for the last minute or two. Take the sauce off the heat and discard any unopened clams. Toss through the pasta and serve topped with shaved parmesan.

Mussels Bianco

Feeds 4 · Prep 10 mins · Cook 40 mins · GF, OP

I once worked in a Perth restaurant for exactly two weeks. My job? Standing at a sink, debearding buckets and buckets and buckets of mussels. My hands stank, my back ached, and it put me off mussels for a very long time. This dish rekindled the love, and it takes mere minutes to pull off. Pure cream (even the long-life kind) adds a touch of decadence, but you can turn this dish dairy-free by substituting it for passata or tinned diced tomatoes instead.

1.2kg (2.5lb) mussels

2 tbsp extra virgin olive oil

2 large garlic cloves, finely sliced

½ red chilli, finely chopped (or 1 tsp dried chilli flakes)

½ cup dry white wine

½ cup vegetable stock

½ cup pure cream

3 tbsp finely chopped fresh parsley (optional)

Debeard and scrub the mussels clean. Heat the olive oil in a wok or large saucepan over medium-low heat and gently sweat the garlic. Stir in the red chilli and add the mussels, wine and stock. Cover the pot and increase to medium heat.

Once the sauce comes to a simmer, the mussels should open in 3-4 minutes. Take the pot off the heat, add the cream and parsley and toss through. Discard any mussels that haven't opened and serve immediately with crusty bread (gluten-free if preferred).

SALTY BITES TO SHARE AT SUNDOWN

Sri Lanka can take the blame for getting me hooked on *bites* – those tasty, deep-fried snacks sold from streetside carts that gather a crowd. Sweaty tropical sailors know only too well that when you've been leather tramping around town, checking out the sights and hauling supplies, nothing takes the edge off quite like a plate of bites teamed with a cold ale and a watery view. I've nibbled curried potato puffs, vegetable samosas, pastry folded around boiled egg and fiery sambal, and delicious balls of lentil dhal fried to crispy perfection. Tasty and cheap (healthy, not so much), Sri Lankan bites are a miraculous salve after a long day in the hot sun. My salty bites mimic these flavour-packed morsels, but with a touch more freshness. Make them for parties, potlucks and beach campfires, or share them with your best mate at sundown.

Quick Fish Bites

Makes 12-14 • Prep 5 mins • Cook 10 mins • QC

2 cups (350g) finely chopped fish fillets

1½ tbsp (30ml) lemon juice

1 large garlic clove, finely chopped

2 spring onions (scallion), finely chopped

1 tbsp finely chopped fresh dill

1 tsp capers, rinsed and chopped

¾ cup breadcrumbs

1-2 tbsp coconut oil for frying

Serve with whole egg mayonnaise mixed with dill and capers.

In a large bowl, combine all ingredients (except the oil) and mix well. Use clean hands to form the mixture into small patties (about 1/4 cup each). Heat a little oil in a non-stick frying pan over medium heat and cook the fish bites in two batches, turning, for 4-5 minutes each. Drain on a wire rack.

Season 1/3 cup of whole egg mayonnaise with finely chopped capers and fresh dill and serve with the fish bites.

Coconut Panko Prawns

Makes 16 • Prep 20 mins • Cook 10 mins • QC

16 raw king prawns (shrimp)

¼ cup plain (all-purpose) flour

½ cup shredded coconut

½ cup panko breadcrumbs

2 free-range eggs, lightly whisked

1-2 cups peanut or coconut oil

Serve with Chilli Peach Jam (see page 211).

Peel and devein the prawns, removing the head but leaving the tail intact.

Sift the flour onto a saucer, and combine the shredded coconut and breadcrumbs on another large plate. Lightly whisk the eggs in a bowl. Dip each prawn in the flour, then egg, then roll it in the coconut and breadcrumb mixture. Refrigerate for an hour (or longer if you like).

When you're ready to eat, heat the oil in a wok or deep pan, and fry the prawns until golden. Drain on paper towel.

Cashew & Coriander Prawn Cakes

Makes 8 • Prep 15 mins • Cook 10 mins

½ cup roasted cashew nuts
600g (1.3lb) cooked, peeled prawns
1 large free-range egg, lightly beaten
zest of a lime
2 spring onions (scallion), finely sliced
2 tbsp finely chopped fresh coriander (cilantro)
½ tsp finely chopped chilli
1 ⅓ cups breadcrumbs
2 tbsp coconut oil
1 lime, cut into wedges to serve

Quick Lime Aioli

½ cup whole egg mayonnaise
½ small garlic clove, crushed
juice and zest of ½ lime
salt and pepper to taste

To make the aioli, combine all ingredients and season to taste with salt and pepper. Refrigerate until ready to eat.

Finely chop (or use a mini food processor) the cashews and pour them into a large mixing bowl. Blitz or finely chop the prawns and add them with the egg, zest, spring onion, coriander, chilli and 1 cup of breadcrumbs. Mix well and shape the mixture into 8 cakes, coat in the remaining breadcrumb and refrigerate until ready to eat.

Heat 2 tablespoons of coconut oil in a frypan and cook the patties in two batches, turning until golden (about 4 minutes). Serve with the Quick Lime Aioli and lime wedges.

Spanish Smoked Paprika Prawns

Makes 1 decent bowl • Prep 15 mins Cook 10 mins • GF

500g (1lb) prawns
⅓ cup (100g) salt
½ cup (75g) cornflour (cornstarch)
½ cup (75g) rice flour
2 tbsp ground smoked paprika
4 cups (1L) coconut oil (or other frying oil)
4 large garlic cloves
3-4 red and green chillies
2 tbsp Spanish sherry (Jerez)

Shell the prawns (leaving their heads and tails intact) and soak them for 10 minutes in a brine made of the salt and 1-litre of water. Drain the prawns well and rest them on paper towel. Sieve the flours and paprika into a bowl and toss the prawns in to coat. Finely chop the garlic and half a chilli and set aside. Slice the remaining chillies into long strands.

Heat the coconut oil and deep-fry the prawns and sliced chillies in small batches until crisp. Drain the pan, lower the heat and return the pan to the stove. Gently sauté the chopped chilli and garlic, add the prawns and sherry and toss quickly to coat and colour the prawns. Drain on paper towel and serve immediately with cold beers and chilled Jerez.

Sesame Salmon Spoons

Makes 8 • Prep 5 mins + Marinading time Cook 10 mins • GF, QC

Make this with the last of the salmon (or any other fillet of firm fish). It's quick to pull off, super tasty and makes a cool little sideliner to chilled ales at sundown. Make a meal out of these by cooking a crisp vegetable stir-fry and serving with steamed rice.

1 salmon fillet (about 260g/0.5lb)

1 tbsp tamari (or soy sauce)

2 tsp rice malt syrup (or honey)

1 tsp finely chopped pickled ginger

1 tbsp peanut oil

1 tbsp sesame seeds

extra oil for frying

Take the skin off the salmon and slice it into 8 cubes. Mix the tamari, rice malt syrup (or honey), pickled ginger and peanut oil, toss in the salmon cubes, and refrigerate for 15 minutes. Toast the sesame seeds and set aside. Warm a little oil in a frying pan over medium heat and pan-fry the salmon pieces for about 2 minutes on each side. Serve sprinkled with toasted sesame seeds.

Basil Leaf Fish Bites

Makes 24 • Prep 10 mins • Cook 10 mins

Aromatic basil leaves might seem an unlikely choice of packaging, but they balance out the heady Thai flavours of this dish perfectly. Most of the flavours here could come from long-life pastes or jars, but you'll need a blooming pot of basil (or a big, fresh bunch from the local market) and a couple of fillets of any firm, white fish.

400g (14oz) firm white fish

⅓ cup plain (all-purpose) flour (or use rice flour to go GF)

coconut or peanut oil for frying

24 large fresh basil leaves

2 tbsp fried shallot

2 tbsp crushed peanuts

extra fresh coriander (cilantro) sprigs (excellent but optional)

1 lemon

Marinade

2 tsp rice malt syrup (or sugar)

1 tbsp sesame oil

2 tsp soy sauce

⅓ cup coconut cream

2 lemongrass stalks (whites only, or 2 tsp from a jar)

2 spring onions (scallion) or 2-3 shallots

1 red chilli (or 1 tsp dried chilli flakes)

1 clove garlic

¼ cup finely chopped coriander
(or 1 tbsp long-life paste)

For the marinade, whisk together the rice malt syrup, sesame oil, soy sauce and coconut cream. Finely chop the lemongrass, spring onions, chilli, garlic and fresh coriander, and stir in. Cut the fish into bite-sized pieces, toss it through the marinade to coat well, and refrigerate for 2-3 hours.

When you're ready to eat, coat the fish pieces lightly in plain (or rice) flour and shallow fry in a pan for 2-3 minutes. Drain them on paper towel before tucking each fish bite into a basil leaf. Top with a sprinkle of crushed peanuts, fried shallots and a sprig of fresh coriander. Drizzle with a little fresh lemon juice and serve.

Bamboo Barramundi

Makes 6 • Prep 10 mins • Cook 10 mins • GF QC

Dreaming of barramundi and shaking out brand-new fishing rods, we gathered on the riverbank, ready to cast. Dad went first, but his line never hit the water, unspooling in a crazy arc of mind-boggling mess. Maya's new birthday rod disintegrated next, so while crocodiles gathered and whoops of barramundi joy rang out upstream, we did far more fixing than fishing.

As the sun dipped low, we called it a day, returning to camp with nothing but missed opportunities. We slunk into our camp chairs clutching tepid beers, joined by dusk-time mosquitoes that even a smoky campfire couldn't chase away. Spraying and slapping as we gulped down bowls of pasta, we went to bed praying for barramundi salvation at dawn. The sunrise was spectacular, but the barras never came, so it was a good thing we had some sneaky fillets on hand to conjure up this herby dish.

400g (14oz) barramundi (or other firm white fish)

2 tbsp extra virgin olive oil

1 tbsp finely chopped lemon thyme

1 tbsp finely chopped flat-leaf parsley

6 bamboo skewers

Cut the barramundi into small cubes and thread them onto 6 skewers that have been soaked in water for about 20 minutes. Combine the olive oil and herbs in a shallow pan, add the skewers and rub the mixture all over the fish. Refrigerate for 20 minutes, then barbecue, grill or panfry and enjoy!

Italian Tuna Bites

Makes 10 • Prep 10 mins Cook • 35 mins

Our first equator crossing was a hectic, squally affair: a huge tuna off the back, Maya dancing in the rain, and me on the helm, steering us into the Equator Isles anchorage, trying to take a photo of said dancing child to convince her pals she'd observed protocol.

Tuna is best eaten fresh, so when you land one, having a crowd on hand is a blessing. Simply grab a sharp knife, some wasabi and a bottle of soy sauce, and shave off wafer-thin slices to serve at sundown. Then turn one decent fillet into these deliciously simple tuna bites, served with a rich tomato and white wine sauce and crusty bread.

250g (0.5lb) tuna fillet, cubed

salt and pepper

3 tbsp extra virgin olive oil

1 free-range egg, beaten

½ cup parmesan cheese

⅔ cup fresh breadcrumbs

2 tsp lemon juice

zest of half a lemon

3 tbsp chopped parsley (or 1 tsp dried)

1 tsp finely chopped fresh oregano (or ½ tsp dried)

2 garlic cloves, finely sliced

1 onion, finely chopped

400g (14oz) tinned tomatoes

1 tbsp tomato paste

¼ cup white wine

Season the tuna generously with salt and pepper. Warm 1 tablespoon of olive oil in a frypan and add the fish, turning for 1-2 minutes. Transfer to a mixing bowl and set aside.

When the fish has cooled, add the egg, parmesan, breadcrumbs, lemon juice, zest, two-thirds of the parsley and half the chopped oregano. Combine well and form into 10 balls, about 5cm (2in) in diameter, adding extra breadcrumbs if required. Refrigerate for 30 minutes.

Warm 1 tablespoon of olive oil over low heat and sweat the garlic and onion for 10 minutes. Stir in the tomatoes, tomato paste, wine, and the remaining parsley and oregano. Bring it to a boil, reduce the heat and simmer, uncovered for 15 minutes, stirring occasionally until the sauce has thickened to your likening.

Heat 1 tablespoon of olive oil in a pan and fry the tuna bites, turning occasionally for 5 minutes or until golden. Stir through the sauce and serve with crusty bread.

The Gatherer

SUNNY DAY SALADS

For All Kinds Of Weather

When markets and stores are within reach, great salads are a breeze. But once you set sail and the fresh things start to dwindle, you need to build salads in a slightly different way. These recipes are the ultimate one-pot-wonders with no interest in sticking to the sidelines. They turn the classic lettuce-tomato-cucumber combo completely on its head, utilising all kinds of ingredients to make truly satisfying, flexible, all-in-a-bowl meals.

Here's how to make one:

Veg Out: In place of lettuce (or in addition to it), build your salads on a bed of finely chopped or grated vegetables that can outlive green leaves by weeks. Choose raw beetroot, sliced fennel or lightly blanched asparagus or broccolini, then add your salad greens if you have them. Try building on a foundation of leftover roast vegetables: pumpkin, sweet potato, red onion, garlic, zucchini, corn and eggplants. Choose a colourful variety because the more vibrant the veggies, the more you ramp up your intake of vitamins and minerals.

Beef It Up: add quick-cook grains such as quinoa, rice or couscous, or toss your salad veggies through blanched rice noodles or wholemeal pasta. Bread salad is a favourite of mine, too; try the Tuscan Tomato Salad on page 138.

Pack It With Protein: add some lightly grilled seafood (fish and prawns work well), tinned tuna, anchovies, slices of marinated barbecued tofu, or crumbled feta cheese.

Get Fruity: strawberries, fresh peaches and watermelon all love balsamic vinegar, while citrus fruits boost the iron absorption of rocket and spinach and instantly dress up greens. Pears, nashi fruit, apples and fresh blueberries partner well with bitter walnuts and parmesan cheese. Even kiwi fruit makes a great substitute for tomatoes when making Mexican-style salsa.

Add Some Crunch: a great salad needs crunch, so just before serving, add a sprinkle of toasted sesame or sunflower seeds, some chopped raw or toasted organic nuts, pan-toasted coconut, crispy fried Chinese noodles, fennel croutons (see page 138), or some crushed toasted rice (see how to make smashed rice on page 140).

Get Pickled: there are always a few jars of Spiced Pickled Vegetables in my fridge, patiently waiting for their chance to shine and add tang to many meals. To make a batch, turn to page 140.

Swap It Out: Substitute bottled dressings for a simple squeeze of fresh lemon or lime juice, a drizzle of cold-pressed macadamia nut oil (or sesame oil for instant Asian flavour), and a little sea salt and cracked black pepper.

Got A Garden Growing? Fresh herbs add potent flavour to salads, so add a little of whatever's growing in your garden: finely chopped Vietnamese mint, coriander sprigs, basil leaves, parsley or dill – whatever suits the flavour of your salad.

Food As Medicine: Give Your Body A Boost

Add **chopped fresh chillies** to rev up a sluggish metabolism, boost the immune system and supply vitamins C and E, folic acid, potassium, beta-carotene and fibre.

Add **mint and lime juice** to stimulate your appetite, refresh the palette, and cleanse and hydrate your body.

Add **rocket, spinach leaves and parsley** to protect against age-related diseases and cancers and for the good amounts of iron, vitamin C, beta-carotene and fibre they supply.

Add **grapefruit and oranges** to boost your absorption of iron from leafy greens and to supply lots of vitamin C and fibre.

Add **fresh fish** for a dose of Omega-3s, important fatty acids that help reduce the symptoms of arthritis, asthma and psoriasis and slow fatty build-up in blood vessel walls, helping to reduce the risk of a heart attack.

Add **pistachio nuts** for protein, vitamin E, fibre and essential fatty acids.

Som Tam Malako (Green Papaya Salad)

Feeds 4 • Prep 15 mins • GF, NC

A slice of ruby-pink papaya tastes like pure sunshine to me, but it's unripened papaya that makes this salad sing. Its magical ingredient is a milky sap called papain, packed with protein-splitting enzymes that aid digestion, relieve insect stings, and even remove stubborn blood and fat stains from fabrics.

In Eastern Indonesia's "Forgotten Islands", where remote-living locals love to trade, home-grown papayas are swapped for T-shirts and hats, sunglasses and goggles, and fishing lures and fins. The last time we visited Wotap Island, a whole week's worth of produce was pushed onto our decks: bananas, bush taro and young drinking coconuts known as kelapa muda. In our bounty were 10 huge green papayas, so as the sun went down, this is what we ate.

Because of Som Tam Malako, I always have green papayas on board, and what escapes the salad bowl slowly ripens for smoothies.

1 medium green papaya (pawpaw) or 2 green mangoes

1 large garlic clove, peeled

1-2 fresh red chillies (or 1 tsp dried chilli flakes)

2 Roma tomatoes (or a handful of cherry tomatoes)

juice of a lime

1 tbsp fish sauce

2 tsp rice malt syrup (or sugar)

2-3 tbsp crushed roasted peanuts

Serve with Sticky Rice (page 160).

Your need very firm green papaya or mangoes for this salad. Grate or julienne the fruit, or shred it Thai-style, using just a knife and a chopping board. To do this, peel your papaya (or mango), then cradle it in the palm of one hand. Using a heavy knife, carefully make lots of fine, deep cuts into the flesh, almost to the core (the Thais do this breathtakingly fast). Turn the papaya on its end on a chopping board, and slice down the fruit, cutting in very thin layers to produce fine shreds of fruit. Cradle the papaya again, and on a fresh, uncut side, repeat the process until you have about three cups of shredded fruit.

Pound the garlic and fresh (or dried) chillies in a mortar and pestle, blitz them in a mini food chopper, or simply finely chop them and scrape them into a large mixing bowl. You can use as many chillies as you can handle or none at all if serving to kids.

Add the shredded papaya and use clean hands to work the garlic and chilli into the flesh. Add the tomato (cut into large chunks) and gently mix it in without mashing it too much. Add the lime juice, fish sauce and rice malt syrup to the bowl, or mix them separately to adjust the seasonings to taste. Mix everything together well and serve sprinkled with crushed toasted peanuts and a serve of sticky rice.

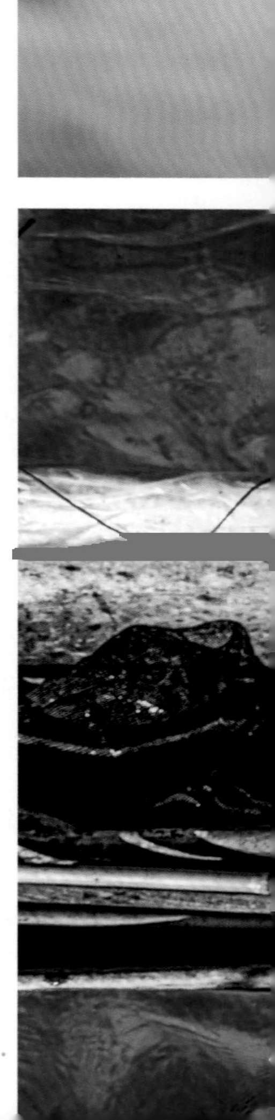

Laab Norhai (Bamboo Laab)

Feeds 2 · Prep 15 mins · Cook 2 min · GF, V, QC

In Luang Prabang, that most beautiful of French-inspired Laotian cities, I learnt to make this fresh, perky salad. Now that I'm cruising through Southeast Asia – where snake beans cost a dollar a bunch – I make it often. It needn't be chilli-hot, so just add whatever your tastebuds can handle. It's also extremely forgiving. If you can't find fresh lemongrass or kaffir (makrut) lime leaves, use lemongrass paste or freshly grated lime zest instead. Laab begs for fresh herbs, though, so if you've got a small garden on board, plant mint, coriander and Vietnamese mint.

3 raw snake beans, very finely sliced

3 lemongrass stalks (whites only), finely chopped

1 tbsp dried crushed chillies

2 tsp vegetable stock powder

½ tsp sea salt

1 tbsp white rice

1 kaffir (makrut) lime leaf, finely sliced

1 carrot, finely sliced

1 cup bamboo shoots, drained and sliced

2 tsp water

4 sprigs fresh mint

4 Vietnamese mint leaves

5 sprigs fresh coriander (cilantro)

½ cup bean sprouts (optional)

Serve with Sticky Rice (page 160) in 4 lettuce cups.

In a large mixing bowl, combine the very finely chopped snake beans, lemongrass, crushed chillies, stock powder and salt. Gently toast one tablespoon of rice in a small pan for 1-2 minutes until lightly coloured. Remove and grind into a powder using a mortar and pestle (or a grinder). This might seem like a strange salad ingredient, but trust me, toasted crushed rice tastes awesome.

Add the crushed rice to the bean mixture and stir in the lime leaf, carrot, bamboo shoots, water, fresh herbs and bean sprouts. Mix well and serve on lettuce leaves with sticky or steamed rice.

Spicy Lao Cashew Salad

Feeds 2 · Prep 15 mins · GF, QC

In Laos, they use a raw vegetable called jambean to make the incredibly tasty salad, Yam Nai Moung Hiana Phan. Use jambean if you can get your hands on it, but if not, nashi pear is a near-perfect substitute. This salad has so much texture, and the taste will blow you away. Serve it with sticky rice or some sticks of Barbecued Fish Laab (see page 87).

4 small, fresh red chillies

1 tbsp raw sugar

1 tbsp cider vinegar

½ bunch fresh coriander (cilantro) leaves

20 sprigs fresh mint

2 handfuls watercress

10 small butter lettuce leaves (or other salad greens)

10 cherry tomatoes, halved (or 1 big tomato)

1 boiled free-range egg, sliced

2 nashi pears, very finely sliced

½ cup roasted cashew nuts

pinch of salt

If you have one, use a mortar and pestle to pound the chillies and raw sugar into a paste, then add the cider vinegar and pound again. Alternatively, finely chop the chillies (or use ready-made crushed chillies or paste), and mash the chillies and raw sugar in a small bowl with the back of a spoon. Pour in the cider vinegar and mix well.

Rinse and dry the coriander, mint, watercress and lettuce leaves and combine them in a large salad bowl with the tomato. Pour in the chilli and vinegar mixture and add the boiled egg, nashi pears and cashews. Season to taste with a pinch of salt, and use your hands to work the paste into the vegetables. Don't worry about bruising the lettuce and herbs; just work on coating the leaves well. Eat with a serve of sticky rice or some sticks of Barbecued Fish Laab.

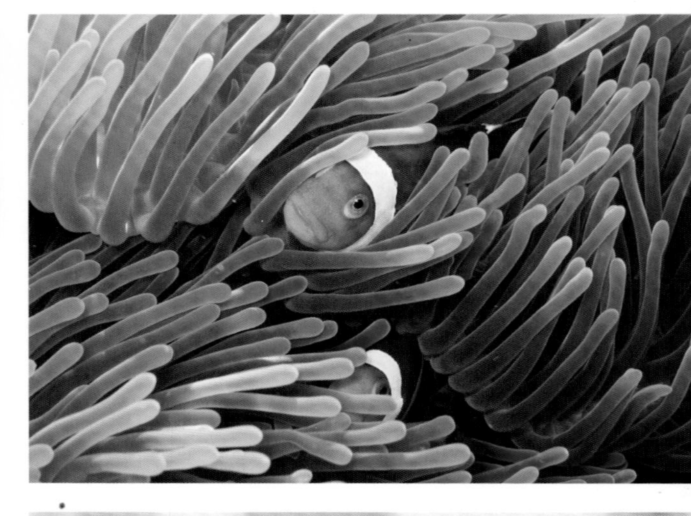

Beetroot, Feta & Quinoa Salad

Feeds 2 • Prep 15 mins • Cook 25 mins • GF

Aussies love beets on burgers in a way that makes us seem a little strange. Really though, it's a match made in heaven because a slice of beetroot imparts a sweet-and-sour flavour that pulls everything together. Bake them, boil them or grate them into a pickle, happy knowing that they're rich in folate, which we need for proper cellular function, and to ward off heart disease and strokes.

2 medium (or 4 baby) beetroots (raw or precooked)

½ cup tricolour quinoa

1 large orange (or other sweet citrus)

¼ cup pistachio nuts, roughly chopped

1 cup baby rocket (arugula) leaves (any salad greens work)

1 cup (125g) crumbled feta

Dressing

½ cup natural yoghurt

3 tsp lemon juice

½ clove garlic, crushed

salt and pepper to taste

If using raw beets, cover them with water in a pot, bring them to the boil, reduce to a simmer and cook until tender. Drain and when cool, peel and slice into segments. If you take the time to cook your own, boil a few extra beets and preserve them (see Spiced Pickled Vegetables on page 140).

Rinse the quinoa under a running tap for 30 seconds (you can use salt water), then drain well to reduce the bitterness from the quinoa's natural coating of saponin. Tip it into a small pot with one cup of water and a decent pinch of salt and bring to a boil over medium-high heat. Reduce the heat to medium-low and simmer, uncovered, until the quinoa is tender (about 10 to 12 minutes). Take it off the heat and leave it to stand, covered, for five minutes, fluff it with a fork and transfer it to a mixing bowl.

While the quinoa cooks, segment the orange (or other sweet citrus) and cut it into pieces. Toast the pistachio nuts in a pan over low heat, and rinse and dry the rocket. Combine all dressing ingredients in a jar, shake well and season to taste with salt and pepper. Add the orange pieces, pistachio nuts, rocket, beetroot and crumbled feta to the quinoa, drizzle the dressing and serve.

Avocado Citrus Salad

Feeds 4 • Prep 10 mins • Cook 2 mins • GF, QC

Ward off scurvy, fight free radicals and protect against premature crinkles. This antioxidant-rich salad (with vitamin C to max out your iron absorption) can do it all. Oranges are full of fibre and last for ages on boats. Buy only firm, ripe, heavy fruit (they won't ripen after picking).

Choose organic fruit if you can, or wash them in warm soapy water and rinse well to remove wax and sprays. Once you get them aboard, store oranges at room temperature, putting them in the fridge only to chill them or to extend their life.

2 avocados, sliced thinly

2 large oranges

2 large handfuls (100g) baby rocket (arugula)

2 spring onions, finely sliced

½ cup pecan halves

Lemon And Honey Dressing

2 tbsp lemon juice

1 tbsp honey

1 tbsp extra virgin olive oil

1 tsp wholegrain mustard

salt and pepper to taste

Serve with shaved parmesan.

For the dressing, combine all ingredients in a glass jar and shake vigorously. Refrigerate until needed.

Gently toast the pecans in a pan over low heat, and slice them into slivers.

Peel the avocados and slice them into thin strips. Cut the oranges into eight wedges, remove the peel and slice each segment in half. Place the avocado, orange, rocket and spring onion in a salad bowl, pour over the dressing and gently toss everything together. Serve topped with toasted pecans and shaved parmesan cheese.

Tuscan Tomato Salad with fennel croutons

Feeds 2-4 · Prep 15 mins · Cook 10 mins

Pulau Misool sits like a stingray in the sea, its tail trailing off to the east in a fractured swirl of towering limestone islets and hidden caves. Steering their boats into snug, rocky amphitheatres, sailors tie up between sheer karst walls and then dive overboard to explore some of Indonesia's most pristine coral reefs. We paddled kayaks, swam with huge, purple moon jellies, and climbed limestone craters to swim in secret, landlocked lagoons. Armed with torches, we dared ourselves into decorated caves sculpted with stalactites and filled with bats and blind cave spiders. Diving and snorkelling until the light finally faded, we hauled out on deck, sunkist and spent, and watched hornbills returning to roost with wild, hooting calls. On days like these, euphoric with all our wondrous natural encounters, we were glad that Misool's unbelievable sanctuary was so well protected. With fresh fish off the menu, we ate this salad instead.

1 tbsp capers, drained and rinsed

4-5 anchovies

⅓ cup Kalamata olives, pitted

4 grilled red capsicums (bell pepper)

small bunch of basil

1 garlic clove, crushed

3 big, ripe tomatoes
(or a punnet of cherry tomatoes)

splash of red wine vinegar

drizzle of extra virgin olive oil

salt and pepper

Fennel Croutons

½ loaf of sourdough or ciabatta bread

2 cloves garlic

2-3 tbsp extra virgin olive oil

1 tsp fennel seeds

1 tsp dried rosemary (or fresh sprigs)

pinch of salt

Serve with parmesan.

For the Fennel Croutons, slice the bread thickly and tear or chop it into small pieces. Finely grate or crush two cloves of garlic and combine them with the olive oil, fennel seeds and rosemary. Season with a good pinch or grind of salt. Toss in the bread and mix well with your hands. Toast the croutons in a heavy-based frypan over very low heat, tossing occasionally until they are crisp and brown. Alternatively, place them on a baking tray under a moderate grill, or bake at about 180°C (350°F) until golden (10 to 12 minutes). Tip into a large bowl and set aside.

While the croutons are cooking, roughly chop the capers, anchovies, olives and two of the grilled capsicums, and tear up the basil leaves. Crush the garlic clove, dice the tomatoes and toss everything together in a large bowl. Add a splash of red wine vinegar and a good drizzle of olive oil, and season with a pinch of salt and pepper.

When ready to serve, slice the remaining capsicum and add it with the fennel croutons, then mix it with your hands. Adjust seasonings to taste and serve topped with plenty of shaved or grated parmesan cheese.

Smashed Rice Salad

Feeds 4 • Prep 10 mins • Cook 5 mins • GF, V, QC

Smashed rice is an intriguing, aromatic topping that adds delicious crunch to this and any other Asian-style salad.

2 tbsp jasmine rice

3 large handfuls (150g) baby spinach leaves

1 Lebanese (or ½ continental) cucumber

½ bunch fresh coriander (cilantro)

1 tbsp sweet chilli sauce

1 tbsp tamari (or other GF soy sauce)

1 tbsp rice wine vinegar

½ tsp sesame oil

To make smashed rice, heat a non-stick frypan over medium heat and gently toast the uncooked rice, stirring for about 5 minutes or until the grains are golden brown. Take it off the heat, and when cool, coarsely grind the rice in a mini chopper, grinder or mortar and pestle. You can also pour the cooled rice into a couple of small plastic bags and crush it with a rolling pin.

Slice the cucumber in half lengthways, then slice diagonally into crescents. Place in a serving bowl and add baby spinach leaves and coriander (trimmed and roughly chopped). Combine the sweet chilli sauce, tamari (or soy sauce), rice vinegar and sesame oil in a glass jar and shake vigorously. Drizzle the dressing over the salad, toss gently and sprinkle with smashed rice just before serving.

Spiced Pickled Vegetables

Fills 2 jars • Prep 15 mins • Cook 10 mins • GF, V, OP

You can use almost any vegetables, especially whatever's abundant and in season locally. Use herbs and spices you like best with any combination of vinegars that are at least 5 per cent acetic acid. I use mostly high-acid apple cider vinegar, but white is also good. Red wine and balsamic impart robust flavours that suit pickling onions.

2 x 500ml (pint) glass jars

1 cup vinegar (apple cider, white, red wine or a mixture)

1 cup water

1 tbsp sugar

2 tsp sea salt

3 cups of veggies (enough to fill 2 jars): red onions, carrots, radishes, beetroots, cucumbers, capsicum (bell pepper), beans and/or asparagus

You Choice of Flavour-Packed Seasonings

2 garlic cloves, thickly sliced

1 tsp fennel seeds

1 tsp dried chilli flakes

4 bay leaves

2 star anise

1 tbsp whole cloves

1 tsp peppercorns

To sterilise jars, bring a pot of water to the boil, add the jars and lids, and boil for 10 minutes. Remove with tongs and upend on a wire rack to cool.

For the pickling brine, add 1 cup each of water and vinegar, the sugar and salt, and stir gently as you bring it to the boil. Take off the heat and set the pot aside.

Peel the onions, wash your veggies and slice them thinly (leave beans, asparagus and baby carrots whole). Add whatever seasonings you like to the jars and fill them with vegetables, adding just enough so that the vinegar can surround them. Fill the jars with hot vinegar mixture, and gently tap the jars on the bench to remove air bubbles. Seal and set aside for a few hours to cool. Veggies are ready to nibble on within 8 hours but are tastiest after 2 or 3 days and will keep for months in the fridge. Serve with Marinaded Feta (page 213) and freshly baked bread.

The Vegie Patch
APPLES $2
PEARS $2
CARROTS $2
ONIONS $2
BEETROOT $3
KALE $2
$1
CAPSICUMS
3 for $2
EGGS $5

NO-FUSS FOOD

For Sailing (& Lazy) Days

Tom Yum in a Jar

Feeds 4 • Prep 15 mins • GF, QC

There's a cool little café in Darwin that makes laksa just the way I like it. It's a generous bowl of noodles in a rich, spicy coconut broth, topped with lots of crisp vegetables and tasty tofu puffs, minus the soggy cabbage. The chunkiness of Chef Alberto's delicious soup inspired this recipe, which I prep in advance in big glass jars ready to be topped up with hot water. It's perfect devoured in the cockpit under sail, taken ashore for picnic lunches or simple beach sunset dinners. Use the biggest glass jars you own because there's a lot to pack in here!

4 x 500ml (pint) glass jars

4 hard-boiled, free-range eggs, halved

40g (1.5oz) dried vermicelli noodles

16 small fried tofu puffs

1 tbsp tom yum paste

1 tsp vegetable stock powder

6 cups (1.5L) litres of boiling water

Your Choice Of Veggies (All Or Any)

4-6 mushrooms, sliced

8 cherry tomatoes, halved

1 small carrot, sliced

⅔ cup bean sprouts

spring onion (scallion), finely sliced

For Flavour

4 slices fresh ginger

4 lemongrass stalks, bashed

1 fresh red chilli, thinly sliced (optional)

1 lime or lemon, quartered

fresh coriander (cilantro) leaves to serve

Divide the boiled eggs, dried noodles, tofu and your choice of veggies between four large glass jars. Add the ginger, lemongrass and chilli (optional). Squeeze a quarter of a lime (or lemon) into each jar to cover the ingredients and pop the lime in for flavour too. Stick the jars in the fridge.

When you are ready to eat, boil up some water (or have a large thermos of hot water ready). Combine the tom yum paste, vegetable stock powder and about 6 cups of hot water. If serving to young kids, you can replace all or some of the tom yum paste with extra stock powder. Pour the soup into the jars, leave for 6 minutes, stir and top with fresh coriander (optional).

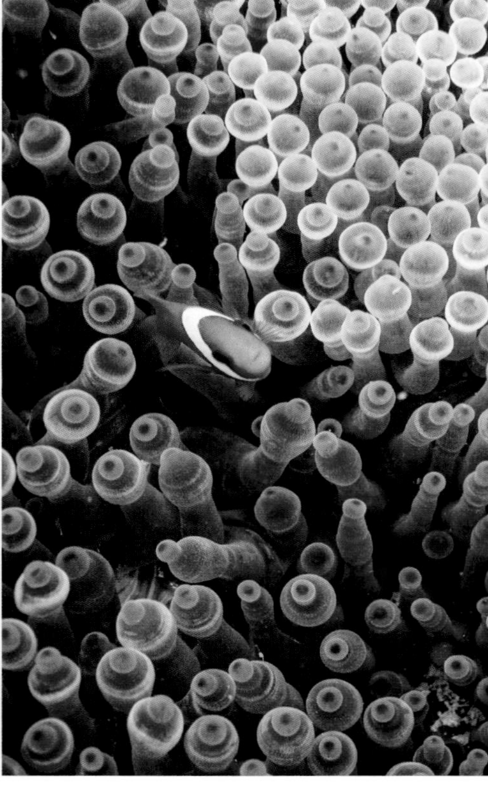

Veg-out Burgers

Makes 6 • Prep 15 mins • Cook 5 mins • QC

Even pescatarians like me need a burger fix once in a while, but I'm a little bit fussy. Far too many vegetarian patties I've tried taste like mashed up baby food with only the crumb coating holding everything together. I want something adult, with real flavour and lots of texture, and I don't want to spend ages at the stovetop, cooking up and cooling down my veggies. These patties can be made in minutes (no precooking required), and once coated, store well in the fridge to be pan-fried whenever you need them.

400g (15oz) tin chickpeas

1 cup grated zucchini (courgette)

2 tbsp basil pesto

1 tbsp toasted pine nuts

1 large slice of roasted capsicum (bell pepper)

1 garlic clove, roughly chopped

1 tsp paprika

1 cup panko breadcrumbs

2 tbsp toasted sesame seeds

1 tbsp extra virgin olive oil

Serve with Pickled Beetroot (page 214) or Quick Pickled Onion (page 88) and Zesty Dill Mayo (page 216).

Use a stick blender to roughly blitz half the zucchini with the pesto, pine nuts, capsicum, garlic, paprika and breadcrumbs (alternatively, finely chop the zucchini and capsicum and mix everything together by hand). Drain and rinse the chickpeas and give them a rough mash. Stir through the mixture with the remaining grated zucchini and sesame seeds.

Form into tablespoon-sized balls and grill, panfry or barbecue the patties in a little olive oil over medium heat for about 2-3 minutes a side. I cook them smaller than burger patties, so they're crispier, and then load a handful on each burger. Serve with Pickled Beetroot or Quick Pickled Onion and Zesty Dill Mayo – or with or without bread buns or wraps.

To turn this recipe vegan, use or make vegan pesto and Dill Mayo.

Cauliflower & Cheddar Fritters

Makes 10 • Prep 10 mins • Cook 15 mins • QC

I committed to a vegetarian diet when I was 20, and since then, my Mum has been hugely supportive. Her fridge is always stocked with things my meat-free daughter and I enjoy. She has always got some excellent new vegetarian recipe to try out when we visit. This is inspired by the fritters she cooked for us one night, morphed a little (so that I can use less oil) but with the same creamy decadence. It might seem like a benign kind of player, but cauliflower contains a little of almost every vitamin and mineral your body needs. It's packed with vitamins C, K, B6 and folate and is rich in a range of antioxidants that help ward off heart disease and protect against many cancers. And since cauliflower can survive for up to 2-3 weeks in the fridge (sealed in a zip-lock plastic bag), it's a very sailor-friendly veg too.

2 generous cups of cauliflower florets (fresh or frozen)

⅔ cup self-raising flour

½ cup milk (any)

2 tbsp natural Greek yoghurt

1 large free-range egg

1 cup grated cheddar cheese

salt and pepper

extra virgin olive oil for frying

1 lemon, cut into wedges

Serve with lemon wedges and 10-Minute Mango Chutney (see page 211).

Steam, boil or microwave the cauliflower (fresh or frozen) until cooked but firm. Drain well. Meanwhile, combine the flour, milk, yoghurt and egg in a bowl and mix well with a spoon. Stir in the cauliflower and cheese, and season well with salt and pepper.

Heat 1 tablespoon of oil in a large non-stick frypan over medium-high heat. Ladle in 1/3 cup of the mixture for each fritter and cook in batches for 1-2 minutes per side until golden. Drain on a wire rack and serve warm with lemon wedges and a dollop of 10-Minute Mango Chutney.

Save-the-day Silverbeet Pastries

Makes 16 • Prep 15 mins • Cook 25-45 mins

Dave invented these pastries on a cycle-touring trip around Tassie when Maya was five and riding pillion. It had been a long, cold, rainy day filled with steep hills and swerving motorists, and I really needed a boost. Dave hit the only grocery shop we could find (while I scanned used car ads outside, dreaming of a possible upgrade). He triumphantly emerged with the makings of these mood-altering snacks, cooked them on a camp stove, and we've been making them ever since. They are flavour-packed, unfussy treats (which is precisely how Dave always cooks), and because Dave loves his proteins, adding scrambled eggs makes them more nutritious, filling, and rather creamy and kid-friendly. Use any green leaves you like – even defrosted blocks of frozen spinach work – and bake them in the oven or very slowly in a heavy-based pan, flipping them over when they turn golden.

1 bunch silverbeet (6-7 large stalks) or 250g (10oz) frozen spinach

½ tbsp extra virgin olive oil

1 small onion, finely chopped

2 garlic cloves, finely chopped

1 tsp powdered vegetable stock

cracked black pepper

4 free-range eggs, whisked

1 ½ cups grated cheddar (or a blend of feta and cheddar)

4 sheets puff pastry

If using fresh silverbeet, wash it well, pat it dry and slice off (and discard) the white stalks. Finely chop the leaves and set them aside. Alternatively, simply defrost a packet of frozen spinach. Heat a large frypan over medium-low heat and warm the olive oil. Gently fry the onion and garlic until soft (4-5 minutes).

Add the silverbeet, increase the heat to medium and cook it down, stirring occasionally, until soft and the moisture has mostly evaporated (about 5 minutes). Skip this step if you're using defrosted greens but make sure they are well-drained. Take it off the heat and stir in the vegetable stock (if you're using feta, reduce the stock by half to even out the saltiness). Season with a good grind of black pepper and set aside to cool.

Whisk the eggs and scramble them in a lightly oiled, non-stick pan. Take them off the heat and stir them into the silverbeet mixture with the cheese.

Lay four sheets of pastry on a clean benchtop to defrost. Slice each sheet into quarters and add a couple of tablespoons of cooled filling to each. Close them with your fingertips to form triangles and press the edges together.

Cook the pastries in batches in a large, heavy-based frypan over very low heat, turning once when the pastry browns. In a conventional oven, bake them on trays at 180°C (350°F) for 10-15 minutes. They are great with Chilli Peach Jam (page 211).

Pumpkin Ravioli

with basil & blue cheese

Feeds 2-3 · Prep 20 mins · Cook 55 mins

My sailing pal Sarah and I were hedging bets on when our pasta would run out. We were a long way from the shops, with a lot of mouths to feed. "We could always make our own," she declared wearily. But I was already tasting this dish. All I needed was some gow gee pastry and a sneaky triangle of frozen blue cheese. Home-made pasta (even this cheats' version) tastes better than anything from a shop. If you're a fan of blue cheese, spend just two minutes making the sauce and pour it over any kind of pasta in your pantry.

800g (1.7lb) pumpkin (any kind)

1 tbsp extra virgin olive oil

½ cup raw pecans

½ cup ricotta

salt and pepper

24 gow gee pastries

Blue Cheese Sauce

200g (7oz) blue cheese

½ cup cream

a handful of basil leaves

Peel and chop the pumpkin into small pieces, place on a tray lined with baking paper and drizzle with extra virgin olive oil. Bake at 180°C (350°F) for 30 minutes. Take the pumpkin off the tray, add the pecans and bake for 4 minutes. Set them aside to cool. Mash the pumpkin, stir in the ricotta, and season to taste with salt and pepper.

This is the finicky part, but it's worth it, trust me: place 12 gow gee pastries on a clean bench, spoon on 1 tablespoon of pumpkin mixture and smear all edges of the wrappers with a little water. Cover with another gow gee wrapper, gently squeezing out the air as you press the edges together to create ravioli squares.

Bring a large pot of water to a rolling boil and cook the ravioli, 4 pieces at a time, for about 5 minutes a batch. Place the cooked ravioli on a tray lined with baking paper and cover it with foil to keep warm while you continue cooking.

Meanwhile, melt the blue cheese and cream in a small pot over low heat for 2-3 minutes. Stir in the basil leaves, then take it off the heat. Serve the ravioli with plenty of sauce and top with toasted pecans.

Super-Green Fritters

Makes about 16 · Prep 15 mins · Cook 20 mins

I am a little bit hopeless at making fritters because I can't bear to plunge healthy food into a pan of simmering oil. These fritters are different: packed with iron-giving greenness and lots of flavour, and dry enough that you don't have to use too much frying oil. Make these if there are kids on board who shy away from greens, and double it on hungry days.

2 large zucchinis (courgette), grated

1 tsp salt

big handful (50g) of baby spinach leaves

½ lemon, zest and juice

1 spring onion (scallion), finely sliced

⅔ cup (100g) feta, crumbled

2 large free-range eggs, lightly whisked

⅓ cup self-raising flour

¼ cup finely chopped fresh parsley

½ tsp curry powder

salt and pepper

extra virgin olive oil for frying

Serve with ½ cup thick Greek yoghurt mixed with a dollop of Chilli Peach Jam (page 211).

In a large mixing bowl, add the zucchini, sprinkle with two good pinches of salt, and leave for 10 minutes. Wilt the baby spinach leaves in a little boiling water, then drain and when cool enough to handle, squeeze them dry and finely chop. Save the veggie juices for stock if you like.

Squeeze the zucchini with clean hands to remove as much moisture as possible. Put it back in the mixing bowl and add the chopped spinach, lemon juice and finely grated zest. Add the spring onion, feta, eggs, flour, parsley, curry powder, a pinch of salt and a good grind of black pepper. Mix well.

Heat 1 tablespoon of olive oil in a non-stick frypan over medium-high heat. Dollop the fritter mixture into the pan and cook in batches for 2-3 minutes a side, adding more oil for successive batches if required. Serve the fritters warm with a dish of thick Greek yoghurt mixed with a dollop of Chilli Peach Jam.

Crispy Bombay Potatoes

Feeds 4 • Prep 10 mins • Cook 20 mins • GF, CC

This is one of those vegetarian side dishes that shines just fine on its own. While there might appear to be a long ingredient list, it's really just potatoes and spice (with a dollop of creamy yoghurt at the end). The only problem with cooking this over a beach campfire is that the aroma is unbelievably nuts, luring in passersby who'll likely target you as the great cook you are and plonk themselves down to say hi. Bring extra plates.

600g (1.3lb) potatoes, boiled
3 garlic cloves
3cm piece of ginger, peeled
1 small, ripe tomato
1 tsp ground turmeric
1 tsp ground coriander
pinch of garam masala
a handful of fresh coriander (cilantro)
2 tbsp ghee or olive oil
1 tsp cumin seeds
1 tsp mustard seeds
2 dried chillies (optional)
salt and pepper

If you're cooking outdoors, prep the flavourings before leaving the boat. Blend the garlic, ginger and ripe tomato and pour it into a jar. Add the turmeric, ground coriander and garam masala. Pick the coriander leaves but set them aside for serving and finely chop the stalks.

When your fire has died down to a hot bed of coals, warm 2 tablespoons of ghee or olive oil in a large camp oven placed directly over the coals but away from any flames. Cut the potatoes into quarters and fry, gently smashing them with a fork. Cook them for about 10 minutes until they're crisp and golden, then add the cumin and mustard seeds and cook for another 1 minute. Your potatoes might need extra time or another shovel-load of hot coals placed underneath to get them nice and crisp.

Stir in the chopped coriander stalks and dried chillies (optional) and cook for 2 minutes. Finally, add the blended tomato mixture and season everything with a pinch of sea salt and some cracked black pepper. Stir well for 3-4 minutes, take it off the heat, and serve with generous dollops of yoghurt and extra coriander leaves.

If cooking indoors, fry the potatoes in a large, non-stick frying pan or wok over medium heat, and follow the steps above.

Charred Corn Chowder

Feeds 4 • Prep 15 mins • Cook 30-40 mins • GF

4 corn cobs
1-2 tbsp extra virgin olive oil
1 large onion, finely chopped
1 large potato, diced
2 garlic cloves, crushed/grated
1 tsp dried chilli flakes
¼ tsp smoked paprika
4 cups (1L) vegetable stock
½ cup pouring cream
4 gluten-free tortillas

Avocado Salsa

1 tbsp lime juice
pinch of smoked paprika
1 large ripe avocado, chopped
¼ small red onion, finely chopped
salt and pepper

For the salsa, combine the lime juice and smoked paprika in a small bowl. Add the avocado and red onion, season with salt and pepper, and gently stir to combine.

Cook the unhusked cobs on a barbecue hotplate, or remove the husks, drizzle the cobs with olive oil and roast them on a baking tray (180°C/350°F for 20 minutes). When they're tender, set them aside until they're cool enough to handle.

Meanwhile, warm a tablespoon of olive oil in a large saucepan over medium-low heat. Slice the kernels off the cobs and add them to the pot with the onion and potato. Cover and cook, stirring occasionally. After about 10 minutes, stir in the garlic, chilli and paprika, and cook for about one minute more. Add the stock and cream and turn up the heat. When the soup comes to a boil, reduce the heat to medium, cover, and cook until the potato is tender (about 10 minutes).

Take the chowder off the heat and blend or process until thick and smooth. Season to taste with salt and pepper. Chargrill the tortillas on a barbecue plate, over a gas stovetop, or in a dry frypan. Serve alongside bowls of chowder topped with a dollop of avocado salsa.

Fox Sushi

Makes 12 · Prep 20 mins · Cook 15 mins · V

The cute name for these delicious, rice-filled Japanese snacks comes from their sweet fried tofu wrappers that foxes are rumoured to adore. You can season your own inari sushi pockets in a simmering dashi-based broth, or buy packets of ready-made inari (or abura-age), a boat-friendly pantry staple with a long shelf life.

2 cups sushi rice

3 cups cold water

2 tbsp rice vinegar

2 tsp caster sugar

½ tsp salt

12 prepared Japanese inari pockets (abura-age)

1 nori sheet

1 ripe avocado

1 tbsp roasted black sesame seeds

Rinse the rice in cold water until the water runs clear, then drain. Place it in a large pot with 3 cups water, boil, then simmer, covered, for 10 minutes until the water has been absorbed. Take it off the stove, cover the pot with a tea towel and set it aside for 10 minutes before transferring the rice to a ceramic or glass bowl.

Over low heat, dissolve the sugar and salt in the rice vinegar. Pour it over the rice and gently fold it through with a wooden spatula. Cover with a damp tea towel and set it aside to cool, lifting and stirring the rice occasionally.

Use scissors to cut the nori sheet into thin strips. Halve, peel and slice the avocado into small pieces, and use a wooden spatula to gently stir the sesame seeds through the cooled rice.

Drain the inari pockets (and rinse if you like), then carefully open and half-fill each with rice. Slip in a small slice of avocado (or any other filling you like), fill with rice, and wrap with a nori strip. Serve with tamari or soy sauce.

Coconut & Kaffir Lime Noodles

Feeds 4 · Prep 15 mins · Cook 20 mins · V

100g (3.5oz) noodles (any kind)

180g (6.5oz) firm tofu, sliced

2 tbsp coconut oil

2 tbsp tamari or soy sauce

⅔ cup water

1 tsp rice malt syrup, honey or sugar

2 small red or green chillies, finely chopped

4 kaffir (makrut) lime leaves (fresh or dried)

3 garlic cloves, finely chopped

½ cup coconut milk powder

1 red onion, sliced into crescents

½ carrot, sliced

1 tomato, cut into crescents

1 cup shredded Chinese cabbage

1 cup bean sprouts

1 cup chopped fresh coriander (cilantro)

2 spring onions (scallions)

1 cup baby spinach leaves

Serve with fried onion and lime wedges.

Boil up your favourite noodles, drain, rinse and set them aside. In a large non-stick pan or wok, shallow-fry the tofu slices (cut 5mm or 1/4in thick) in a little coconut oil until golden. Drain on a wire rack (or paper towel) and set aside.

Pour off the oil and return the pan or wok to medium-high heat. Bring the tamari and 2/3 cup water to the boil. Reduce to a simmer and stir in your choice of sweetener, chopped chillies, whole lime leaves, garlic and coconut milk powder (mixed into a paste with a little water). Add the onion, carrot and tomato, and simmer for 3 minutes.

Stir in the cabbage, bean sprouts, coriander and spring onions (sliced into 10cm/4in lengths), and toss everything together for 1 minute. Add the noodles and baby spinach leaves and heat until the noodles are warmed through. Serve the noodles topped with slices of tofu, some fried onion and wedges of fresh lime.

Walnut & Cheddar Risotto

Feeds 2-3 · Prep 10 mins · Cook 35 mins · GF

This is a dish that can go two ways. Eat your risotto topped with a generous dollop of walnut and cheddar pesto, or double the recipe and turn leftovers into tasty arancini balls. Stuffed with a generous scoop of walnut pesto and a chunk of mozzarella, they make great snacks for sailing days or to serve at sundown.

4 cups (1L) vegetable stock

1 tbsp butter

1 tbsp extra virgin olive oil

1 onion, peeled and finely chopped

1 ⅓ cups (250g) Arborio rice

¼ cup (25g) vintage cheddar

salt and pepper

Walnut & Cheddar Pesto

1 large bunch of basil leaves, rinsed and dried

⅔ cup walnut pieces, toasted

1 garlic clove, chopped

½ cup extra virgin olive oil

½ cup (50g) vintage cheddar, grated

salt and pepper

Get your pesto going first. Blitz together the basil, toasted walnuts, garlic and extra virgin olive oil. Stir through the cheese and season to taste with salt and pepper. Transfer to a jar, seal the pesto with a drizzle of extra virgin olive oil and refrigerate for up to 5-7 days.

To begin the risotto, melt the butter and olive oil in a pan over low heat and add the finely chopped onion. Sweat the onion for 15 minutes until soft, then increase the heat to medium and stir in the Arborio rice, coating the grains in oil and butter. Meanwhile, pour the stock into a seperate pan and bring it to a slow boil.

Gradually ladle in the simmering stock, one scoop at a time, waiting until all the liquid has been absorbed before adding more. Continue cooking and frequently stirring until your stock pot is empty and the risotto is nice and tender (about 15-20 minutes). Take it off the heat, crumble in the cheddar cheese, season to taste, and serve topped with a generous dollop of pesto.

If you're making arancini, set it aside to cool, forgoing the pesto topping for now.

Arancini Balls

Makes 12 · Prep 15 mins · Cook 10 mins

1 batch of cooked and cooled risotto

⅓ cup Walnut & Cheddar Pesto

50g mozzarella, chopped into 12 chunks

150g plain (all-purpose) flour

2 large free-range eggs, beaten

1 ½ cups (200g) fine, dried breadcrumbs

extra virgin olive oil for frying

Take a batch of cooled risotto and roll a tablespoonful between wet palms to form a small ball. Poke a hole in the middle and add a tiny spoonful of pesto and a small piece of mozzarella. Cover the hole and continue until you have about 12 balls.

Place the flour, egg and breadcrumbs in separate dishes, and dip the arancini in each (flour, then egg, then roll in breadcrumbs). Heat 1/2 cup of olive oil in a deep pan over medium heat. Shallow fry the arancini in batches for 3-4 minutes, turning occasionally, until golden brown. Remove with a slotted spoon, drain on paper towel and serve hot or cold.

Wok-tossed Miso Eggplant

Feeds 4 • Prep 10 mins • Cook 35-40 mins • GF, V

2 red onions (or a big handful of shallots), thinly sliced

3 tbsp peanut or coconut oil

2 tsp balsamic vinegar

2 tbsp gluten-free kecap manis

1 large globe eggplant (aubergine)
or 2-3 thin Chinese or Japanese eggplants

½ red capsicum (bell pepper), thinly sliced

2 garlic cloves, finely chopped

1 tsp grated (or crushed) ginger

1 ½ tbsp gluten-free miso paste

1 tsp sesame oil

¼ cup warm water

Serve with sliced spring onions (scallions)
and toasted sesame seeds.

Warm 1 tablespoon of oil in a wok or large frypan over low heat and cook the onions, stirring occasionally, until soft (about 15 minutes, or 10 minutes for shallots). Stir in the vinegar and 1 tablespoon of kecap manis and cook for another 10 minutes or until the onions caramelise. Take the wok (or pan) off the heat, remove the onions and wipe the wok clean.

Quarter the globe eggplant lengthways and slice into 1cm (1/2in) thick pieces (or slice thinner Chinese or Japanese eggplants into 1cm-thick rounds). Heat 1 tablespoon of oil over medium-high heat and fry the eggplant in batches, tossing or turning frequently for about 5 minutes a batch. Remove from the wok, add just a touch of oil and cook the capsicum strips for 2 minutes.

Stir in the garlic and ginger, and return the eggplant and onion to the wok. Toss, cooking, for 2 minutes, until everything is warmed through. Combine the miso paste, 1 tablespoon of kecap manis, sesame oil and 1/4 cup warm water, mix well and pour into the wok. Toss everything together gently and serve topped with sliced spring onions and toasted sesame beside fried or steamed fish and rice.

Gluten-free Eggplant Schnitzels

Feeds 4 • Prep 15 mins • Cook 15 mins • GF

There was a stint in my life when I practically lived on rice cakes. Then one day, I woke up and realised they taste like cardboard. This recipe proves that rice cakes *can* taste good, and it's the only reason I still buy them. The crunch they give to these schnitzels is out-of-this-world, and I make them this way always, even though gluten and I are firm friends.

2 medium eggplants (aubergine)

6 thin organic rice cakes

2 tsp dried mixed Italian herbs

½ tsp smoked paprika

2 eggs

½ cup chickpea flour

salt

extra virgin olive or coconut oil for frying

Serve with Avocado Citrus Salad (page 137).

Cut the eggplants lengthways into 1cm wide slices (about 4-5 slices per eggplant). Cut off and discard the skins and generously salt both sides of the sliced eggplant. Set aside for 5-10 minutes, then rinse and pat dry with some paper towel.

Break up the rice cakes and blend or process with the Italian herbs and smoked paprika to form crumbs. Lightly beat the eggs and pour the chickpea flour onto a plate.

Coat the eggplant slices with seasoned chickpea flour first, dip them into the egg, and then coat well with crumbs. Heat enough oil in a pan to shallow fry the schnitzels (be sure it's hot) for 4-5 minutes, turning once. Serve with Avocado Citrus Salad.

Honey-glazed Halloumi

Feeds 2-4 · Prep 5 mins · Cook 10 mins · QC

Halloumi is the reason I am no longer a vegan because, really, who could possibly resist a plate of fried cheese? All halloumi needs is a squeeze of lemon and some cracked black pepper, but this recipe takes things to a whole new level. Salty and herby, it might be a savoury snack, but add butter, honey and lemon, and it shuffles a little closer to dessert. Give it pride of place on any cheese platter or eat it all yourself (you deserve it).

1 tbsp extra virgin olive oil

180g (7oz) halloumi, sliced

2 tbsp honey (or rice malt syrup*)

1 tbsp butter

1 tsp dried thyme

¼ cup roughly chopped raw walnuts

1 lemon

Serve with lemon wedges and bread toasts.

** Using rice malt syrup instead of honey turns this dish fructose-free.*

Heat 1 tablespoon of olive oil in a large, non-stick frypan over medium heat. Fry the halloumi on one side until it browns. Add the honey (or rice malt syrup), butter and thyme, and flip the halloumi over.

Add the walnuts and a good squeeze of lemon juice and toss the pan gently, cooking until the halloumi browns on the other side and the sauce caramelises (it won't take long). Serve sizzling, straight out of the pan with lemon wedges and bread toasts.

Cheats' Pizza

with roast pumpkin & pine nuts

Feeds 4 · Prep 10 mins · Cook 35 mins

Sometimes, you just need a shortcut.

1kg (2lb) peeled pumpkin

1-2 tbsp extra virgin olive oil

⅓ cup sour cream

4 large pita or pizza bases (page 202)

1 tbsp plain (all-purpose) flour

Handful (50g) baby spinach leaves

1 ⅓ cup (200g) crumbled marinated or regular feta (see page 213)

⅓ cup pine nuts

Cut the pumpkin into chunks, place on a baking tray and drizzle with olive oil. Bake in a preheated oven at 200°C (390°F) for about 25 minutes until tender. Remove from the oven and leave to cool slightly, then mash with a fork and stir in the sour cream.

Lightly dust the bottom of each pizza base with flour. Spread the pumpkin mixture over the bases and top each with baby spinach leaves, crumbled feta cheese and a sprinkle of pine nuts. Bake for 10-12 minutes.

Sticky Rice

Feeds 4 • Cook 40 mins + Soaking time • GF, V

Glutinous rice needs to be soaked overnight and then steamed the following day for 40 minutes. It really has no substitute, and once you try it (teamed with som tam or topped with fresh ripe mango and drizzled with honey and coconut milk), there is no going back.

Measure 2 cups of glutinous rice into a bowl, adding enough water to cover the rice by 5cm (2in). Soak overnight, then rinse thoroughly. When you're ready to cook, line a bamboo or ordinary saucepan steamer with muslin cloth and add the drained rice. Fill the bottom pot to a depth of 10cm (4in), add the steamer with the rice and cover firmly with a lid. Bring to the boil and steam the rice for 40 minutes. Take off the heat and wrap it in a towel to keep the rice warm until you are ready to eat.

Coconut Rice

Feeds 2-3 • Prep 5 mins • Cook 35 mins • GF, V, OP

1 tbsp coconut oil

1 large red onion, finely sliced

3 cardamom pods

½ tsp ground cinnamon

1 tsp turmeric

1 lemongrass stalk, finely chopped

1 cup basmati rice, rinsed well

375ml (13 fl oz) coconut milk

½ cup water

Preheat the oven to 180°C (350°F). Heat the oil over low heat in a large saucepan and gently fry the red onion. Stir in the cardamom pods, cinnamon, turmeric and lemongrass, and cook for 1 minute more. Add the rice and stir briefly, then slowly pour in the coconut milk and water and bring to the boil.

Pour the rice into an ovenproof dish and bake, covered, for 25 minutes. Alternatively, place your camp oven into a hole on the fire's edge, cover it with hot coals and leave it to bake. Check and stir the rice about halfway through cooking; remove from the oven or coals and fluff with a fork before serving.

PREPPING FOR PASSAGE

Ready-To-Go Meals For Big Adventures

The storm was still raging when David woke me for my 1am shift. I climbed fully clothed out of our salty bed, struggled into my raingear and tied myself into *Footprints* – 31 feet of timber and sail being hurled eastward across the Gulf of Carpentaria. Fighting off sleep and nausea after three days under stormy skies, I focused my addled mind on maintaining our course, catching my breath as each bolt of lightning illuminated unimaginably huge waves rising up from behind.

There were no familiar comforts – no horizon separating sea and sky, no blinking stars, no seabirds, no chatter on the radio – nothing but the wind screaming across a heaving sea, the boom of thunder, and sails flogging beneath squalls. Our open-decked Wharram catamaran rode the sea like she was on rails, but she offered almost no separation from it. So, when at 4am, a ship's lights appeared to starboard, I flew into action to illuminate the boat. There was a frustrating radio silence (this was before AIS) and gauging the ship's heading from the crest of each wave proved absolutely impossible.

I grabbed the radio and called my 'unidentified ship', begging for a heading in progressively more urgent tones. Finally, reluctantly, there was a voice on the line, and with our positions determined, we slipped past each other into the storm. A day later, anchored safely in the lee of Cape York Peninsula, I drank my first meal in days and swore over a bottle of bubbles that I'd never do it again. We did, of course (another four times actually), but on a bigger chunk of fibreglass with lots of ready-made meals like these.

Pesto & Parmesan Bread Soup

Feeds 4 · Prep 10 mins · Cook 30 mins

So easy to make, this tasty one-pot wonder is teamed with olive oil toasts to scrape bowls clean. There are no fussy ingredients, and it's flexible enough to take any veggies you have (even wilting ones). I rarely make this the same way twice, swapping eggplant or beans for zucchini, adding chilli or olives, and when there's no wine left on board, using extra vegetable stock instead. It doesn't *need* toast (crusty bread will do), but they really make the dish.

3 tbsp extra virgin olive oil

1 medium onion, diced

1 medium carrot, finely chopped

1 medium zucchini (courgette), finely chopped

2 garlic cloves, crushed

400g (14oz) tin diced tomatoes

¼ cup dried, sliced mushrooms (or a handful of fresh)

4 cups (1L) vegetable stock

½ cup dry white wine (or extra stock)

3 tbsp tomato paste

4-5 sprigs fresh basil (or 1 tsp dried basil)

cracked black pepper

2 sourdough (or other) bread rolls, sliced

Serve with basil pesto, parmesan and fresh basil leaves.

Gently warm a drizzle of olive oil in a large saucepan. Add the onion, carrot, zucchini and garlic, and cook for about 5 minutes, stirring. Add the tinned tomatoes, dried or fresh mushrooms, vegetable stock, white wine (if using), tomato paste and fresh or dried basil. Cover the pot and bring to a simmer, then cook, stirring occasionally, for about 20 minutes. Season with cracked black pepper.

Meanwhile, drizzle the bread slices with olive oil and bake under a grill until crisp (5-10 minutes). Serve the soup in four bowls topped with a dollop of basil pesto, some shaved or grated parmesan cheese, fresh basil leaves and your home-baked bread toasts. To prep this dish for passage, make the soup in advance and freeze or refrigerate it. When ready to eat, warm up your soup and toast off the croutons.

Roasted Garlic & Tomato Soup

Feeds 4 · Prep 10 mins · Cook 45-50 mins

5 large ripe tomatoes

2 onions

6 garlic cloves

1 red capsicum (bell pepper)

extra virgin olive oil

salt and cracked black pepper

1 tsp dried chilli flakes

2 tbsp fresh rosemary, thyme or basil (or 2 tsp dried)

2 cups pure tomato juice

2 tbsp basil pesto

Serve with a drizzle of cream and crusty bread.

Preheat the oven to 200°C (390°F). Halve the tomatoes and onions and place them on a large baking tray with the unpeeled garlic cloves. Slice and deseed the capsicum and add to the tray. Drizzle with olive oil and season well with salt, pepper, chilli flakes and your choice of fresh or dried herbs. Bake for 40-45 minutes, then set aside to cool.

Peel the skins off the tomatoes, capsicum strips, onion and garlic and discard. Transfer the roasted veggies to a large pot and add the tomato juice and pesto. Use a stick blender to puree the soup and simmer it on the stove for 5 minutes. Season to taste with salt and cracked black pepper. Serve with a drizzle of cream and chunks of fresh crusty bread, or freeze for your next passage.

Power-charged Tabouleh

Feeds 4 • Prep 10 mins • Cook 15 mins • GF, V

1 cup quinoa

¾ tsp salt, divided

¼ continental cucumber, sliced

1 punnet cherry tomatoes, halved

1 bunch flat-leaf parsley, leaves only

½ cup fresh mint leaves

2 spring onions, thinly sliced

2 tbsp pine nuts, toasted

salt and pepper

Dressing

2 tbsp lemon juice (about 1 lemon)

1 garlic clove, grated or minced

½ cup extra virgin olive oil

Quinoa needs to be rinsed well first to reduce the bitterness from its natural coating of saponin. Rinse it under a running tap for 30 seconds – you can use salt water – then drain well and use.

In a medium saucepan, bring the quinoa, 1/4 teaspoon of salt and 2 cups of water to a boil over medium-high heat. Reduce the heat to medium-low and simmer, uncovered, until the quinoa is tender (10-12 minutes). Take off the heat and leave to stand, covered, for 5 minutes, then fluff with a fork and set aside to cool.

Combine the sliced cucumber and tomato in a medium bowl and stir through about 1/2 teaspoon of salt. Leave for 10 minutes to remove excess juice. Meanwhile, make a dressing by whisking the lemon juice and garlic together in a small bowl. Gradually whisk in the olive oil and season to taste with salt and pepper.

Transfer the quinoa to a salad bowl and pour over 1/4 cup of the dressing. Toss to mix. Drain the cucumber and tomato mix (discard the salty brine) and add to your bowl. Pick the leaves off the mint and parsley and toss through with the spring onion and toasted pine nuts. Season to taste with salt and pepper, and drizzle over the remaining dressing. Serve immediately, or leave to rest for 15 minutes to allow flavours to fuse.

Stored in the fridge, quinoa tabouleh will keep for up to four days. Make a double batch of the dressing before you head out (or during a calm moment at sea) and tuck it in the fridge to quickly dress any salad.

Easy Persian Pilau

Feeds 4 • Prep 10 mins • Cook 20 mins • GF, OP

This easy stovetop creation takes only marginally longer to put together than cooking plain rice. It uses just two main ingredients – sweet potato and tinned lentils – jazzed up with spices and served with some crumbled feta. That qualifies it as food you can cook on passage, but on shorter, multi-night trips, I whip it up before we set sail and stick it in the fridge to be reheated and topped with cheese when needed.

3 cups peeled, small diced sweet potato (kumara)

1 tbsp extra virgin olive oil

½ tsp ground cumin

½ tsp ground coriander

½ tsp ground cinnamon

½ tsp ground turmeric

1 cup basmati rice

1 ½ cups vegetable stock

400g (15oz) can brown lentils

¾ cup (100g) crumbled feta

Serve with fresh coriander sprigs and 1-2 tablespoons toasted black sesame seeds.

Heat a large, heavy-based pan over medium heat. Warm 1 tablespoon of olive oil and fry the sweet potato for 5 minutes, stirring as needed. Add the spices and stir well for 30 seconds (add extra oil if needed to ensure they don't burn). Stir in the rice, then the stock and bring to the boil.

Reduce the heat to low and simmer, covered, for 10 minutes until the rice is tender. Set aside to allow the rice to steam. Rinse and drain the lentils and gently fork them through the rice. Serve topped with crumbled feta, toasted sesame seeds and fresh coriander sprigs.

Mushroom, Feta & Lentil Rolls

Makes 8 • Prep 25 mins • Cook 40 mins

Filo is fussy, and while it's not my go-to pastry, its irresistibly flaky, bakery-fresh taste just wins me over when we've been a bit too long in the wilds. You can make your own filo, but a box in the freezer is a convenient choice. To prep these for passage, make and bake them in advance and refrigerate them, ready for munching. Alternatively, roll them up and freeze them, ready to be popped in the oven when you're underway (they will keep for a month). Some chefs say filo shouldn't be refrozen because it will crumble upon re-entry into the world. I say filo will crumble anyway. Simply defrost it in the fridge, and keep it covered with a damp tea towel while you assemble these treats.

10 sheets filo pastry, defrosted
1-2 tbsp extra virgin olive oil
½ tsp sumac

The Filling

1 tbsp extra virgin olive oil
1 medium onion, chopped
2 garlic cloves, crushed or grated
2 ½ cups (250g) mushrooms, sliced
400g (15oz) tin brown lentils
1 medium carrot, grated
⅓ cup coarsely chopped cashews
pinch of hot paprika
1 ½ tsp ground cumin
¼ tsp ground cinnamon
¼ tsp dried chilli flakes (optional)
1 free-range egg
½ cup (80g) crumbled feta
salt and pepper

Serve with natural Greek yoghurt.

For the filling, warm the olive oil in a frying pan over medium-low heat. Cook the onion until translucent, then add the garlic and cook for 2-3 minutes more. Increase the heat a little, add the mushrooms and stir until the mushrooms are soft and any liquid has evaporated.

Preheat the oven to 200°C (390°F) and line an oven tray with baking paper. Place the rinsed and drained lentils in a mixing bowl and add grated carrot, cashews, all the spices and a lightly beaten egg. Stir in the mushroom mixture and crumbled feta, and season to taste with salt and pepper.

Layer five sheets of filo on top of each other, brushing or spraying each layer with olive oil as you stack. Keep the remaining sheets of filo covered with a clean, damp tea towel to prevent them from drying out. Spoon half the lentil mixture along the long side of the pastry stack and roll it up. Cut it into four pieces and place them on the baking tray.

Continue with the remaining pastry stack and lentil mixture. Brush or spray the rolls with olive oil and sprinkle with sumac. Bake for 30 minutes or until golden. You can freeze these pastries uncooked and bake them directly from frozen when on passage (about 35 minutes in a preheated oven at 200°C/390°F). Serve with natural Greek yoghurt.

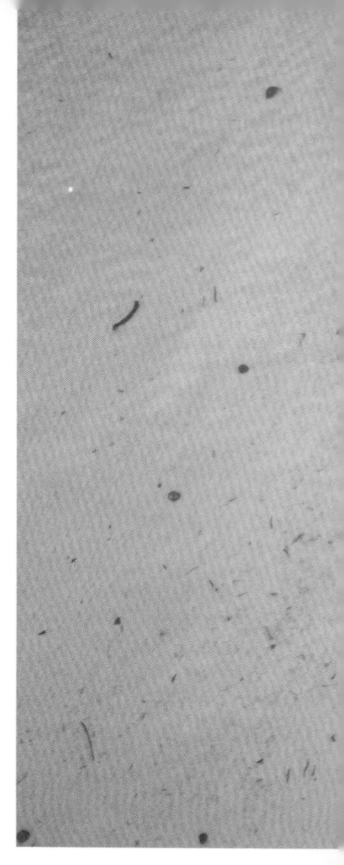

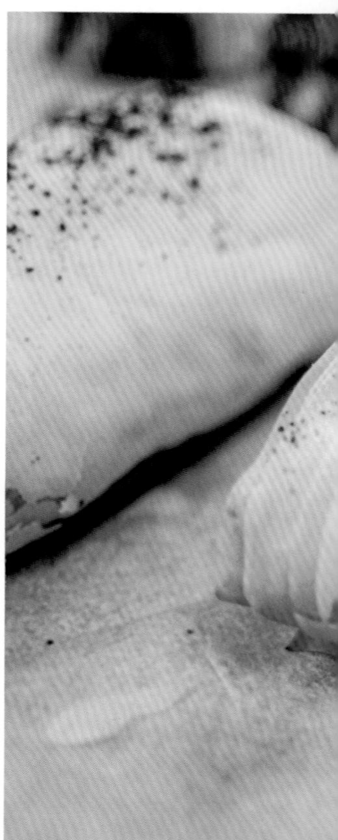

Red Lentil Bolognese

Feeds 4 · Prep 10 mins · Cook 40-50 mins · GF, V

This is by far our favourite meal. The red lentils break down to create a Bolognese-like texture, adding a nutty flavour that even meat-eaters enjoy. The sauce freezes perfectly to be defrosted on passage and generously accepts any vegetables you have in the fridge.

1 tbsp extra virgin olive oil

1 medium onion, finely chopped

3 garlic cloves, finely chopped

3 cups chopped eggplant (aubergine), carrot, mushroom and zucchini (courgette)

2 heaped tbsp tomato paste

¾ cup red lentils, sprouted, soaked or rinsed well

2 x 400g (14oz) tins diced tomatoes

1 cup vegetable stock

1 cup water

4-5 bay leaves

a handful of fresh basil (or 1 ½ tsp dried mixed Italian herbs)

salt and pepper

Serve with 500g (1lb) of gluten-free (or regular) pasta and parmesan cheese or nutritional yeast flakes (if vegan).

Warm 1 tablespoon of extra virgin olive oil over a low heat and sweat the onion and garlic for 2 minutes, stirring occasionally. Stir in the chopped vegetables and cook for 3-4 minutes, then add the tomato paste and stir for 1 minute. Rinse the red lentils (whole or split) before adding them to the pot, or soak unhulled red lentils overnight or sprout for 1-2 days before using. Add tinned tomatoes, stock, water and herbs and turn up the heat.

When the sauce comes to the boil, reduce the heat to low, cover the pot and simmer for about 30-40 minutes, stirring it occasionally. Take the lid off for the final 10 minutes of cooking and stir well to help break down the lentils into a thick sauce, and season well with salt and pepper,

While the sauce simmers, bring a large pot of water to the boil. Cook your choice of pasta until al dente. Drain well, toss with the sauce, and serve topped with parmesan cheese (or vegan nutritional yeast flakes) and some fresh basil leaves.

Ramp up the flavour. This sauce is super versatile. Add some chopped Kalamata olives or anchovies towards the end of the cooking time (reduce the salt if you do), a dash of good red wine, some chopped red chillies or grilled capsicum strips.

Caponata

Feeds 4 · Prep 5 mins · GF, V, QC

Nearly everything for this is in your cupboards. Keep a jar in the fridge to perk up meals on passage, toss over pasta or spread on bread. Serve it when friends come for sundowners with crisp toasts and a wedge of cheese.

150g (5.5oz) chargrilled eggplant (aubergine) slices

1 tbsp capers, rinsed and drained

4 anchovies

5 sun-dried tomatoes

2 ripe tomatoes, diced

1 tbsp chopped fresh parsley (or 1 tsp dried)

¼ cup toasted pine nuts

cracked black pepper

squeeze of lemon

Finely chop (or throw into a mini food processor) the eggplant, capers, anchovies and sundried tomatoes. Scrape into a mixing bowl, add the fresh tomato, parsley and pine nuts, and season with cracked black pepper and a squeeze of lemon. Toss everything together and refrigerate in a glass jar, or serve on toasted bread or spoon over pasta.

Rustic Pumpkin Pie

Feeds 4 · Prep 20 mins · Cook 50-55 mins

I don't often make pastry from scratch, but this rustic pie doesn't call for perfection, and is so forgiving, you can cook it on the stove and finish it under the grill. This is another 'day-before-sailing' bakes, stored in the fridge and reheated (or served cold at midnight) when the seas are rough, and you don't want to be in the galley long.

half a butternut pumpkin (about 800g/28oz)

1 large red onion, cut into wedges

6 garlic cloves

2 tbsp extra virgin olive oil

8 cherry bocconcini balls (or 340g/12oz chopped mozzarella, fresh or frozen)

½ cup (75g) crumbled feta

fresh or dried herbs (basil, thyme, rosemary)

Pastry

2 cups plain (all-purpose) flour

150g (1 ⅓ sticks) cold butter, diced

1 medium free-range egg

½ tsp salt

Cut the pumpkin into small chunks (about 4cm/1.5in), removing, and discarding the skin (save the seeds for sprouting and nibbling). Place the pumpkin pieces on a baking tray with the onion and garlic cloves (crush them a little and leave the skins on). Pour over a drizzle of olive oil and bake at 200°C (390°F) for 20-25 minutes, until just tender. If using the stovetop, cook the veggies in a heavy-based pan, uncovered, over medium heat until tender, adding as much oil as you need to stop the pumpkin from sticking, and turning them occasionally. When tender, set the veggies aside to cool, and remove the onion and garlic skins.

For the pastry, pour the flour into a bowl, stir in the salt and butter, and rub it through the flour with your fingers until it resembles breadcrumbs. Crack in an egg, bring the pastry together and knead gently on a floured bench for one minute. Form the dough into a flat disk and refrigerate it for 20 minutes. Don't worry too much about getting a perfect texture.

When the veggies have cooled, roll out the pastry to fit your pan or tray, leaving a nice edge to fold over the filling. Pour in the cooled pumpkin mixture and add the torn bocconcini balls (or roughly chopped mozzarella), crumbled feta and some herbs (a handful of fresh or a tablespoon of dried). Fold over the pastry edge and bake at 200°C (390°F) for about 30 minutes, until golden. If you don't have an oven, cook it on the stovetop over low heat and finish it to crispy perfection under the grill.

Puttanesca Pantry Bake

Feeds 4 · Prep 10 mins · Cook 20 mins

Almost everything needed for this quick pasta bake comes straight from your cupboards. Throw it together when fresh stores have dwindled, and freshen with a handful of herbs from your blooming boat garden. Pre-make the sauce and freeze it in advance, ready to be tossed through pasta, topped with cheese and popped under the grill. But really, this super-quick sauce can be ready and waiting in the time it takes for the pasta to reach al dente.

1 tbsp extra virgin olive oil

1 medium onion, finely diced

2 garlic cloves, crushed or chopped

2 anchovies, finely chopped

½ cup pitted Kalamata olives, roughly chopped

¼ chilli, finely chopped

1 tbsp baby capers, rinsed

4 sundried tomatoes, roughly chopped

handful of fresh basil or parsley or both (optional)

2 tbsp tomato paste

2 x 400g (14oz) tin tomatoes

1 cup vegetable stock

1 tbsp lemon juice

1 tbsp cream (fresh or long-life)

cracked black pepper

400g (14oz) penne pasta

⅓ cup grated parmesan cheese

Bring a large pot of water to the boil and add your pasta. While it cooks to al dente, heat 1 tablespoon of olive oil in a large frypan (capable of fitting under your grill) and gently sweat the onion and garlic over medium heat. Add the anchovies, olives, chilli, capers and sundried tomatoes, and stir for 2 minutes. Tear up the fresh herbs (if you have them on hand) and stir through.

Add the tomato paste, tinned tomatoes, vegetable stock and lemon juice, and stir and simmer uncovered for 5 minutes. Add the cream, cook the sauce for 2 minutes more, then season with cracked pepper and take off the heat. Drain the pasta, tip it into the pan and toss everything together well. Sprinkle parmesan over the top and place under a preheated grill for 5 minutes, until the cheese has melted and browned.

Want to reduce salt? Leave out the anchovies and rinse the olives and caper well before using. Choose 'no added salt' tinned tomatoes and tomato paste too.

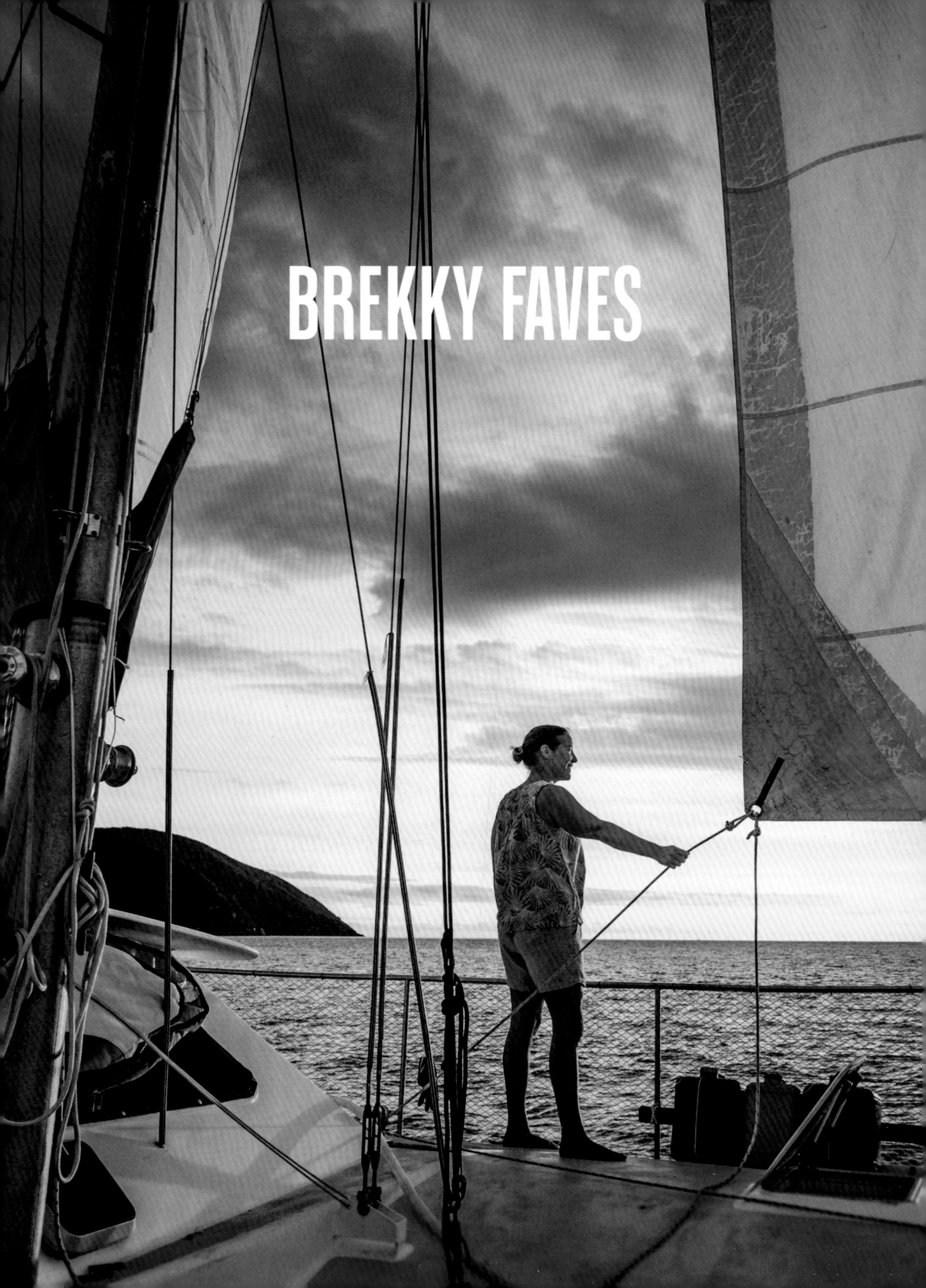

BREKKY FAVES

Nepalese Chiya

Makes 4 · Prep 5 mins · Cook 20 mins · GF, OP

After tackling lots of family treks in Nepal's Himalayan mountains, this aromatic spiced tea is what rouses sleepyheads on our boat, to gather in the bridgedeck and dream about heading back to those hills. Chai (or Chiya as Nepalis call it) can be made a hundred different ways, but this is how we like it best. When I wake early in Kathmandu and hit the streets, I follow my nose to the local chaiwala's stall for a cup of tea that's 'pulled' before serving. To do this, simply pour your brewed tea from one pot into another (do it over the sink). This aerates, cools and infuses the tea with a massive flavour hit before it's served and sipped outside, watching the world awaken.

2 cups water

2 cups milk

4 whole cloves

1 tsp ground cardamon (or 3-4 pods, crushed open)

1 cinnamon stick (or 1 tsp ground cinnamon)

3-4 slices of fresh ginger

2 tbsp black tea leaves

1-2 tbsp rice malt syrup or sugar (optional and to taste)

In a large saucepan, gently heat the water and milk. Before it comes to a simmer, add the spices and stir well. Add the tea and turn down the heat when the milk comes to a gentle boil. Stir in some sweetener if you like, and simmer the tea for 3-4 minutes. Then, take off the heat, strain, pull and serve.

Nutty Mocha Granola

Makes 5-6 cups · Prep 5 mins · Cook 15 mins

This recipe is considerably flexible, easily adjusting to any dietary desires. Need it gluten-free? Use rice or corn-based cereals. Avoid dairy? Swap butter for oil. Or make it fructose-free by using rice malt syrup instead of maple syrup and leaving out the brown sugar. Keep the quantities the same but use any nuts, seeds or dried fruit you like.

3 cups rolled oats
1 cup puffed rice
¼ cup raw cashews
¼ cup walnuts
¼ cup pepitas
2 tbsp pistachios
2 tbsp sunflower seeds
2 tsp instant coffee powder
1 tbsp cacao or cocoa powder
1 tsp ground cinnamon
¼ cup rice malt (or maple) syrup
1 tbsp brown sugar (optional)
60g chopped butter
½ cup dried cranberries

In a large mixing bowl, combine the oats, puffed rice, nuts and seeds. In a small pot, dissolve the instant coffee in 1 tbsp of warm water. Add the cacao or cocoa, cinnamon, rice malt (or maple) syrup, brown sugar (optional) and butter, and warm over very low heat, stirring until smooth and combined (2-3 minutes).

Pour the hot syrup over the oat and nut mixture, stir well to combine and tip onto a baking tray lined with baking paper. Place in a preheated oven and bake for 15 minutes at 180°C (350°), stirring every 5 minutes. Add the cranberries to the tray and bake for 2 minutes more, then set aside to cool and store in an airtight container.

No oven? Place the tray under a low-heat grill and gently bake until lightly toasted, stirring the mixture every 5 minutes. Alternatively, cook on the stovetop in a heavy-based frypan over low heat.

Sunshine Smoothie Bowl

Feeds 1 · Prep 10 mins · GF, V, NC

This recipe takes fruit salad to the next level. It's packed with protein and antioxidants, and although I use dairy-free soy milk and yoghurt here, you can substitute regular dairy products or use coconut or rice milk instead. Experiment with different fruits, flavours and textures using whatever is fresh and juicy at your local market, and put as many colours into your smoothie bowl as possible.

1 cup frozen mango
1 frozen banana
¼ cup vanilla soy or coconut yoghurt
½ cup soy milk (or other milk)
¼ cup fresh or frozen blueberries

Serve with roughly chopped pistachios, shredded coconut and fresh mint leaves.

Blitz together the mango, banana, yoghurt and milk until smooth. Pour into a bowl and top with blueberries, chopped pistachios, shredded coconut and mint leaves.

Eggs in Hell

Feeds 4 · Prep 5 mins · Cook 20 mins · GF, OP

This is Dave's kind of breakfast: a hearty, protein-packed meal with heaps of veggies that keeps him going well beyond lunchtime. It makes an excellent, lazy dinner, too, served with chunky slices of toasted homemade bread.

1 tbsp extra virgin olive oil

½ medium brown onion, chopped

2 garlic cloves, finely chopped

½ large red capsicum (bell pepper), chopped

8-10 mushrooms, sliced

400g (14oz) tin whole tomatoes, roughly chopped

440g (15oz) tin baked beans

½ tsp ground cumin

¼ tsp smoked paprika

freshly cracked black pepper

handful of cherry tomatoes, halved

4 large free-range eggs

Serve with chopped flat-leaf parsley.

Over medium heat, warm 1 tbsp of olive oil in a large, heavy-based frypan. Sauté the onion until it softens, and add the garlic, capsicum and mushrooms. Cook for 4-5 minutes.

Add the tinned tomatoes, baked beans and spices. Simmer and stir for 5 minutes, then toss in the cherry tomatoes. Make four small wells in the mixture with a spoon and crack in the eggs. Cover the pan and cook for about 5 minutes or until the eggs are set. Take off the heat, sprinkle with chopped parsley and serve.

Stovetop Cyclone Pie

Feeds 4 · Prep 10 mins · Cook 25-30 mins

We'd sailed halfway up Cape York when the season's last cyclone crossed the Coral Sea. It chased us out of our snug Flinders Island anchorage, where dugongs surfaced mere metres from the boat, and dinners were a smorgasbord of queenfish and mackerel, golden trevally and delicious flowery rock cod. Into the mangroves we went, deep into Princess Charlotte Bay, to tie the boat off sturdy riverside trees, strip the decks clear and begin the nervous wait for wild winds. Cyclone Ann whipped us into action, but she made us wait too. We caught barramundi, filmed crocodiles sidling past, and, in readiness for a hefty blow, baked up this stovetop treat we now call Cyclone Pie. Fortunately for us, Ann quickly ran out of puff, crossing the coast as a tropical low, but it was all good practice. If not for Ann, we would never have discovered our beautiful river anchorage or enjoyed our post-blow breakfast of simply delicious pie.

7 large free-range eggs

2 sheets of puff pastry

handful of cherry tomatoes, halved

1 spring onion, finely sliced

½ cup grated cheddar cheese

Grease a large, heavy-based frypan and cover the base and sides of the pan with pastry, overlapping the edges to get a good seal. Whisk the eggs and pour over the pastry. Top with tomatoes, spring onion and cheese. Cover the pan with a lid and cook over very low heat for 15-20 minutes, until you begin to smell that the base is browned.

Take off the stove and cook under a grill at medium heat until the egg is set and the cheese browns (about 10 minutes). If you have an oven, bake the pie at around 180°C (350°F) until it's crispy and golden.

Mango Lassi

Makes 2 · Prep 5 mins · GF

It's a perfectly balanced combination of yin and yang: cool, hydrating and protein-rich. According to traditional Chinese medicine, yin foods – mangoes, melons, limes and more – are easy on your digestive system and keep you cool and refreshed. If lactose doesn't love you, swap for coconut or soy yoghurt instead.

2 large mangoes (or 2 cups frozen)

1 cup (250ml) orange juice

¾ cup (200g) natural yoghurt

1 tsp rice malt syrup (optional)

If using fresh mangoes, peel, slice and freeze the flesh for 2-3 hours (overnight is best). Combine the frozen mango, orange juice, yoghurt and rice malt syrup in a blender, and puree until smooth. If you can't wait for your mango to freeze, simply blitz it with 1-2 cups of ice cubes.

Iced Green Tea

Makes 4 · Prep 15 mins + Time to cool · GF, V

2 tbsp roughly chopped fresh ginger

4 cups (1L) of water

½ tsp ground mixed spice

½ tsp ground cinnamon

¼ cup rice malt syrup (or honey)

2 tbsp green tea leaves

Serve with ice, lemon slices and fresh mint.

Place the fresh ginger in a large pot with 1 litre of water and bring to a simmer. Add the ground spices and rice malt syrup (or honey), simmer gently for 10 minutes, then take off the heat and add the tea. Set aside to infuse for 10 minutes.

Strain the tea, discard the ginger, and set aside to cool. Refrigerate or chill to room temperature, and serve over ice with slices of fresh lemon and mint sprigs.

Coconut Strawberry Shakes

Makes 2 · Prep 5 mins + 12 hrs to soak · GF

½ cup blanched almonds

2 tbsp dried cranberries

1 cup UHT coconut drinking milk*

2 tbsp Greek yoghurt

1 cup strawberries (fresh or frozen)

1 tsp chia seeds

** Coconut drinking milk is thinner and lighter than tinned coconut milk and is usually combined with water, brown rice milk and sea salt. Swap with regular coconut milk if you prefer.*

Soak the almonds in filtered water overnight. Add the dried cranberries about 30 minutes before preparing this breakfast shake, and drain well. Combine with coconut milk, Greek yoghurt, strawberries and chia seeds. Blend until smooth and serve chilled or over ice.

Passionfruit Chia Pudding

Makes 4 · Prep 5 mins + 6 hrs to soak · GF, V

Need to power up with protein? The chia seeds used here contribute more omega-3 fatty acids than 300g of fresh salmon. It's also vegan and packed with vitamin C, but you can use regular dairy products and any fruit you like.

200ml (7fl oz) UHT coconut drinking milk*

1 cup coconut yoghurt

¼ cup chia seeds

3-4 fresh passionfruits

⅓ cup shredded coconut

4 mint sprigs to serve (optional)

Combine the coconut milk, yoghurt and chia seeds, stir well, cover and refrigerate for at least 6 hours (or overnight). When ready to serve, gently toast the coconut. Divide the pudding into four glasses or bowls and serve topped with passionfruit pulp, toasted coconut and mint sprigs (optional).

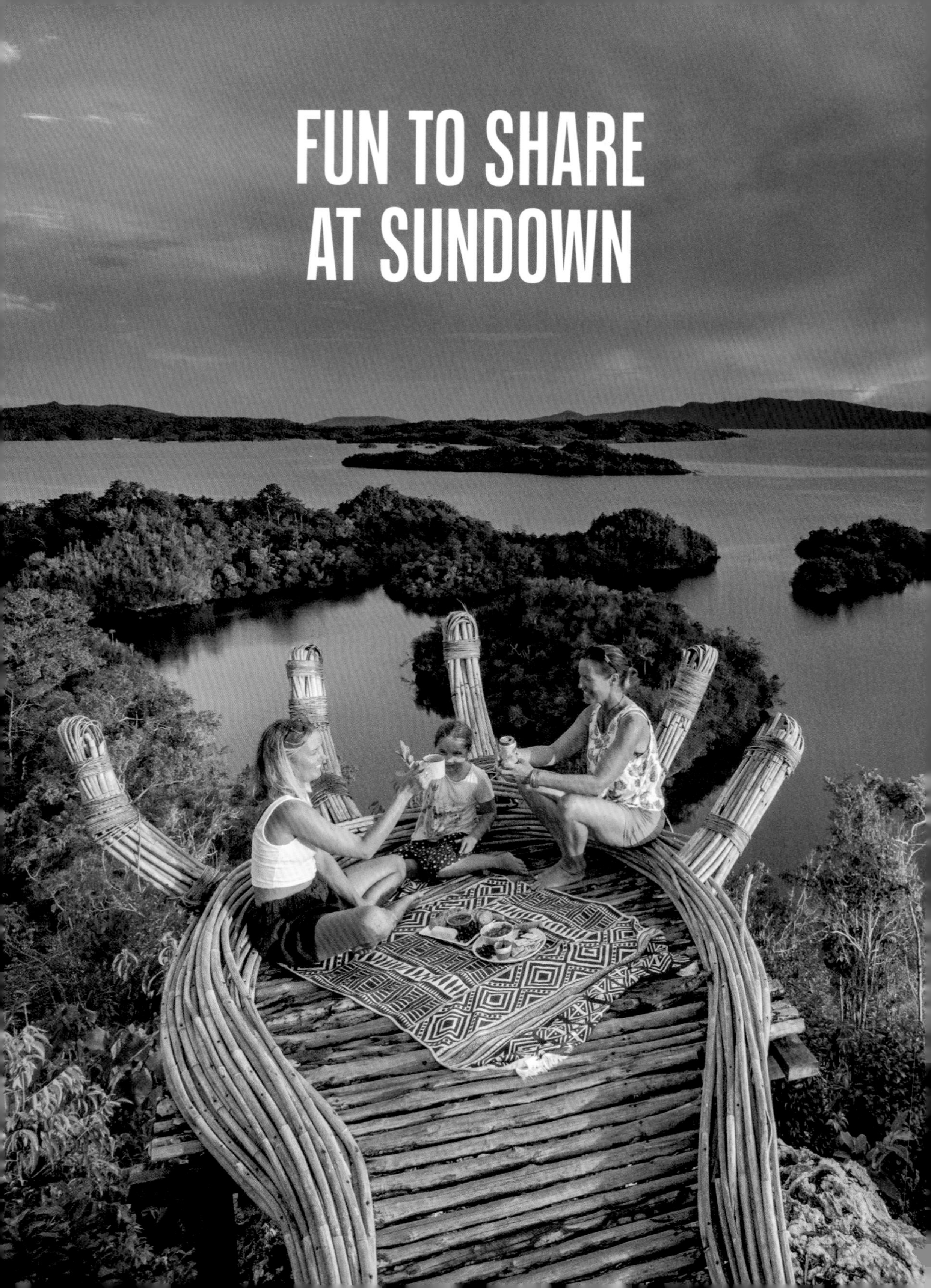

FUN TO SHARE AT SUNDOWN

Honey-baked Brie

Feeds 4-6 • Prep 5 mins • Cook 15 mins • GF, QC

2 x 125g (4.5oz) rounds of brie (or camembert)

2 tsp honey

4 sprigs of fresh thyme

½ tsp dried crushed chillies (optional)

Preheat the oven to 180°C (350°F). Line a baking tray with a crumpled piece of baking paper. Unwrap the cheese, place it on the tray and use a sharp knife to score a criss-cross pattern on each round. The crumpled baking paper elevates the cheese while it's in the oven and then helps to transfer it for serving.

Drizzle each round of brie with a little honey, and sprinkle with thyme and some crushed chilli if you'd like some extra sting. Cover the tray with foil and bake for 10 minutes. Uncover and bake for a further 5 minutes or until the cheese melts slightly. Serve immediately with bread toasts or crackers.

Guacamole Fresca

Makes 2 cups • Prep 10 mins • Cook 5 mins • V, QC

3 tsp ground cumin

2 large ripe avocados

1 ½ tbsp lime juice

1 spring onion, finely chopped

⅓ cup finely chopped fresh coriander (cilantro) or a squeeze of coriander paste

½ tsp crushed dried red chillies (optional)

salt and pepper

4 sheets mountain bread (or corn chips if gluten-free)

Over low heat, gently warm the ground cumin in a non-stick pan until aromatic (about 30 seconds) and tip it into a mixing bowl. Halve the avocados, remove the seeds and scoop the flesh into the bowl. Add the lime juice and mash well with a fork.

Stir in the finely chopped spring onion, coriander and crushed chillies (optional). Season to taste with salt and pepper. Slice the mountain bread into thin, short strips and toast in batches on the barbecue or in a frypan sprayed with olive oil until crisp, turning once.

Steamed Nepali Momos

Makes about 75 • Prep 30-45 mins (depending on the number of helpers) • Cook 30 mins • V

This spicy little snack is what Nepalis order when they meet up with friends to sip chiya and chat. From the backstreets of Kathmandu to the highest reaches of the Himalayas, you'll find momos on just about every menu, stuffed with vegetables, buffalo, and even nak cheese or chocolate. This recipe is one of my favourites, and the reason it makes so many is because they are highly addictive and quickly gather a crowd. Serve them with Chilli & Ginger Sauce (page 217) or a simple dish of soy sauce.

3 ⅓ cups wholemeal plain (all-purpose) flour

1 ½ cups warm water

coconut oil or ghee

Fill with

3 spring onions (scallions), finely chopped

1 tomato, finely chopped

1 cup finely chopped Asian greens or wombok cabbage

2 garlic cloves, finely chopped

1 tsp minced ginger

1 tsp ground cumin

½ tsp ground turmeric

½ tsp ground coriander

1 tsp momo (or Nepali) masala

½ tsp chilli flakes (optional)

½ bunch of fresh coriander (cilantro), finely chopped

salt to taste

Place the flour in a large mixing bowl and slowly add the warm water, mixing just enough to form a soft dough. Knead well (for about 10 minutes), roll the dough into a ball, rub with a little coconut oil or ghee, and place in a sealed container for 30 minutes.

For the filling, combine all ingredients, mix well with your hands and season to taste with salt.

Briefly knead the dough to warm it up. Nepali cooks pinch out little balls of dough, flatten them on a board with the palm of their hand, and use a rolling pin, and then their fingers, to shape the dough into small disks. Until you get the knack, try rolling out the dough on a floured benchtop to a thickness of 2-3mm (1/8in), and using a circular cookie cutter or a glass to cut out rounds about 7cm (3in) wide.

The art of making momos is all in their folding. Hold a circle of dough in one palm and add a couple of heaped teaspoons of vegetable mixture. With your free hand, bring the edges of the dough together, crimping them closed and making little pleats along the centre of the momo to seal it tightly shut. It takes a little practice, but there is no such thing as a bad momo! Continue until all the pastry has been cut and filled, then steam the momos in batches on a well-oiled rack for 10 minutes each.

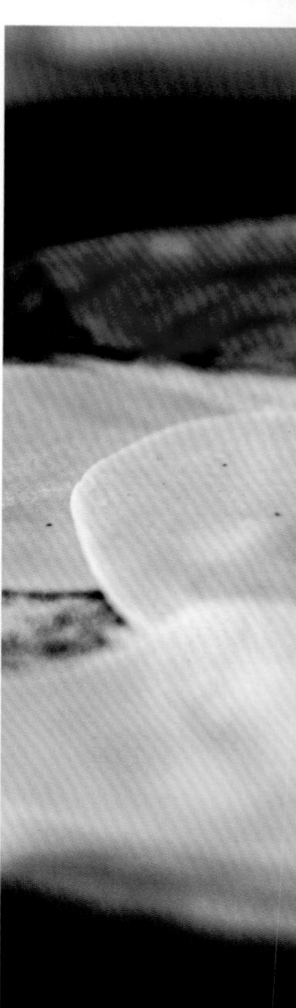

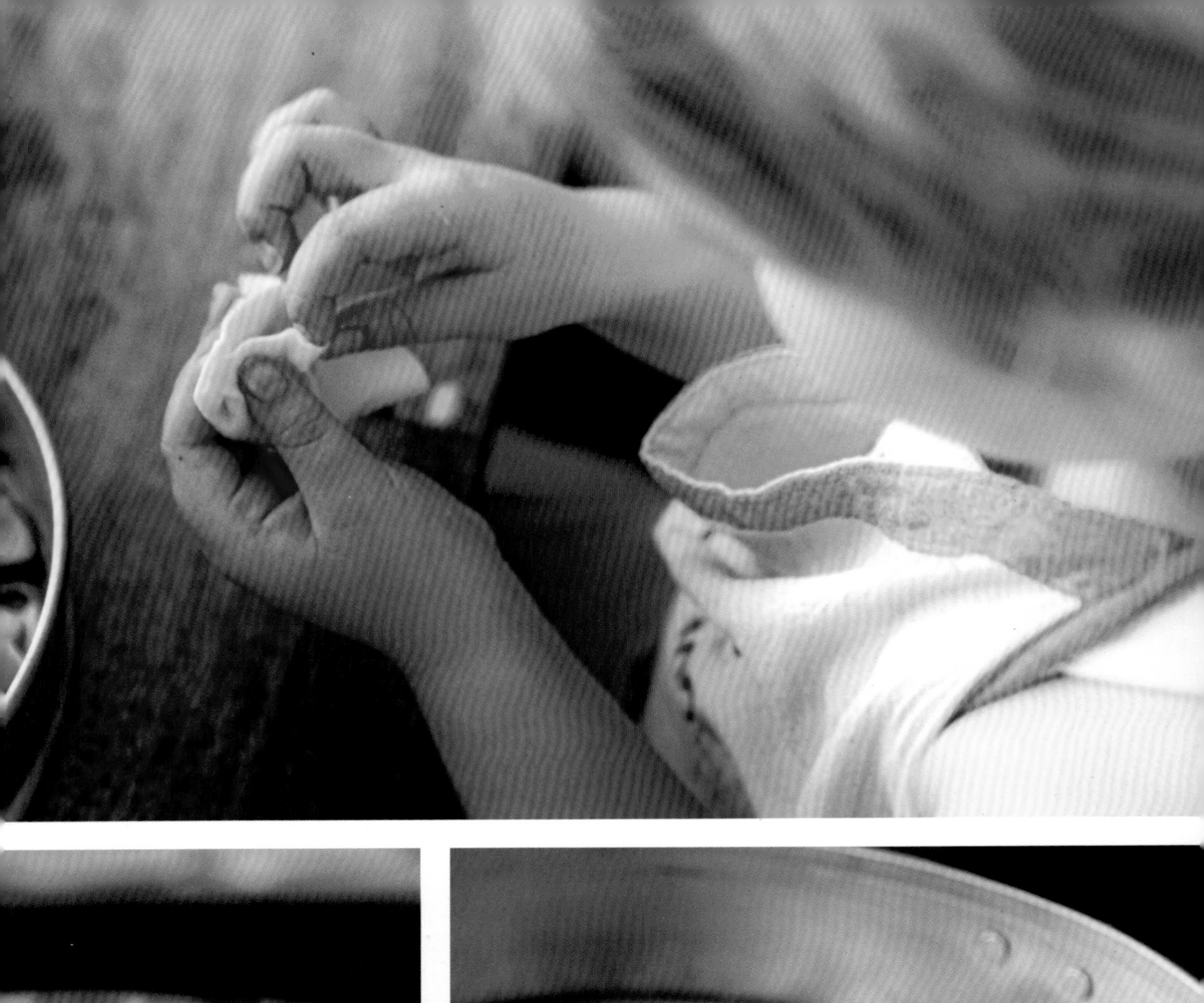

Red Onion Bhajis

with coriander yoghurt

Makes 20 • Prep 15 mins • Cook 10 mins

Friends were coming aboard, and the snack situation was dire. There'd already been a week of sundowners and lots of late-night munchies on the helm. We'd run out of cheese, chips and vegetables to dip. What I did have was a pile of aging onions, a pot of homemade yoghurt, and a clump of coriander that I hadn't managed to kill. A few shakes of spice and a quick plunge into some hot oil later, and we were ready to munch and chink icy brews in front of a killer, red-sky sunset.

2 large red onions

⅔ cup plain (all-purpose) flour

½ tsp baking powder

¼ tsp ground cumin

½ tsp ground turmeric

½ tsp chilli powder

½ tsp sea salt

⅔ cup cold water

coconut (or peanut) oil

coriander (cilantro) sprigs to serve

Coriander Yoghurt

½ bunch coriander, rinsed

1 cup natural Greek yoghurt

½ lemon, juiced (about 1 tbsp)

1 small garlic clove, roughly chopped

2 tsp extra virgin olive oil

pinch of pepper

Halve, and then thinly slice the onions and place them in a large bowl. Cover with cold water and set them aside while you prepare the yoghurt.

For the yoghurt, pick off the coriander leaves and blitz them with yoghurt, lemon juice, garlic and olive oil. Process until smooth and season with a pinch of pepper. Pour into a serving bowl and refrigerate.

Back to the bhajis, sift the flour, baking powder and spices into a mixing bowl. Add the salt and cold water and whisk to form a thick batter. Drain the onion, add it to the batter and stir well.

Heat a generous amount of coconut oil in a deep frypan or wok. When hot, add heaped spoonfuls of the onion mixture, cooking each batch for 1-2 minutes until golden. Drain on a wire rack and serve scattered with coriander leaves and a dish of coriander yoghurt.

Roast Vegetable Dip

with dukkah

Makes 2 cups • Prep 15 mins • Cook 45 mins • GF

750g (1.5lb) carrots, peeled

1 red capsicum (bell pepper)

8 garlic cloves

1 tbsp ground cumin

2 tsp ground coriander

½ tsp fennel seeds

½ tsp ground turmeric

good pinch of hot paprika

good pinch of dried chilli flakes

¼ cup extra virgin olive oil

3 tbsp pine nuts

½ cup natural Greek yoghurt

½ lemon (zest and juice)

salt and pepper

1 tbsp dukkah, to serve

Preheat the oven to 190°C (375°F). Roughly chop the carrots and capsicum and place them in a mixing bowl. Smash the garlic cloves with the back of a knife but leave them unpeeled. Add the garlic, spices and extra virgin olive oil to the bowl, toss everything together, and spread on a baking tray lined with baking paper. Roast for about 45 minutes, adding the pine nuts for the final 10 minutes of baking.

Set the tray aside to cool. Peel the garlic cloves and discard the skins. Blend or mash them together with the roasted vegetables, pine nuts, yoghurt and the zest and juice (4 teaspoons) of half a lemon. Season to taste with a good grind of salt and pepper. Serve garnished with dukkah.

Iced Tamarind Juice

Makes 4 · Prep 10 mins · GF, V

After a hectic Gulf-of-Carpentaria crossing (they always are), Nhulunbuy is a well-deserved reward. There's an endless sweep of turquoise coves and an intriguing historical site at Garanhan. Behind 250-year-old tamarind trees in a Macassan bêche-de-mer fishing camp (which predates the arrival of James Cook), the 170-year-old Wurrwurrwuy Stone Arrangements depict dugout canoes, fireplaces and boats. They preserve a harmonious history between Indonesians and the local Laramirri (Yolngu) who traded hunting rights for dugout canoes and stone tools.

This Sulawesi fleet arrived on the northwest monsoon every December, returning when the winds changed, often with intrepid Yolngu men sharing the 1600km journey. Today, old bêche-de-mer camps can be found along Australia's north, marked by aging tamarind trees planted to ward off scurvy and add flavour to food. The tree's fruit imparts a tangy sour flavour to seafood dipping sauces, curries and sweet treats, too. When the heat gets too much to bear aboard our boat, a jug of this tea never fails to cool things down.

½ cup tamarind pulp (about 150g/5.5oz)

2 ½ cups hot water

⅓ cup rice malt syrup

1 lime

Serve with muddled mint sugar, fresh mint and ice.

Combine 1 cup of hot water with the tamarind pulp (only use 1/3 cup if your pulp is seedless) and stir until dissolved over medium heat. Pour the mixture through a mesh strainer to remove the seeds, then return it to the heat with another 1 ½ cups of water and the rice malt syrup. Stir until the syrup dissolves. Adjust the flavour suit your tastes: add a squeeze of lime to sour it up or a little more rice malt syrup to sweeten it. Refrigerate until chilled.

Pound together 1 tablespoon of sugar and some fresh mint leaves. Rub a cut lime over the rim of four glasses and dip each into the mint sugar. Fill the glasses with ice and extra mint leaves, pour in the tamarind juice and serve.

Iced Moroccan Tea

Makes 2 · Prep 10 mins + Chilling time · GF, V

Nepalis like it spicy, and Russians drink it with a sugar cube on the tongue. Moroccans are all about the mint, and drinking tea is an integral part of their culture. It forms the cornerstone of almost all interactions, and everything from retail purchases to business deals and all family concerns are discussed and decided over a cup of mint tea. Drink it hot or pour it over ice with slices of lemon and lots of fresh mint.

1 heaped tbsp gunpowder (Chinese green) tea

large handful of fresh mint sprigs

2 tbsp rice malt syrup (to taste)

3 cups water, divided

2 cups ice

½ lemon, sliced

extra mint sprigs

Use a teapot if yours can go on the stovetop, or simply boil 1 cup of water in a saucepan, add the tea and swirl well. Tip away the brewed tea (it's a little too bitter) but retain the leaves and return the pot to the stove. Add 2 cups of water and bring it to a boil. Let the tea simmer for a minute before adding the mint leaves, and when the water beings to bubble again (allow 1 minute), take the pot off the heat, add the rice malt syrup and stir well. Let the tea cool slightly, then strain it into glasses filled with plenty of ice. Add lemon slices and fresh mint sprigs to serve.

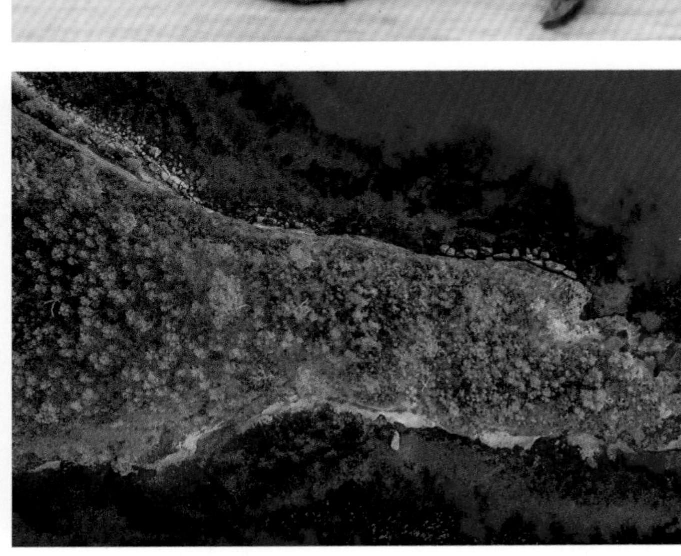

Agua Fresca

Makes 4 • Prep 10 mins • GF, V

Sunsets are for dreaming and for adding new, wild ideas to our Sailing Bucket List. It's a wish list for watery encounters, offbeat experiences and dare-you challenges that invariably take us to places we might never otherwise discover. Like in search of blind cave crabs and Indonesia's most surprising, underwater mermaid. To plunge into lakes swarming with jellyfish, tackle precarious tree climbs and eyeball enormously gentle whale sharks: all ticked off from our collective *Wild One* bucket list that keeps growing and growing the longer we sail.

Agua Fresca is perfect sunset-dreaming juice. This Mexican favourite is fresh and alcohol-free, making it ideal for balmy afternoons and for serving to kids. Its name means 'fresh water', and it's pretty darn delicious.

1 small, ripe papaya (pawpaw)

2 cups cold water

1 cup of ice

2 tbsp rice malt syrup (to taste)

1 lime, juiced

Serve with extra ice and mint sprigs.

Peel and chop the papaya, discarding the seeds. Blend all ingredients and pour into 4 glasses filled with extra ice. Add a few mint sprigs and serve.

Lemon-lime Barley Cooler

Makes 3 cups • Prep 5 mins • Cook 35 mins • V

1 cup pearl barley

4 cups (1L) water

1 cup mixed lemon and lime juice

½ cup rice malt syrup (or sugar) to taste

2 cups sparkling mineral or soda water

Serve with extra slices of citrus and ice cubes.

Rinse the barley first, place it in a saucepan with the water and bring it to a boil. Reduce the heat and simmer for 30 minutes or until the liquid is reduced by half. Strain out the barley and discard but keep the water, and add the lemon and lime juice and sweeten to taste with rice malt syrup (or sugar), stirring until it's dissolved. Set it aside to cool, and then refrigerate until chilled. To serve, fill glasses with ice and citrus slices, then add equal quantities of the barley syrup and sparkling mineral or soda water.

Strawberry Fizz

Makes 4 • Prep 10 mins + Brewing time • GF, V

3 tsp tea leaves (any choice)

¼ tsp mixed spice

¼ tsp grated fresh ginger

¼ tsp ground cinnamon

¼ tsp ground nutmeg

2-3 tbsp rice malt syrup (to taste)

2 large strawberries, sliced

Serve with ice, orange juice and soda water.

In a small pot, boil 2 cups of water and your favourite tea, all the spices and enough rice malt syrup to suit your tastes. Reduce the heat and simmer for 5 minutes. Take off the heat and leave to brew for 15 minutes. Strain the tea, then set it aside to cool. Divide the cooled tea between four large glasses. Add ice cubes and sliced strawberries, and top up each glass with orange juice and soda water, then simply stir and serve.

Lemon Curd Cocktails

Makes 2 · Prep 5 mins · GF

Taste-testing this one (at 9am, no less) kick-started one of the best 'work' days in my galley, ever! I made it with superb, homemade curd (created by a true-blue Canadian sailor from home-grown backyard citrus), and I think that makes all the difference.

90ml (3 fl oz) lemon vodka

4 ½ tbsp Lemon & Lime Curd (page 212)

3 tsp lemon juice

Lemon foam

2 free-range egg whites

2 tsp caster (superfine) sugar

juice of a large lemon

In a cocktail shaker, combine the lemon vodka, lemon curd and lemon juice with ice, shake well and strain into martini glasses.

For the lemon foam, use a stick blender to blitz together the egg whites, caster sugar and lemon juice for 45 seconds. Pour it over the top and serve. If you don't love the idea of raw egg, simply dress the cocktail with a dollop of cream.

Tropical Sour

Makes 4 · Prep 5 mins · GF, V

a handful of mint leaves

2 cups cranberry juice, chilled

½ cup Malibu liqueur

juice of 1 lime

4-5 cups ice cubes

1 cup lemonade

Rinse the mint leaves and place them in a large jug. Add the cranberry and lime juice with Malibu and stir well. Pour it into 4 (or more) glasses filled with ice, top with lemonade and serve.

Blueberry G&T

Makes 2 • Prep 5 mins • GF, V

Sailors and gin just go together, even when we aren't sailing. I have a travel tradition when I fly that involves a sneaky bottle of Bombay Sapphire at 35,000 feet. When the plane's finally airborne, and it's just me and a G&T, I can celebrate that the drama of airport check-in is finally behind me and let the adventure begin. Intrepid cruisers who love their gin are frequently onboard distillers. We've had more than one gin tasting on our boat's back deck, and for a while, we cruised with a boat we nicknamed Gin-Toc because their gin was actually pretty good. I'm always quick to compliment these boat-made creations (especially at sundown,) but I've never had the heart to say out loud that gin just tastes better at 35,000 feet. This blueberry G&T recipe comes to the rescue and makes even rather ordinary, boat-made gin taste sublimely good at sea level.

½ cup blueberries (fresh or frozen)

1 tbsp lime juice

¼ tsp vanilla bean paste

¼ cup gin

⅔ cup tonic water

2 cups crushed ice to serve

In a jug or cocktail shaker, mash the blueberries with lime juice and vanilla paste (if using frozen blueberries, give them a few minutes to defrost first). Add the gin and shake well. Fill your two favourite glasses with ice, strain the gin mixture into the glasses and top with tonic water. Enjoy with sunset.

SAILING STAPLES FROM SCRATCH

There is always something to do on a boat: an endless list of things to stow, things to fix, things to clean, and sometimes, kids to teach, amuse and stow/fix/clean too. Then there are meals to cook, snacks to prepare and lots of washing up. Now I really love to cook (washing up, not so much), so I don't mind getting busy in the galley. But, and it's a big but, sometimes the world outside just tugs for my attention (hello coral reef!).

So, I take shortcuts. I don't make everything from scratch, just the things that really count when I'm cruising, like fresh yoghurt, sourdough bread, and home-brewed beer (obviously). Maya jokes that my sourdough starter gets more attention than she does. I will also happily grate my own coconuts because freshly grated coconut added to smoothies and my Mum's famous 5-ingredient Coconut Cake (page 245) is my kind of bliss. I do find that the farther I get from 'civilisation', when all my ready-to-go 'instant' food has been used up, I spend a lot more time in the galley, putting meals and snacks together.

But, there are some things I don't do too. I don't make my own stock (although I'd be impressed if you did) because if I did have a lazy hour to spare, I'd prefer to jump overboard and look at fish rather than cook up their bones. Feel free to create as much from scratch as you like, but don't feel bad if you take a shortcut when cooking dinner and go look at fish instead. I'll see you down below.

Maya's Papaya Scones

Makes 12 · Prep 10 mins · Cook 15 mins · QC

- 3 cups self-raising flour
- ⅓ cup caster sugar
- 1 pinch of salt
- 1 tbsp softened butter
- 1 ¼ cups papaya
- 1 egg, lightly whisked

Preheat the oven to 200°C (390°F). Measure flour, sugar and salt into a bowl. Rub in the butter, using your fingertips, then make a well in the centre. Roughly blend the papaya (I use half chopped and half pureed) and add it to the flour mixture along with the lightly whisked egg. Use your hands to gently bring the wet and dry ingredients together to form a soft dough.

Turn it out onto a lightly floured bench and gently knead only until the dough comes together. Pat the dough into a disk about 3cm (1in) thick. Dip a 6.5cm (2.5in) cookie cutter or glass into flour and cut out the first round of scones. Bring the dough scraps back together and repeat until you have 12 scones. Bake them on a tray lined with baking paper for 15 minutes or until browned.

Yoghurt Flatbreads

Makes 6 · Prep 25 mins · Cook 15 mins · QC

- 1 ½ cups self-raising flour
- ¾ cup thick natural yoghurt
- 1 tsp baking powder
- 2 generous pinches of salt
- 1 tbsp oil (extra virgin olive or coconut)

Measure the flour, yoghurt, baking powder and salt into a mixing bowl, stir with a spoon and use clean hands to bring it all together. Form the dough into a ball and leave it in a covered bowl for 20 minutes.

Divide the dough into six equal pieces and form each into a ball. Flatten each with the palm of your hand. Use an oiled rolling pin (or glass bottle) to roll the dough on a lightly oiled bench to a thickness of about 3mm (1/8in). Heat a dry frypan over medium heat and fry each flatbread for about 1 minute per side. Serve as breakfast wraps with fried eggs and grilled tomatoes, to mop up a bowl of Charred Corn Chowder (page 151) or to dip into Quick Sri Lankan Curry (page 89).

Sailing Catalpa's Sourdough

Makes 1 loaf • Prep 15 mins + Rising time
Cook 45-60 mins • V

I spent decades baking yeast bread before I was gifted my first jar of sourdough starter. Thanks to Tera of *@sv_nalukai* and Sara from *@sailingcatalpa*, I lost hours learning the art of sourdough before finally perfecting a loaf that feeds us daily. Until you find your bread-making groove, this daily ritual can seem daunting. The quirky tradition of naming your sourdough starter is testament to the amount of time you'll spend together. Mine is descended from a starter called Rosie, that Sara has been sweet talking every morning for five years. When Maya asked what we would call ours, the bubbles just weren't happening. "What rhymes with pain?" I asked. "Shane?" Sailors are great gifters of wisdom, tips and starter, and after that, all you need is this recipe, a cool name, and a little sweet talking too.

I feed my starter every night, and by morning, when it's bubbling away, I use it to make a new batch of dough. Mornings are also for baking yesterday's dough, pulled straight out of the fridge, all puffy and gorgeous.

Feeding my starter at night works best for me in the tropics because the it reacts more slowly in the cooler hours. In chillier regions, your starter may need more daytime heat to rise, so experiment to find what works.

To feed starter, mix 3 tablespoons (60ml) of starter with half a cup of water and 2/3 cup of flour, and leave it overnight. To test it, drop a tiny pinch of starter into a glass of water. It's ready to use when it floats. If it doesn't, feed it again and set it aside for another 6 to 12 hours.

As a backup in case of forgotten feeds or other galley disasters, I keep a small jar of starter in the fridge. It will keep for months, which is essential if you leave the boat for a while. To reactivate your backup starter, bring it to room temperature, feed it once every 12 hours until it resumes its normal bubbling, and then continue once every 24 hours as usual.

4 cups plain (all-purpose) flour (about 500g)

½ cup sourdough starter

1 ¼ cups water

After 1 Hour, Add

1 tbsp water

2 tsp salt

1 tbsp raw sunflower seeds

2 tsp raw sesame seeds

Optional

fresh or dry herbs

sultanas (sultana raisins)

ground cinnamon

rice flour

sesame seeds

Measure the flour into a large bowl, add the starter and water, and mix it with a large spoon. Use wet hands to combine and briefly knead the dough to bring it together. Cover the bowl with a tea towel and set it aside. After one hour, add 1 tablespoon (but up to 3 tablespoons if needed) of water, salt and the seeds. At this point, you can also add some fresh or dried herbs or toss in a handful of sultanas and 1 teaspoon of ground cinnamon. Mix the dough with wet hands until well combined, and set the dough aside. After 30 minutes, stretch the dough three times by pulling it apart with your hands. Wind the dough back into a ball and set it aside. After another 30 minutes, stretch the dough three times, form it into a ball, and cover and refrigerate it overnight or for 24 hours.

When it's ready to bake, preheat the oven and upend the dough onto a well-oiled tray or transfer it to a loaf tin or a Dutch or camp oven. Score the top of the dough deeply with a knife and sprinkle with rice flour or brush with a little water and top with sesame seeds. Baking time will depend entirely on your boat oven. In my galley oven, I bake bread for 45-60 minutes at around 180°C (350°F), but my more efficient Weber barbecue browns a loaf in 35 minutes at around 200°C (390°F).

I also roll out this this dough for pizza bases and flatbreads.

STORYTELLER
DARWIN

Easy Cheesy Monkey Bread

Feeds 4 • Prep 25 mins + 35 mins Rising time Cook 30-35 mins

Hankering for something more decadent than focaccia, I baked this bread on one of those drizzly days when you need to make your own sunshine. My daughter Maya did all the messy mixing and stirring, which is how I know that other mini chefs will want to get their sticky fingers into this too. It tastes far more sophisticated than its name might imply. Make it with kids or when you crave real bakery treats a long way from the harbour.

3 ¼ cups plain (all-purpose) flour

1 tsp salt

2 tsp (7g) dried yeast

1 tbsp rice malt syrup

1 large free-range egg

1 cup (250ml) warm water

2 tbsp extra virgin olive oil

Monkey Mix

1 cup grated cheddar

⅔ cup (100g) crumbled feta

¼ cup (50g) cold butter, coarsely grated

2 garlic cloves, finely chopped

¼ cup finely chopped coriander (cilantro) (optional)

½ tsp chili flakes (optional)

salt and pepper

For the dough, combine the flour, salt, yeast and rice malt syrup in a mixing bowl. Add one egg, the warm water and the oil, and stir to combine. Turn the dough onto a lightly floured surface and knead for 10 minutes (or until mini-chefs lose interest). Wrap in a large beeswax sheet (or reusable plastic bag) and stick in the fridge. You can make this any time in advance.

For the Monkey Mix, combine all the ingredients in a large mixing bowl. Transfer a third of the mixture to the fridge for later. Cut the cold dough into four equal chunks, and cut each of these into eight pieces. Roughly shape the dough into balls, toss them each in the cheese mixture to coat, and arrange them in a greased ovenproof skillet (or camp oven if cooking on the fire). Top with any cheese you have left in your bowl.

Put the bread in a warm place for 30-40 minutes. Preheat the oven to 180°C (350°F), or get your campfire coals ready, and bake the bread for about 20 minutes. Top with the extra cheese mixture from the fridge and bake for another 10-15 minutes until golden. Eat immediately or take it on a picnic.

Roti Canai

Makes 10 • Prep 25 mins + Resting time Cook 20 mins

Making roti takes a bit of practice, but don't get hung up on looks. The proof is in the eating, and this bread tastes fine, however it looks. To make my favourite Malay-style breakfast, have a pot of red lentil dhal ready for dunking, and pour your coffee rich and sweet.

4 cups (500g) plain (all-purpose) flour

1 tsp salt

1 large free-range egg, beaten

pinch of sugar

1 cup warm water

½ cup coconut oil or ghee for rolling

Serve with red lentil dhal or vegetarian curry.

Combine the flour and salt in a mixing bowl (sifting is optional). Make a well in the centre and pour in the beaten egg, a pinch of sugar and up to 1 cup of warm water, adding just a little at a time until the dough is soft. Form into a ball and knead for about 5 minutes until elastic and soft. Divide into ten small balls and coat each with coconut oil or ghee. Cover well and rest the dough in a cool spot for a few hours.

When ready to eat, roll the balls out one at a time on a clean benchtop. Using generous dobs of oil or ghee and the palms of your hands, stretch the dough out on the bench until very thin and transparent but don't worry if you get the odd hole or tear. Carefully pick up the dough by one edge and let it hang and stretch into a long ribbon. Lay the dough back down, roll it up into a round coil (it will look like a pastry scroll), and then flatten it with your palm into a 20cm wide disc. Set aside, cover it with a tea towel and continue until you have all ten.

Heat a frypan over medium heat, add about a teaspoon of oil and fry the roti, one at a time, for 1-2 minutes per side, adding a little more oil before you flip it. When golden, take it out of the pan and cover it with a tea towel while you continue to cook your rotis.

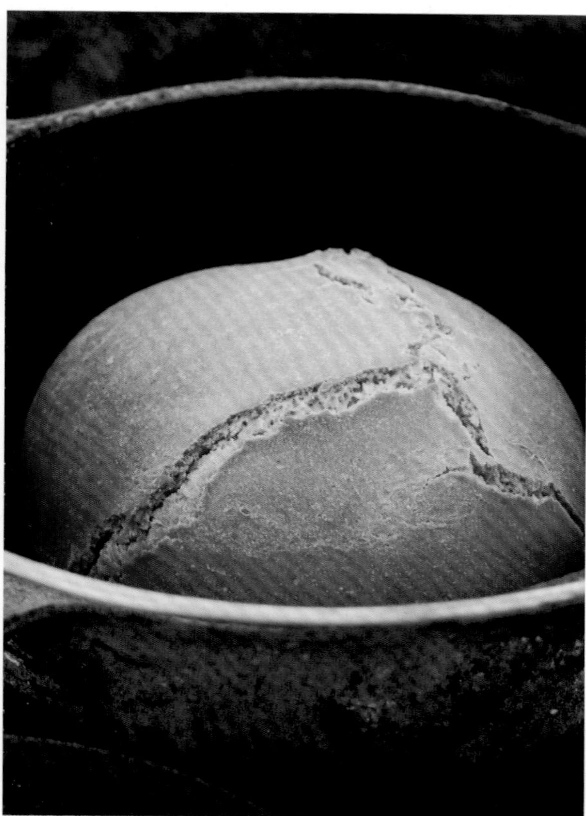

Campfire Bread

Feeds 4 · Prep 15 mins + 2 hrs Rising time Cook 20-25 mins · V, CC

You can oven-bake this bread, of course, but when you are going ashore to stretch your legs and dig your toes into the sand to toast the sunset, you might be tempted to get a fire going and let it bake your bread. The dough needs an hour to rise before it goes into the camp oven and another hour to rest while your gather kindling, build a fire and let it burn down to a nice bed of coals. Baking bread over a fire infuses it with an amazing flavour, plus your boat doesn't overheat, you save on gas, and you get to cook your bread sitting down. That sure works for me.

1 cup warm water

1 tsp sugar

2 tsp (7g) dried yeast

2 tbsp extra virgin olive oil

1 tsp salt

3 cups plain (all-purpose) flour

Pour 1 cup of warm water into a large bowl and sprinkle in the sugar and yeast. Set it aside for 10 minutes. When frothy, add the olive oil and salt and sift in the flour. Mix well. Turn the dough onto a lightly floured bench and knead for 5-10 minutes with floured hands until it is soft and elastic. Place it in an oiled bowl and leave it to rise in a warm place for about an hour.

When the dough has risen to about twice its size, punch it down, knead for a minute and form it into a ball. Place it in an oiled camp oven and take it with you to the beach, leaving it in a warm spot to rise for another hour (or more). When the campfire has burned down to a good bed of coals, dig a shallow pit on the edge of the fire away from any flames, put the lid on your camp oven and shovel a few hot coals on top. Baking time will depend on the heat of your fire but allow around 20-25 minutes.

If you aren't building a fire, place your bread dough on a large baking tray lined with baking paper and bake in a preheated oven at 210°C (410°F) for about 20-25 minutes until golden.

Lemon Pepper Damper

Feeds 4 · Prep 20 mins + 40 mins Rising time Cook 20 mins · CC

2 cups self-raising flour

1 tsp salt

1 tsp lemon zest

2 tsp cracked black pepper

2 tbsp (40g) chilled butter, chopped

1 tbsp chopped fresh chives

⅔ cup grated cheddar

2 tsp lemon juice

⅔ cup milk

Pour the flour and salt into a large mixing bowl, and stir through the lemon zest and black pepper. Using your fingers, rub in the butter until the mixture resembles breadcrumbs. Stir in the chopped chives and grated cheese.

Pour the lemon juice into the milk, then add to your bowl, mixing until you have a nice, soft dough. If the dough is too stiff, add a little more milk. Turn the dough onto a lightly floured surface, knead for one minute, and divide it into two pieces.

Damper is best cooked on fire, so press each piece of dough into a circle about 1 inch thick and place it in two lightly-oiled, small camp ovens (or pool your dough into one big camp oven and cook for 5 minutes longer). Score the dough with a knife into six wedges and dust lightly with rice flour. Dig two shallow pits on the edge of the fire away from any flames, shovel a few amber coals into the holes, place the camp ovens inside (with lids firmly in place), and shovel a few hot coals on top of the pots. Bake for 20 minutes or until golden and the damper sounds hollow when you tap the base. Serve warm with plenty of butter.

In the oven: Place the dampers on oven trays that have been either greased or lined with baking paper. Bake in a preheated oven at 210°C (410°F) for about 20 minutes until golden.

DIY Pizzas

Makes 2 large or 4 small pizza
Prep 20 mins + 40 mins to rise • Cook 10 mins

'Pizza' is one of the few words understood just about everywhere. And because we love pizza, it always finds its way onto the menu. I've eaten it en route to Everest Base Camp, had the 'Happy' kind in Cambodia, and stood on a street corner in San Francisco stretching an enormous triangle of Margherita between my hand and mouth. Here's how to make it from scratch.

2 tsp (7g) dry yeast

1 cup warm water

1 tsp sugar

2 cups plain (all-purpose) flour

1 tsp salt

¼ cup extra virgin olive oil

Combine the yeast, warm water (not too hot) and sugar in a pot and leave it in a warm place until it starts to foam (about 10 minutes). Combine the flour and salt in a mixing bowl, pour in the olive oil and the yeast mixture, and stir to combine.

Turn the dough onto a floured benchtop, knead for about 5 minutes until the dough is soft and elastic, roll into a ball and place in an oiled pot. Leave it, covered, in a warm place for 40 minutes until the dough has doubled in size.

Punch the dough down, knead for 5 minutes, then break it into four pieces and roll each out. Add toppings and oven bake at 220°C (430°F) for 10 minutes or until golden. If you don't have an oven, cook one side of the bases in a large pan over low heat until the underside is golden. Top the cooked side, slide it back into the pan, and cover it so that the cheese melts. Or place it under a medium-hot grill until golden and bubbly.

Garlicky BBQ Pizzas: Toast your bases and garlic cloves on the barbecue. Smear them with the garlic and top with tomato slices, sun-dried tomato, capsicum, and very thin strips of barbecued carrot and zucchini, crumbled marinaded feta cheese (page 213), Kalamata olives and fresh basil.

Rocket & Ricotta Pizza: Blend 100g of wilted baby rocket leaves with ¼ cup ricotta and 1 garlic clove. Smear it on and top with cherry tomatoes, extra ricotta, pepper and basil, and bake.

Yeast-free Sun Bread

Makes 1 loaf • Prep 15 mins • Cook 30 mins • V

2 cups plain (all-purpose) flour

pinch of salt

1 tsp bicarbonate of soda (baking soda)

2 tbsp sun-dried tomatoes, chopped

1 tbsp Kalamata olives, chopped

¼ cup fresh chopped basil (or 1 tbsp dried)

cracked black pepper

1 cup warm water

2 tbsp extra virgin olive oil

1 tbsp sunflower seeds

1 tsp sesame seeds

In a large bowl, sift together the flour, salt and bicarbonate of soda. Add sundried tomatoes, olives, fresh or dried basil, and a couple of good grinds or pinches of black pepper. Mix the water and oil together, pour into the flour mixture, and combine to form a soft dough. Turn onto a lightly floured board or benchtop and press the dough into a disk about 3cm (1in) thick and 15cm (6in) in diameter.

Score with a knife into six segments and place in a camp oven (or on an oiled or paper-lined tray). Brush the top of the dough with a little extra oil and press on your choice of seeds (I like sunflower and sesame).

Baking on the fire: build a small fire and let it burn down to a nice bed of hot coals. Place your camp oven on hot coals briefly while you dig a shallow pit on the edge of the campfire, away from any flames. Place the camp oven in your pit, secure the lid, cover with hot coals and bake for 25-30 minutes or until golden (when baked, your bread will sound hollow when tapped).

In the oven: Preheat your oven to 220°C (430°F). Bake your bread on a tray lined with baking paper for 25-30 minutes until it's golden.

Home-made Yoghurt

Makes 4 cups · GF

1 cup powdered full-cream milk mixed with 3 cups of water

or 1 litre (4 cups) UHT milk

or 1 litre (4 cups) fresh milk

Plus ⅓ cup natural yoghurt (as a starter)

In an Easi-Yo yoghurt kit (or similar): Boil enough water to fill the thermos to the correct water level. In an insert container, mix the powdered milk and water together (or use UHT milk), add the yoghurt starter and shake well. Insert the yoghurt container into the thermos and screw the lid tight. Leave for 8 to 10 hours until the yoghurt is firm, then refrigerate. If your yoghurt doesn't set (or is a little runny), leave it in the thermos for up to 12 hours or more.

In sterilised jars: Gently heat either UHT or powdered milk (made with 3 cups of water) in a pan until you can dip a clean finger in the milk and hold it there for 10 seconds. Take the milk off the heat and pour half of the warm milk into a jug. Mix in the yoghurt and stir in the rest of the milk. Pour into sterilised and warmed glass jars, seal with lids and stand the jars in a pan of hot water. Cover with a towel to keep warm, and leave in a warm spot for 6 to 8 hours or until cooled and set.

In a 1-litre thermos: Heat the milk as above, stir in the yoghurt and pour the warm mixture into a clean, pre-warmed, wide-mouthed thermos flask. Close and set aside for 8-10 hours (or until set)

If using fresh milk: Bring fresh milk to the boil until the froth rises, then reduce the heat and simmer for two minutes to kill off any unwanted bacteria. Take the pot off the heat and leave the milk to cool until lukewarm (about half an hour). Stir in the yoghurt and continue with any of the methods above.

Ricotta and Indian Paneer

Makes 3 cups · Cook 10 mins + Resting time · GF

Fresh and delicately flavoured and so simple to make, ricotta and paneer are both made by adding acid and heat to fresh, whole milk. Warm milk is curdled, and the curds are squeezed dry in a cloth to make ricotta, which can then be pressed and solidified to create a block of paneer. Use paneer in the place of tofu in any vegetarian dish: sliced and deep-fried or threaded onto skewers and marinaded in Indian spices and olive oil for 20 minutes before barbecuing. Crumble it into curries, add to samosa fillings, or turn it into creamy spinach palak paneer. Paneer will keep for up to five days in the fridge.

3 litres (quarts) full cream milk

90ml (⅓ cup) lemon juice

1 tsp salt (optional)

In a large saucepan, bring the milk to a simmer over medium heat, stirring to stop it sticking to the bottom of the pan. When it begins to foam (but before it comes to a boil), add the lemon juice to make the milk curdle, stir and take it off the heat. Add another tablespoon of lemon juice if your milk doesn't separate. Set the pot aside for 10 minutes to rest.

To separate the curds and whey, cover a large mixing bowl with muslin cloth and carefully pour in the curds, letting the whey drain through into the bowl. Save the whey, if you like, to use in place of water for sourdough, soups or for soaking seeds and pulses to sprout. Squeeze the muslin cloth tight to remove any extra liquid. What you have in your cloth is fresh ricotta.

For paneer you can add 1/4 teaspoon of salt at this point, but it's optional. If I'm making paneer for salty Indian dishes, I tend to leave it out. Place the muslin-covered curds in a square-shaped dish covered with a heavy weight to produce a neat square of cheese. Alternatively, sit the cloth of curds on a plate and put a stack of plates on top. Leave for 2-3 hours and refrigerate it for 30 minutes to firm it up before slicing.

***Tip:** UHT (ultra-high temperature) milk doesn't work in this recipe because it won't separate into curds and whey (on account of being treated to an ultra-high temperature). Use fresh milk or powdered milk made with a ratio of 1 cup milk powder to 2 cups water.*

Home-brewed Ginger Beer

Makes 20 litres · GF, V

Russians shoot vodka, *Thais* love whisky, *Mexicans* swig tequila, *Swedes* savour aquavit, *Spaniards* sip sherry, *Greeks* go for ouzo, and *Chinese* and *Koreans* sip scotch and cognac. *Sailors* brew it themselves

Brewing our own beer and ginger beer is something we've been doing aboard for 20 years now. It's a cost-effective way of enjoying a sundowner, and we never need to hunt for alcohol at a new port. Ginger beer is our brew of choice because it's completely preservative-free and produces zero waste, so there's no more worrying about how to deal with an excess of empty bottles and cans in places without proper recycling.

There is considerable room to experiment with all kinds of flavours, and you can vary the alcohol content of your ginger beer too. We keep ours at around 3 per cent. In our current sailing grounds, where a kilo of ginger costs $2, we can make approximately 24 bottles of brew for the grand price of about $4. There are lots of different ways to brew all kinds of beer, and we are always adjusting flavours, but this is the recipe that works for us.

How alcoholic is my brew?

To work out the alcoholic content of any brew (the ABV or alcohol by volume), use the hydrometer that (most likely) came with your brew kit. By taking a small sample of your brew and measuring its gravity, you can work out its density and alcohol content. Take a reading on the first day of brewing, before fermentation begins, by filling the hydrometer with a little of your brew (this is your original gravity). Take another reading 6 or 7 days later when fermentation has finished (your final gravity). The difference between the two, multiplied by 131.25, gives you the ABV percentage of your brew.

1kg (2.2lb) fresh (or frozen) ginger

1-1.6kg (2.2-3.5lb) sugar (depending on desired ABV)

2 tsp yeast

24 PET bottles (740ml/25 fl oz)

Flavourings

8 cloves

zest of 4 limes (avoid the pith)

1 cinnamon stick

1 tsp vanilla extract (or 1 bean)

Scrub the ginger well and roughly chop it (and peel it if you have the patience). Use a stick blender to blitz it with a little water into a pulp. Pour the ginger into the largest pot you've got, add sugar and your choice of flavourings, and fill the pot with water, allowing room for the mixture to boil up. Bring to a boil, reduce the heat and simmer for 15 minutes.

Using 1.6kg of sugar should produce a beer with an alcohol content of around 5 per cent (give or take). Reducing the sugar to 1kg brings the buzz down considerably, to just over 3 per cent. Our boat buddies, *@theovenscrew*, add chopped lemongrass, cloves and a cinnamon stick to their beer. There are no hard-and-fast rules about flavour, so add whatever interests you.

Take the pot off the heat and pour it into your sterilised fermenter. Add enough water to reach 20 litres, skim away the ginger skin that floats to the top of the fermenter, and allow it to cool to room temperature before stirring in 2 teaspoons of yeast. Cover and leave the brew for 24 hours, then stir every day for 6 more days. We use 740ml PET bottles and add a heaped teaspoon of sugar to each before filling with beer and capping. Ideally, store the brew for two weeks before drinking.

EXCELSIOR

POTS OF FLAVOUR

When Maya was tiny, preserving anything other than our sanity was utterly laughable, so pickling vegetables was never on my radar. Instead, my in-laws – Val and Richard – plied us with jars of their homemade tomato chutney, and chilli-pickled green tomatoes and eggplants made fresh from their garden.

But our love of sailing really far away (and staying there long after the fresh veggies have all been eaten) brought me back to pickles. Although reluctant, I soon discovered how these little pots of wonder can really rev things up when markets and stores are distant memories. And, even better, cooking from scratch didn't hold me in the galley all day.

The trick to making great pickles and preserves is to get your hands on the ripest, tastiest produce and fresh herbs and spices you can, and cook them up *before* they start to wilt. The world is full of recipes for relishes, sambals, chilli jams and chutneys, but the ones included here are simple, tasty, quick to prepare, and flexible enough to handle whatever fresh things and spices you decide to add to your mix. I use a variety of vinegars, depending on the flavour I'm shooting for, but apple cider vinegar is my go-to.

During the Middle Ages, wealthy Greeks and Romans paid more for cinnamon than its weight in gold. Highly prized peppercorns were used as currency, so that very high rents were called 'peppercorn rents' (kind of like marina rents, but with less sting).

When choosing spices, add those that partner well with your produce, bearing in mind what these potent powerhouses can do for your health too. Cinnamon balances blood sugar levels and combats fatigue, nutmeg helps to relieve joint pain, and pepper aids digestion by increasing the flow of gastric juices. Chillies, mint and cloves all stimulate sluggish appetites.

Store dried spices in your galley's coolest, darkest corner (not on the bench where heat and sunlight can degrade their freshness). Replace them every six months. Although it's preferable to grind whole spices just before using (in a mortar and pestle or a coffee grinder), you can freshen already ground spices and release their aromatic oils by gently toasting them in a dry pan over very low heat.

Sterilising jars

Throughout this chapter you'll be using a lot of jars. To make sure they don't turn into petri dishes, wash jars and lids in hot, soapy water. Submerge them in a pot of boiling water for 10 minutes then invert on a wire rack to air dry. Alternatively, place upright jars and lids, well-spaced, on a baking tray and pop into a preheated oven heated (at 120°C/250°F) for 20 minutes.

Dave's Coconut Sambal

Makes 1 large jar • Prep 10 mins
Cook 15 mins • GF

This is hands-down the best sambal I have ever tasted, but the chilli aroma evacuates the boat when it's frying on the stove. Dave is probably not alone in his 'shake-and-dash' cooking style, so this recipe has a bit of flex when it comes to measuring and balancing the sweet, salty and sour ingredient flavours. You'll need a set of bulletproof lungs to stand over the stove and fry this up without sneezing and coughing and completely losing the plot. The reward for those who tough it out is a big jar of sambal that will transform your fish-and-rice dinners for months.

10 red chillies (whatever heat you can handle)

3-5 garlic cloves

2 tbsp coconut oil

1 large, ripe tomato

glug of apple cider vinegar

splash of fish sauce

1 tsp tamarind pulp (or tamarind paste)

1 tsp sugar

shake of paprika

½ cup salted peanuts

1-2 tbsp freshly grated (or dried) coconut

extra coconut oil

Blitz the chillies, garlic and coconut oil, and gently fry the paste in a pan over low-medium heat. Meanwhile, blitz together the tomato, vinegar, fish sauce, tamarind paste or pulp (remove and discard the seeds from the pulp first), sugar and paprika, and pour into the pan. Continue frying and stirring to simmer off the excess moisture.

Blitz together the salted peanuts and coconut and stir into the pan. Mix well and take the pan off the heat. Stir through some extra coconut oil to get the consistency you like, and spoon into 1 or 2 sterilised glass jars and refrigerate for up to a month. This recipe freezes well.

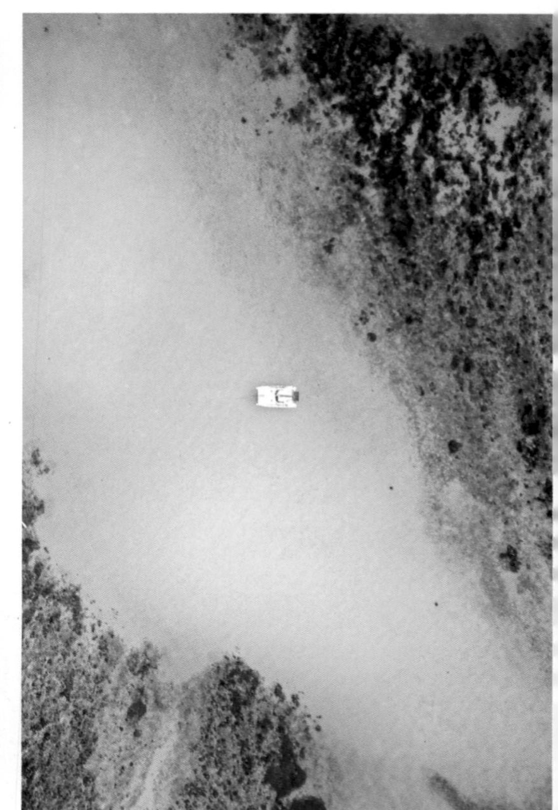

10-minute Mango Chutney

Makes 2 cups · Cook 10 mins · GF, V, QC

There's an anchorage in West Papua we call 'Mango Madness' for the uninhabited shoreline of wild mango trees that hang out over the sea. Come Christmas time, when the mangoes ripen and fall, they litter the banks and the shallows in their hundreds, waiting to be gathered by the bucket load. Far too stringy for fruit salad, they are best frozen for mango smoothies and Nice Cream (page 226) or simmered into a batch of this quick-cook chutney.

⅔ cup (165ml) apple cider vinegar

1 small onion, finely diced

1 garlic clove, finely chopped

1 tsp cumin seeds

1 tsp mustard seeds

½ tsp chilli flakes

½ tsp salt

4 ripe mangoes, peeled and diced (about 600g)

⅓ cup (60g) loose packed brown sugar

Place the vinegar, onion, garlic, spices and salt in a large saucepan and boil rapidly until the liquid has reduced by half. Add the mango and simmer. When it begins to soften, add the brown sugar and stir occasionally, cooking for five minutes more Take it off the heat, pour it into sterilised jars and refrigerate.

Serve it with fried halloumi, fish or Cauliflower & Cheddar Fritters (page 145).

Chilli Peach Jam

Makes 2 cups · Prep 10 mins · Cook 1 hr · GF, V, OP

This is one of the first recipes I ever designed, and I still make it to this day (albeit with less sugar and salt than I used to). I've made it with all kinds of fleshy fruit over the years, depending on what's in season: papaya, nectarines, peaches, mango, strawberries, and sometimes with a little passionfruit too. This recipe has considerable wriggle room, so use the fruits you like best in any combination. If adding acidic fruits, such as pineapple, reduce the amount of vinegar slightly and increase the sweetness a little to taste. I eat this with fried halloumi, on vegetarian patties and smeared on just-baked bread topped with pickled eggplant.

5 cups diced peaches

1 cup chopped strawberries

¼ cup fresh lime juice

2 garlic cloves, finely chopped

1-2 fresh red chillies, finely chopped

1 tbsp tamari (or soy sauce)

¼ cup firmly packed brown sugar

100ml (3.5fl oz) apple cider or white wine vinegar

½ tsp salt

Peel and dice the peaches and strawberries (or any other sweet fleshy fruits) and place them in a saucepan. Add the lime juice, garlic, chopped chillies, tamari (or soy sauce), brown sugar, vinegar and salt. Cover and bring it to the boil, then reduce the heat and simmer uncovered for one hour or until the jam has thickened. Sterilise two jam jars, pour in the jam, seal, and leave to cool before refrigerating. Serve with a batch of Dave's Save-the-day Silverbeet Pastries (page 147).

Pear & Rhubarb Relish

Makes 3 cups • Prep 15 mins • Cook 15 mins • GF, V

This surprising relish stars on any cheese platter but is equally at home in a dessert bowl, teamed with mascarpone cream, thick Greek yoghurt, or ice cream.

4 firm pears, peeled, cored and chopped

2 tbsp caster (superfine) sugar

1 tbsp water

4 sticks of rhubarb, cut into 1cm/0.5in peices (about 4 cups)

½ cup sultanas (sultana raisins)

1 tbsp balsamic vinegar

1 tsp finely grated ginger

Combine pears, sugar and water in a pot over medium heat, cover and cook for 7 minutes, stirring occasionally. When tender, add the rhubarb, sultanas, balsamic vinegar and ginger. Cover, increase the heat and bring to the boil. Cook uncovered until the rhubarb is soft and the liquid is almost absorbed (about 7-8 minutes). Pour into sterilised jars, seal with lids and leave to cool before refrigerating.

Lemon & Lime Curd

Makes 3 jars • Prep 5 mins • Cook 15 mins • GF

6 large lemons and/or limes

1 cup butter

2 cups caster (superfine) sugar

6 free-range eggs plus 6 egg yolks

Finely zest the lemons and limes (either fruit works, as does a combination of both), then juice them. Combine the butter and sugar in a large saucepan over low heat. Stir until the butter melts and the sugar dissolves. Whisk the eggs and yolks together, then whisk into the butter mixture. Add the juice and zest and stir over low-to-medium heat until the mixture thickens slightly (it should stick to the back of a spoon and will thicken more when cooled).

***Tip**: Keep the unused egg whites for Lemon Curd Cocktails* *(page 192)*.

Harissa

Makes about 1 cup • Prep 10 mins • GF, V

- 2 tbsp crushed dried red chillies
- 2 tbsp hot water
- 2 tbsp extra virgin olive oil
- 2 cloves garlic, chopped
- 3 tsp ground coriander
- 1 tsp ground cumin
- 1 spring onion, finely chopped
- ½ bunch of fresh mint leaves
- a handful of flat-leaf parsley
- 1 tbsp lemon juice
- sea salt

Soak the dried chillies in hot water for a minute until soft, combine with all remaining ingredients and season with a generous grind of salt. Use a stick blender or food processor to create a smooth paste. Store harrisa in a sterilised glass jar in the fridge, and brush sparingly on skewers of fish, prawns or tofu before barbecuing, grilling or pan-frying over moderate heat for five to six minutes.

Marinated Feta

Fills 1 large jar • Prep 10 mins • GF

Barely a Greek meal is served without some of this salty sheep's milk cheese. Marinading it stretches its shelf-life and injects its intense flavour with serious wow factor. Crumble it over pizza, stir it through pasta with lemon zest, basil and olive oil, or use it to transform any ordinary salad into something special.

- 350g (12oz) feta
- 2 fresh red chillies
- 1 tsp cracked black pepper
- 2 tsp dried oregano
- 4 garlic cloves, roughly chopped
- 4 fresh rosemary sprigs
- 1 cup extra virgin olive oil

Dice the feta and cut the chillies into thin strips, removing and discarding the seeds. Sterilise and dry a large jar, then add the pepper and dried oregano. Add the feta, chillies, chopped garlic cloves and rosemary sprigs, and pour in enough extra virgin olive oil to cover it all. Marinaded feta is flavoursome after 48 hours and lasts for up to 2 months in the fridge.

Pickled Beetroot

Makes 2 cups • Prep 10 mins • Cook 30 mins • GF, V

It takes a seasoned cruiser to gather just the right amount of supplies to see them through any long stint at sea. Not too much, not too little, because while you don't want to weigh down your boat, you certainly don't want to run out of coffee and toilet paper on the high seas. I have a reputation for stockpiling ridiculous amounts of fresh produce on board. And for spending long days in the galley afterwards, chopping and roasting, pickling and marinading, and working hard to preserve my fresh things for the long weeks ahead. I do this because we invariably spend far longer than expected hanging off some lonely shore, diving and dinghy exploring, working and learning, fixing and fussing over the boat, and swiftly gnawing our way through my hauls of fruits and veggies. This is one of my favourite preserves that's quick to cook and has an extraordinarily long shelf life. Eat it on burgers, team it with sharp cheddar cheese, or tuck it into fish tacos.

4-5 raw beetroot, peeled and grated (about 3 packed cups)

1 large, firm pear, grated

½ onion, finely chopped

½ tsp cumin seeds

⅔ cup red wine vinegar

⅓ cup caster (superfine) sugar

salt and pepper

Place the grated beetroot, pear, onion, cumin seeds and vinegar in a large saucepan over medium-high heat. Cover and bring to the boil. Reduce the heat to low and simmer, stirring occasionally, for 10 minutes or until the beetroot has softened.

Stir in the sugar until dissolved, bring to a simmer and cook uncovered, stirring occasionally for 15 minutes or until it's reduced and thickened. Season with salt and pepper. Scoop into sterilised jars, seal tightly and set aside to cool before refrigerating. You can eat it straight away, although deeper flavours develop after a couple of weeks. Unopened, pickled beetroot will last up to 6 months in the fridge. Once opened, it's best consumed within 1 month.

Tropical Almond Pesto

Makes about 1 cup • Prep 10 mins • GF

The quantity of oil used here makes a nice paste for spreading on baked baguettes or as a coating for fish or prawns. For a really smooth pasta sauce, add a little extra olive oil. Pesto is at its best as soon as it is made. To store, transfer to a clean jar, drizzle with enough olive oil to cover the pesto, and refrigerate for up to a week, or store it in the freezer.

2 cups (125g) herbs like basil, coriander (cilantro) and a little parsley

2 garlic cloves

½ cup tropical (or regular) almonds

1 tbsp sunflower seeds (optional)

½ cup (60g) freshly grated parmesan or pecorino

½ cup extra virgin olive oil*

pinch of sea salt

** Add zing and maximise mineral absorption by swapping 1 tbsp of olive oil for 1 tbsp of freshly squeezed lemon juice.*

Wash and shake dry the herbs, then set them aside. In a small pan, gently toast the almonds for about one to two minutes, then add the sunflower seeds and toss the pan occasionally, so they don't burn. Cook for one minute more or until just golden. Use a mortar and pestle, a stick blender or a food processor to pound or blend the herbs, garlic, almonds, sunflower seeds, cheese and a good pinch of sea salt. Slowly add the olive oil until the pesto thickens.

Coriander Pesto

Fills 1 small jar • Prep 5 mins • GF, V

1 bunch fresh coriander (cilantro)

½ fresh red chilli

1 garlic clove

1 small red onion

2 tbsp almonds, chopped

2 tbsp lime juice

1 tbsp extra virgin olive oil

pinch of salt

Combine all ingredients and blitz until smooth. If you've got the time and a mortar and pestle on board, pounding this pesto gives it a lovely, chunky texture. Serve it with fish, spread it on pizza bases, or stir through pasta for easy, instant meals. If you're making it for later, spoon into a glass jar, cover with olive oil and freeze it, or keep it refrigerated for up to a week.

Zesty Dill Mayo

Makes 1/2 cup • Prep 5-10 mins • GF

1 free-range egg

½ cup extra virgin olive oil

1 tbsp seeded mustard

½ lemon, zested and juiced

salt and pepper

1 tbsp chopped fresh dill

Use a stick blender to beat the egg, oil, mustard and lemon juice and zest together for 1 minute, slowly lifting the blender through the mixture as you go. Season to taste with salt and pepper, then stir in the chopped dill.

If you'd rather do it by hand, whisk the egg, mustard, lemon juice and zest, then slowly add the oil, a little at a time, until the mixture becomes thick and creamy. Season to taste with salt and pepper, then stir in the chopped dill.

Kalamata Tapenade

Makes 1/2 cup • Prep 5 mins - GF, V

¾ cup pitted Kalamata olives

3 tsp balsamic vinegar

1 tbsp extra virgin olive oil

1 garlic clove, chopped

black pepper

Use a stick blender to process the olives, vinegar, olive oil and garlic to a smooth paste. Season well with cracked black pepper. Keep in a jar in the fridge and serve spread on bread toasts.

Chilli & Ginger Sauce

Makes 1/2 cup • Prep 10 mins - GF, V

125g (4.5oz) fresh red chillies

2 tbsp grated fresh ginger

1 tsp sesame oil

2 tbsp rice wine vinegar

1 tsp salt

Wash and trim the chillies and remove (and discard) the seeds. Peel and grate the ginger, then blend all ingredients until smooth. Keep refrigerated and serve with Baked Prawn & Noodle Rolls (see page 96) or Steamed Nepali Momos (see page 184).

Sweet Treats & Sea Snacks

THE THING ABOUT SUGAR

When Sarah Wilson (of 'I Quit Sugar' fame) made a bad guy out of sugar, sweet-loving foodies were divided in the same way that humans have always reacted to the sudden revelation that we might be doing it all wrong. Some got swiftly on board, embracing stevia and rice malt syrup, while others found this new, uncomfortable truth a bitter pill to swallow.

Regardless of where your tastes lie on the sweetness spectrum, we can all agree that there's a massive industry around feeding us sweet stuff. And the endless mud-slinging between those for and against sugar doesn't help us clear the fog. As a health-conscious foodie, I want my recipes to be as nutritious as they are delicious, but I'm certainly not averse to enjoying a slice of the good life. As sailors, we know better than anyone that life is all about keeping your balance.

I'm not going to try to pull you onto any bandwagon, but if you already steer clear of sugar or are interested in shifting along that sweetness spectrum in search of more healthful substitutes, I hope this will be helpful. If you prefer to bake with regular sugar (at least until you taste my delicious Avocado Chocolate Mousse, page 224), rest assured that there's something delicious here for you too. I use all kinds of sweeteners in this section and explain how to swap them to suit what you have at hand.

The Fuss About Fructose

All natural sources of sweetness – cane sugar, honey, agave and rice malt syrup – are made up of a range of sugars such as glucose, fructose, sucrose, maltose and more, which are all digested (or metabolised) differently in the body. Glucose (which features heavily in rice malt syrup) can be metabolised by all cells in the body. But fructose makes a beeline for your liver, where it is processed in one big, tremendous hit. For that reason, it's linked to metabolic syndrome, high blood pressure and insulin resistance. But fructose does its worst when it enters your bloodstream, reacting with protein molecules (amino acids) and altering their structure to form AGEs (advanced glycation end-products). Stick with me; this is where it all starts to make sense.

If antioxidants don't step in to tackle repairs (thank-you blueberries), or if an excess of fructose swamps the body, AGEs gradually accumulate and lead to cell damage and disease. Other factors also create AGEs – smoking, a lack of exercise, even living long enough – but high fructose consumption remains a big factor. Cane sugar and corn syrup are 50 per cent fructose, which is why they get singled out as the bad guys (although agave is another high roller), but also because they're both cheap and excessively appear in processed foods.

Foods rich in fructose are also highly addictive, because fructose raises levels of the hormone ghrelin, which keeps you feeling hungry so that you keep eating more. High-level consumption has been linked to everything from Alzheimer's to infertility, and significantly for sailors, accelerated aging and susceptibility to sun damage. Add higher risks of developing diabetes, heart disease, blood sugar imbalances and tooth decay, and you begin to get the distinct impression that sugar ain't, perhaps, the best thing on the shelf.

Now fruit naturally contains fructose, so put down that apple! (said no mother, ever). Fruit is excellent stuff, providing you with lots of other nutritious goodies that make bodies sing. So, before we dive down that rabbit hole, let's agree that there's a big difference between fruit and donuts and get to the good stuff.

Top Swaps

Of all the natural sugar alternatives on the market, only two – rice malt syrup and stevia - are actually fructose-free. My recipes use a liberal amount of rice malt syrup (also known as rice syrup or brown rice syrup) because it's such an easy swap for sugar in any recipe I want to try. For every cup of sugar required, you can substitute between one and one and a quarter cups of rice malt syrup and reduce the amount of other liquid in the recipe by a quarter of a cup. There are lots of seemingly *healthy* sweeteners on the market, so here's what I choose to use.

Rice Malt Syrup: Derived from fermented organic brown rice and made up of complex carbohydrates, maltose (which the body easily metabolises) and a little glucose, rice malt syrup has a honey-like consistency but is a little less sweet.

Stevia: Derived from a liquorice-tasting South American herb, stevia is more than 200 times sweeter than sugar, so you don't need to use much. It's calorie-free and invokes a very mild effect on blood sugar levels, making it a good choice for people with diabetes.

So-So Sugar Swaps

Honey: In ancient times, a beer made from fermented honey, served at Babylonian weddings, lent its name to the 28-day moon cycle that marked the post-marriage period, the *honeymoon*. This liquid gold has been prized as a source of concentrated sweetness ever since. It's been offered to the gods and used as a currency, but as natural as it is, it still contains around 40 per cent fructose.

In its defence, honey (especially dark varieties) supplies flavonoids and phenolic acids that act as antioxidants in the body, chasing down cancer-causing free radicals. Honey also contributes small amounts of vitamin C, riboflavin, thiamine, niacin, iron and manganese.

Maple Syrup: Packed with flavour but containing around 60 per cent sucrose (of which half is fructose), maple syrup regains some ground by offering your body good levels of vitamins and minerals: zinc and manganese, plus calcium, potassium, iron and thiamine. Using honey or maple syrup in place of sugar is an easy swap: for every cup of sugar called for, replace with two-thirds of a cup of either honey or maple syrup, and reduce the amount of liquid in the recipe by a quarter of a cup.

No-Go Sugar Swaps

Coconut and Palm Sugars: Despite my love of all things coconut, the sugar contained in this 'tree of life' serves up around 40 per cent fructose, making it a less-than-perfect choice. Palm sugar, often called for in Southeast Asian recipes, has a similar makeup. Swap both out rice malt syrup instead.

Agave: With up to 90 per cent fructose, this product of the Mexican agave cactus is best left on the shelf.

The 'I've Sailed Too Long' Swap

If you sail long and far enough away, cupboards eventually empty of all those wholesome, healthy staples we rely on back home. Pretty soon, you find yourself standing in a market where sugar is the only sweet option on the shelf. But because all kinds of celebratory cakes simply must be baked for birthdays, equator crossings and farewell potluck dinners, regular old sugar may be the sweetener of choice. Use it whenever you need to (#noguilt).

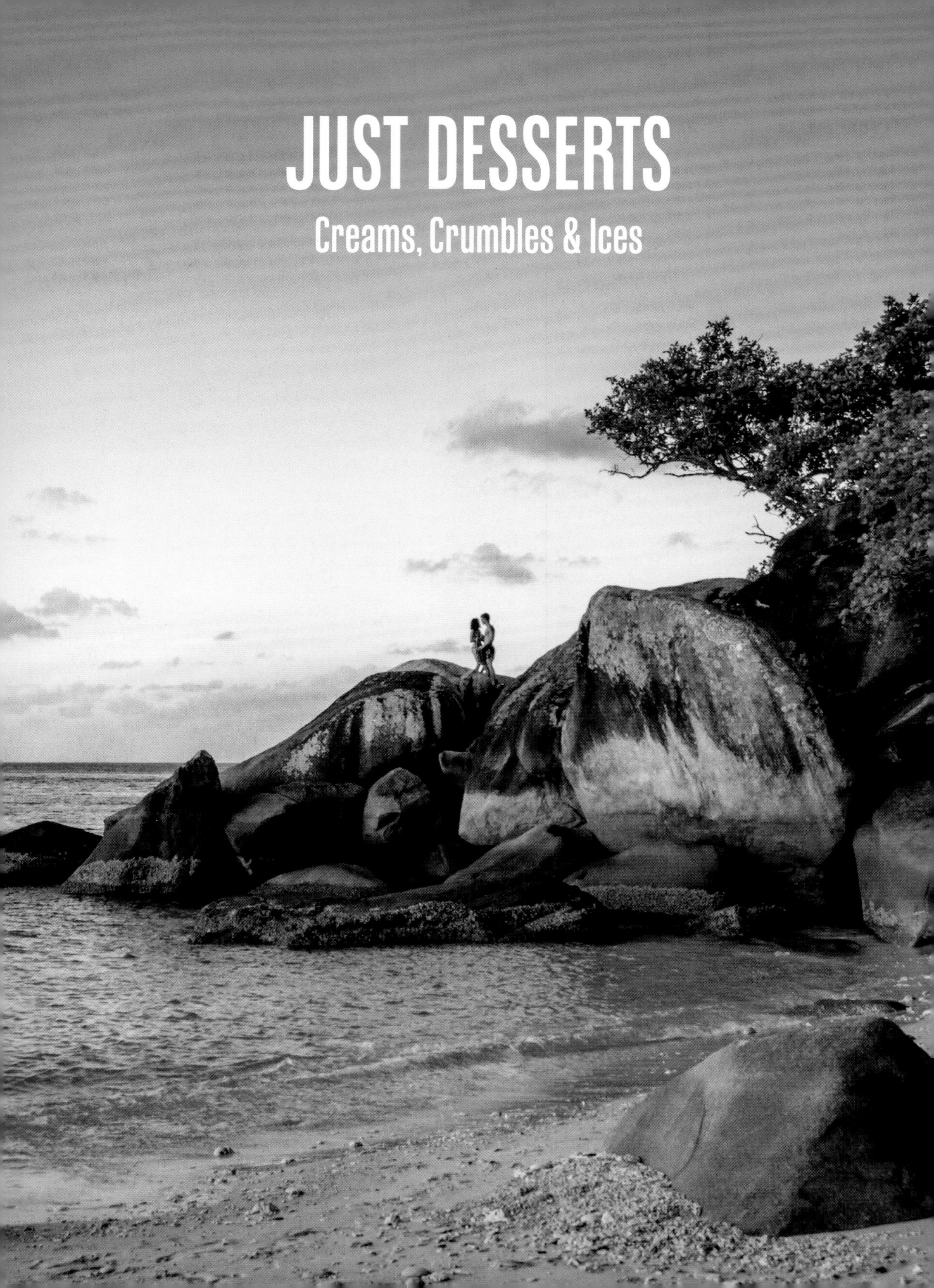

JUST DESSERTS

Creams, Crumbles & Ices

Berry Smash

Feeds 4 · Prep 20 mins · Cook 5 mins · QC

2 cups ripe fruit (berries, sliced peaches and plums)

⅓ cup rice malt syrup

1 cup moscato (I like sparkling best)

200ml (7fl oz) thickened cream

⅔ cup (150g) natural yoghurt

2 cups (200g) crumbled shortbread biscuits

Combine the fruit, rice malt syrup and moscato in a saucepan over medium heat. Bring it to a boil, keep it there for 1 minute, and then take the pot off the heat. Scoop out the fruit with a slotted spoon and set it aside.

Return the pot to the stove, reduce the heat, and simmer the sauce for 15 minutes or until it thickens to a syrup. Pour the syrup back over the fruit and set it aside to cool. When ready to eat, mix the cream and yoghurt together, and add layers to tall glasses between spoonfuls of cooled fruit and crumbled shortbread.

Chilli Lime Ice Cream

Feeds 4-6 · Prep 10 mins + Freezing time · GF, V, OP

1 ⅔ cups water

1 ⅓ cups caster (superfine) sugar

400ml (13.5oz) coconut cream

1 fresh red chilli, finely chopped

3 tsp lime zest

Combine the water and sugar in a saucepan and bring it to a boil. Take it off the heat and set it aside. When cool, blend the sugar syrup and coconut cream together (with a hand blender or whisk), and stir through the chilli and lime zest. The coconut cream and lime zest dramatically temper the red chilli, pulling it back from a hit to a hint.

Pour it into a non-reactive metal bowl or tray and freeze until the mixture is almost set. Break up the mixture and blend it again, then refreeze, preferably overnight. Serve in tiny bowls, or use a small spoon to fill ceramic Asian soup spoons. Place them on a tray and freeze them until you are ready to serve.

Salted Caramel Trifle

Feeds 4 • Prep 10 mins • Cook 10 mins

My birthday falls on Christmas Day, which I love for three excellent reasons: firstly, I get spoilt rotten; secondly, I get double the gifts; and thirdly, Dave handles the cooking. That might sound strange coming from someone who's just written a cookbook, but honestly, my Christmas birthday is for sitting back with a glass of bubbles, chatting with mates and playing with Maya's new toys. It's not for baking a pudding in an overheated galley. This is one of my favourite birthday desserts. It's not fussy, fruity or healthy (so you know it came from Dave). Serve it anytime, with sparklers on top.

½ cup caster (superfine) sugar

3 tbsp (40g) unsalted butter, cubed

¾ tsp sea salt

1 ¾ cups (425ml) double cream

⅔ cup mascarpone

250g (0.5lb) ginger cake
(or 5-minute Lemon Cake, page 239)

Serve with shaved dark chocolate.

Heat a non-stick frypan over medium heat and add the sugar. Cook, stirring with a wooden spoon, for 3 minutes or until the sugar melts and turns golden. Add the cubed butter, sea salt and 1/2 cup of the double cream. Reduce the heat to low and cook, stirring for 6 minutes or until smooth. Set aside to cool.

Combine the remaining cream and mascarpone in a bowl. Cut the cake into chunks and divide half of it between four big, tall glasses or jars. On top of the cake, share out half of the cream mixture and half the caramel sauce. Add another layer of cake, cream and sauce, and serve topped with lots of shaved dark chocolate.

Avocado Chocolate Mousse

Feeds 4 • Prep 5 mins + Chilling time • GF, V, NC

I took this to the 17th birthday dinner for the much-loved Ali off *@sv_nalukai* and served it to a bunch of famously healthy cruisers and excellent boat cooks. Nervous much? You bet, because making a dessert taste decadent while staying wholesome and healthy is a tough gig. This mousse tastes far too good to be this good for you, and it is my favourite by far. Serve it to sweet tooths and wait for the compliments.

1 large ripe avocado

4 tbsp cacao or cocoa powder

3 tbsp rice malt syrup, or maple syrup, or honey

½ cup coconut cream

1 tsp vanilla extract

pinch of salt

Scoop out the avocado flesh and use a stick blender or mini food processor to blend it smooth. Add the cacao (or cocoa), rice malt syrup (or substitute), coconut cream, vanilla an a pinch of salt and blend well. Refrigerate for 2 hours and serve on its own or topped with raspberries, a dollop of cream and some toasted coconut.

***Tip:** Use rice malt syrup to keep this dish fructose-free.*

Raspberry Nice Cream

Feeds 2-3 • Prep 5 min • GF, V, NC

I rarely keep ice cream on board. Partly because it hogs so much freezer space, but mainly because this is so easy to make and infinitely better for you. I started making this when Maya was tiny, and still whip it when we need a sweet fix. It's so nutritious you could eat it for breakfast, and it works with any frozen fruit you like (try bananas, papaya and peaches). When the weather is hot and humid, I freeze small portions of yoghurt and coconut milk to add to the fruit, which helps it stay frozen in our bowls for longer.

1 cup frozen raspberries

3 frozen bananas

¼ cup coconut milk or coconut yoghurt

Use a stick blender to blend everything together and serve immediately.

Grilled Pistachio Plums

Feeds 4 • Prep 5 mins • Cook 5 mins • GF, V QC

Known in China as 'happy nuts' because their half-open shell resembles a smile, pistachios are one of the three most nutritious nuts. Eat them for their powerful phytonutrients, which reduce cholesterol and protect against many cancers.

4 ripe plums

1 tbsp honey

2 tbsp crushed pistachio nuts

Serve with thick coconut yoghurt, chilled coconut cream or Raspberry Nice Cream.

Halve the plums and remove the stones. Place them on a baking tray lined with baking paper and drizzle with honey. Grill for about 5 minutes or until tender. Serve topped with crushed pistachio nuts and a dollop of yoghurt, cream or nice-cream.

Gluten-free Berry Crumble

Feeds 4 • Prep 10 mins • Cook 40 min

Have you got 10 minutes to whip up the kind of baked dessert that makes people adore you? That is literally how long it takes to get this one into the oven. It's so easy you could do it on passage.

2 cups mixed berries (fresh or frozen)

1 apple, peeled, cored and chopped small

2 tbsp rice malt syrup

1 tbsp cornflour (cornstarch)

dash of vanilla extract

Crumble

½ cup rolled oats

½ cup finely chopped almonds

2 tbsp rice malt syrup

pinch of salt

2 tbsp unsalted butter, melted

1½ tbsp plain yogurt

Preheat the oven to 180°C (350°F). Rinse and drain the fresh berries (or defrost if using frozen ones). Pour them into a baking dish and combine with the chopped apple, rice malt syrup, cornflour and vanilla.

For the crumble, combine the oats, chopped almonds, rice malt syrup and a pinch of salt in a mixing bowl. Stir in the melted butter and yoghurt, mix well and dollop on top of the berries. Bake for about 40 minutes or until bubbling and golden. Rest the dish for 5 minutes, then devour it with Greek yoghurt, cream or Nice Cream (page 226).

Coconut Mango Puddings

Feeds 4 • Prep 10 mins + Setting time • GF

Humans and mango trees have something in common. It's not that we both love the tropics, but that we share the same life expectancy. Juicy mangoes are, by far, my favourite fruit, and they work so well in this delicious tropical pudding that's dairy-free too.

2 large ripe mangoes (1.5 cups puree)

3 gelatin leaves (or 2 tsp gelatin powder)

⅓ cup cold water

⅓ cup rice malt syrup

1 cup premium coconut milk

Serve with extra chopped mango.

Peel the mangoes, slice off the flesh and use a stick blender (or food processor) to blitz it until smooth. If using gelatin leaves, soak them in cold water for about 5 minutes, then squeeze the water out of the leaves and place them in a small pot with 1/3 cup of cold water. If using powdered gelatin, sprinkle it over 1/3 cup of cold water in a small pot.

Very gently warm the pot over low heat, whisking until the gelatin has dissolved (you can also do this in a bowl over a pan of hot water). Take off the heat and whisk in the rice malt syrup until dissolved. Blend with the mango and coconut milk until smooth, pour into individual glasses (or one fridge-friendly dish) and refrigerate the pudding for 3 hours (or overnight). Serve with extra chopped mango.

Using agar: seaweed-based agar (or agar-agar) is a vegetarian setting agent derived from red algae. To use it in this dish, sprinkle 2 teaspoons of powdered agar over 1/3 cup of water, leave for 5 minutes, then gently bring the water to the boil and simmer for 2 minutes. Take off the heat, stir through the rice malt syrup and continue with the recipe.

Stovetop Caramelised Peach Crumble

Feeds 4 · Prep 10 mins · Cook 20 mins

Here's one for sailors who keep things simple and whose galleys are compact, stovetop affairs. I sailed for decades on four different oven-free homes, so I know how nice it is to discover recipes you can make entirely on a stovetop. This is the crumble that Dave likes the most, and you can make it with all kinds of different fruits; try plums, nectarines, apples or firm pears.

2 tbsp (30g) butter

5-6 ripe freestone peaches, sliced into crescents

¼ cup brown sugar (or ⅓ cup rice malt syrup)

1 tsp mixed spice

2-3 tbsp water

Almond Crumble

⅓ cup self-raising flour

⅓ cup brown sugar

½ cup roughly chopped almonds and walnuts

½ cup quick-cook oats

3 ½ tbsp (50g) butter

Serve with honey ricotta or yoghurt.

For the almond crumble use your hands to mix all the ingredients well in a large bowl. Transfer to a heavy-based pan over low-medium heat, and stir the mixture occasionally until golden. Alternatively, spread the crumble onto a baking tray and place it under a grill (low-medium heat for 10 minutes or until golden).

Melt 30g of butter in a large frypan over medium heat. Add the sliced peaches and cook, turning occasionally, for 2-3 minutes until tender. Add the brown sugar or rice malt syrup and mixed spice, pour in the water and turn the peaches to coat. Simmer for 5 minutes or until nicely caramelised. Divide the peaches between 4 bowls or glasses, and serve topped with a generous heap of almond crumble and a dollop of double cream or yoghurt.

To make honey ricotta, gently swirl 1 tablespoon of honey and 1 teaspoon of vanilla extract through 250g (1 cup) of ricotta.

ONE-HANDED HELM SNACKS

Blissful Balls

Makes about 30
Prep 20 mins - GF, V, NC

1 cup dried pitted dates (or a mix of dates and sultanas)

1 cup raw walnuts or almonds

1 cup shredded coconut (fresh or dried)

2 tbsp raw cacao (or cocoa powder)

1 tbsp organic coconut oil

1 tsp vanilla extract

extra shredded coconut for rolling

Of all the ways you can make these tasty chocolate balls, this is the way I like best. Made using antioxidant-rich walnuts (which also supply omega-3 fatty acids and the amino acid arginine), they keep for ages in the fridge, ready for sailing days, helm snacks, shore hikes, and dinghy adventures. If you've got kids on board, rope them in to roll the balls in shredded or desiccated coconut, some crushed peanuts or sprinkles.

Soak the dates for 10 minutes in hot water, then drain them. Combine them with the nuts, coconut, cacao (or cocoa) powder, coconut oil and vanilla, and blitz together well using a stick blender or food processor. Roll into small balls (about 2 teaspoons worth) and coat with coconut. Store in the fridge.

Vegan Chocolate Cupcakes

Makes 12 · Prep 10 mins · Cook 20 mins · V

Wickedly rich and chocolatey, this recipe doesn't steal from your precious stash of actual chocolate, and comes to the rescue in sailing grounds where dairy products are absent or expensive. It uses coconut oil instead of butter and lemon juice in the place of milk. It tastes so good no one will ever believe it's dairy-free.

3 cups self-raising flour

⅔ cup cocoa powder (or cacao)

2 tsp bicarbonate of soda (baking soda)

½ tsp salt

1 cup sugar

2 cups water

½ cup coconut oil

2 tbsp lemon juice

1 tbsp vanilla extract

Preheat the oven to 180°C (350°F) and grease a 12-hole muffin tray. Sift the flour, cocoa or cacao, bicarbonate of soda and salt into a large mixing bowl. Add the sugar and stir. In a jug, combine the water, oil, lemon juice and vanilla extract, and stir well. Pour over the dry ingredients and whisk the mixture for 2 minutes until smooth.

Spoon the batter into the muffin tray and thump the tray on the bench to bring any air bubbles to the surface. Bake for 20 minutes. Set aside for 5 minutes, remove from the tray, and cool the cakes on a wire rack. Serve topped with soft icing or a dusting of icing (powdered) sugar.

No-bake Fruit & Nut Bars

Makes 1 tray · Prep 20 mins · NC

I've been (not) baking variations of this slice for years, and it always just works. As long as I stick to the formula, 1 cup each of nuts (and seeds), coconut and dried fruit, plus 3 cups of cereal, the nut butter just holds it all together. Use gluten-free cereals or a dairy-free butter substitute if you like, and swap rice malt syrup for honey if that's what on your shelf.

½ cup raw nuts (almonds, walnuts, cashews)

¼ cup sunflower seeds

¼ cup sesame seeds

3 cups cereal (gluten-free muesli or oats, or puffed rice if required)

1 cup toasted, shredded coconut

1 cup dried fruit (chopped apricots, dates, cranberries, sultanas)

½ cup rice malt syrup

½ cup peanut (or other nut) butter

½ cup (125g) butter (or dairy-free substitute)

Toast the nuts and seeds over gentle heat until golden, adding the big nuts first and toasting the sesame seeds only briefly. Transfer to a large mixing bowl and add your choice of cereals, plus coconut and chopped dried fruit.

Combine the rice malt syrup, nut butter and butter in a saucepan and stir over low heat until melted. Bring the mixture to the boil, then reduce the heat and simmer, uncovered and without stirring, for 4-5 minutes. Pour this over the dry ingredients, mix thoroughly and press into a paper-lined baking tray (roughly 22cm/9in square). Drizzle with melted dark chocolate (if you like); otherwise, refrigerate until set, then cut into squares or bars.

Mexican Hot Chocolate

Satisfies 4 • Prep 10 mins • GF, QC

6 cups milk

180g (6.5oz) dark chocolate

⅓ cup sugar

1 tsp ground cinnamon

½ tsp vanilla extract

Place all ingredients in a saucepan and bring to the boil, stirring continuously. Beat well with a whisk until the mixture stops boiling. Return to the boil and beat again. Bring to the boil a third time and beat over the heat to froth up the milk. Pour into mugs or fill a thermos to get you through the night.

Kei Island Coconut Chips

Fills a bowl • Prep 1 hr + Drying time • Cook 5 mins • GF, V

1 mature coconut

pinch of salt or powdered vegetable stock

Choose a slightly yellowing coconut and remove the husk. Crack the nut into pieces and carefully use a paring knife to pry the coconut flesh from the hard shell. Use a vegetable peeler (and fill a lazy hour under sail) to shave strips of coconut onto a metal tray. Place the coconut in the sun to dry, then toast briefly in a pan over gentle heat, tossing occasionall with a wooden spatula. Eat plain or seasoned with a generous pinch of sea salt or powdered vegetable stock. Serve with drinks.

Nut Fix

Makes 3 cups · Cook 10 mins · V, QC

1 cup mixed nuts (walnuts, cashews, almonds)

1 cup cereal

½ cup sunflower seeds and pepitas or both

¼ cup sesame seeds

½ cup sultanas

1-2 tbsp kecap manis

Gently toast the nuts, cereal, seeds and sultanas in a frypan over low heat, adding the sesame seeds 2 minutes into cooking time and stirring until lightly coloured. Take them off the heat and stir through the kecap manis, pour onto a tray and set aside to cool. Keep a jar handy by the helm.

Chilli Mint Pineapple

Feeds 4 · Prep 10 mins · GF, V, NC

1 ripe pineapple

⅓ cup caster (superfine) sugar

handful of fresh mint

pinch of ground dried chilli

pinch of salt

Serve with ½ cup coconut yoghurt or crème fraiche (optional).

Peel and quarter the pineapple, discard the core and slice thinly into long ribbons. Pound together the caster sugar, mint, ground chilli and salt. Assemble the pineapple on a plate and sprinkle over the spiced sugar. Serve on its own or with a dipping pot of coconut yoghurt (or crème fraiche)

BAKES & CAKES

If you sail long and far enough away, cupboards eventually empty of all those wholesome, healthy staples we rely on back home. Pretty soon, you're standing in a market where sugar is the only sweet option around. But because birthday cakes simply must be baked, these bakes and cakes keep celebrations on track. Bake them for birthdays, equator crossings and potluck dinners, for long hikes, and for midnight snacking when you're flying solo on the helm.

5-minute Lemon Cake

Feeds 12 • Prep 5 mins • Cook 30-35 mins

We were a long sail north of Cairns and desperate for cake. A beach party was brewing at our secluded Cape Flattery anchorage: the firewood was piled up, fishing rods were in the water, and the beer was chilling, but our 40th birthday girl Nikki needed something for all those candles. With no oven on board it was time to get Mum's best-ever lemon cake recipe into the camp oven. Using the last of our fresh eggs and lemons, I put my bush cooking skills to the test, turning flour, oil, sugar and milk powder into a lusciously zesty cake batter poured into a well-greased camp oven.

After burying it in just the right amount of coals, I hovered around the fire until that telltale, just-baked aroma wafted along the beach. That night, after devouring fresh mackerel curry mopped up with chunks of camembert-stuffed damper, Nikki blew out the candles on one of the lightest, fluffiest lemon cakes ever baked on a beach, served with a dusting of icing sugar and a dollop of long-life cream.

1 ½ cups self-raising flour

1 cup sugar

½ cup (125g) softened butter

2 free-range eggs

pinch of salt

grated rind of 1 lemon

½ cup milk (any kind)

Yoghurt And Cream Cheese Frosting

⅔ cup of cream cheese

1 tbsp vanilla yoghurt

½ cup icing sugar

Serve topped with shredded coconut and lemon zest.

Preheat the oven to 180°C (350°F). Combine all the cake ingredients in a mixing bowl and beat for 5 minutes. Pour into a greased cake tin (about 25cm/10in diameter) and bake for 30-35 minutes. Cool on a wire rack, then add a dusting of icing sugar or spread with frosting.

For the yoghurt and cream cheese frosting allow the cream cheese to soften, then beat with the yoghurt and sifted icing sugar until smooth. Spread over your cooled cake and sprinkle with shredded coconut and lemon zest.

Gluten-free Brownies

Makes 15-18 • Prep 20 mins • Cook 40 mins • GF

The world's very first chocoholics were the Mexican Aztecs, who used the beans of the cacao tree to make a wonderfully rich hot drink. After the Spanish Invasion, the explorer Cortez introduced cacao beans to Europe, and all the world's chocoholics lived happily ever after.

150g (1.5 sticks) unsalted butter

150g (5.5oz) dark chocolate, roughly chopped

⅓ cup cocoa powder

⅓ cup hot water

1 ⅓ cups firmly packed brown sugar

¾ cup roughly chopped pecans, toasted

⅓ cup almond meal

⅓ cup rice flour

⅓ cup gluten-free plain (all-purpose) flour

150g (5.5oz) small white chocolate buds

4 free-range eggs, lightly beaten

extra 50g (1.5oz) dark chocolate

extra 1 tsp butter

Candied Pecans

1 cup pecan halves

2 tbsp sugar

Preheat the oven to 180°C (350°F). Lightly grease a baking tray and line it with baking paper. Use a double boiler or heatproof bowl over a pot of boiling water to melt the butter, dark chocolate, cocoa and hot water. Stir until smooth, and then set aside for 10 minutes.

Combine the brown sugar, toasted pecans, almond meal, combined flours, white chocolate buds and eggs in a large mixing bowl. Add the melted chocolate and stir. Pour the mixture into the tray and bake for about 45 minutes. Set aside to cool.

For the candied pecans, heat a frypan over medium heat. Add a cup of pecans, sprinkle with 2 tablespoons of sugar and stir until caramelised. Set aside to cool.

To serve, melt 50g of extra dark chocolate, 1 teaspoon of extra butter and a teaspoon of water in a double boiler or in a bowl over boiling water. Slice the brownie slab into small squares, top with candied pecans and drizzle with dark chocolate. Chill before serving.

Honey & Port Fig Tarts

Makes 12 · Prep 45 mins · Cook 20 mins

12 dried figs (about 200g/7oz)

1 lemon for the juice and rind

⅓ cup rice malt syrup

⅓ cup port

2 sheets of shortcrust pastry

Serve with double cream.

Wash the figs and snip off the stems, then place them in a small saucepan and cover them with cold water. Add a strip of lemon rind and 2 teaspoons of lemon juice. Bring to the boil, reduce the heat and gently simmer for about 25 minutes until the figs are soft. Drain the figs and place them in a bowl. Warm the rice malt syrup and port and pour over the figs. Cover, cool and refrigerate overnight.

When the figs are ready, preheat the oven to 180°C (350°F). Thaw the pastry and use a large glass to cut out rounds. Push the pastry rounds into a 12-hole, greased tart tray, add a fig and fold the pastry around each fig. Bake for about 18 minutes. Serve with a dollop of double cream.

One-bowl Banana Cake

Feeds 10 · Prep 10 mins · Cook 45 mins

125g (4.5oz) butter

1 cup sugar

1 large free-range egg

2 ripe bananas, mashed

1 ½ cups self-raising flour

1 tsp bicarbonate of soda

3 tbsp milk (any kind)

Quick Vanilla Glaze

2 tbsp milk

½ tsp vanilla extract

1 cup icing sugar, sifted

Preheat the oven to 180°C (350°F). Cream the butter and sugar, add an egg and beat well. Stir in the mashed bananas, then the flour. Combine the milk and bicarbonate of soda, add to the mix and stir well to combine. Pour into a well-greased cake tin and bake for 45 minutes. Rest on a cake rack, then turn out and leave to cool before icing with vanilla glaze.

For the vanilla glaze, sift the icing sugar into a small bowl and whisk in the vanilla extract and milk until smooth. Use to drizzle over cooled banana cake.

Blueberry Bread 'n' Butter Puddings

Feeds 6 • Prep 15 mins • Cook 35 mins

6 slices raisin bread (sourdough or regular)

2 tbsp softened butter

2 tbsp berry jam

½ cup blueberries (fresh, frozen or tinned)

1 free-range egg

½ cup natural yoghurt

¼ cup sugar

Serve with extra blueberries and double cream.

Preheat the oven to 180°C (350°F). Slice the crusts off the raisin bread. Butter both sides of each slice, then spread jam on just one side. Cut each piece into 4 triangles. In a standard 6-muffin tray, layer 4 bread triangles into each muffin hole, jam side up, adding small dollops of blueberries between the layers (if using tinned blueberries, drain them first).

Beat the egg, yoghurt and sugar, and pour the mixture over the puddings. Place the muffin tray in a baking dish half-filled with water, and bake for about 35 minutes. Allow the puddings to cool, then gently run a knife around the edge of each pudding and lift out. Serve on their own or with extra blueberries and a dollop of double cream.

Baked Strawberry Pudding

Feeds 4-6 • Prep 15 mins • Cook 55 mins

½ cup (125g) butter

2 large free-range eggs

1 cup caster (superfine) sugar

½ cup milk (any kind)

1 cup plain (all-purpose) flour

1 tsp baking powder

pinch of salt

1 cup strawberries, pureed

2 tbsp cornflour (cornstarch)

½ cup orange juice

Serve with cream or Nice Cream (page 226).

Bring the butter and eggs to room temperature. Preheat the oven to 180°C (350°F) and grease a 2-litre (2-quart) ovenproof pudding dish. In a separate bowl, cream the butter and half the sugar until pale, then beat in the eggs, one at a time. Stir in the milk and fold in the flour, baking powder and a pinch of salt.

Pour the strawberry puree into the prepared pudding dish and spoon the batter over the top. Combine the cornflour and the remaining sugar and sprinkle over the batter. Pour over the orange juice and 1 cup of boiling water. Bake for 55 minutes or until browned and serve with cream or Rasberry Nice Cream.

Portuguese Tart

Feeds 6-8 · Prep 15 mins + Setting time Cook 30 mins

There's a tiny bakery in Kathmandu's Thamel district that sells flaky, creamy Portuguese tarts, which we'd pass by on our regular backstreet wanders. In a weak moment, I strayed in on the heels of Dave and Maya, who swiftly inhaled a delicious plateful. Back on the boat, I set out to create a simple, one-pan version, which was quickly devoured at an Easter brunch with friends in record time. You could fuss with real pastry if you want, but that's not what woos Portuguese tart-lovers. It's the silky, baked custard that gets people hooked and sends them off on secret tart-eating missions in the backstreets of Kathmandu.

1 sheet puff pastry

4 large free-range eggs

1 cup sugar

½ cup cornflour (cornstarch)

¾ cup thickened cream

3 cups milk

2 tsp vanilla extract

Line the base of a 20cm (8in) pie dish with baking paper. Partially defrost the pastry and press it into the dish. Crack the eggs into a mixing bowl and add the sugar, cornflour and cream. Whisk until smooth.

In a saucepan, combine the milk and vanilla, place over medium heat and bring to a simmer. Take the milk off the heat, whisk into the egg mixture and return the custard to the pan, whisking continuously for about 2 minutes or until the mixture thickens.

Take the pan off the heat and pour the custard into the pastry dish. Refrigerate the tart until the custard forms a skin (about 20 minutes), then bake it in a preheated oven at 220°C (430°F) for 30 minutes or until the top is nicely caramelised. Set aside until the custard firms, then serve.

5-ingredient Coconut Cake

Feeds 12 · Prep 5 mins · Cook 40-45 mins

This one-bowl recipe belongs to my Mum, but it's Maya who whips this up before every multi-day passage. I've reworked the recipe to reduce the sugar, and I sometimes add ginger to calm troubled tummies, but it's just as moist as Mum's and lasts for days (well, perhaps technically, just not on our boat). It's super quick to prepare, impossible to get wrong, and uses just one bowl and five ingredients. Throw in whatever dried fruit you have on board, including some finely chopped ginger to ward off seasickness on passage.

1 cup shredded coconut

1 cup self-raising flour (wholemeal works well)

½ cup sugar

¾ cups chopped dried fruit (ginger, dates, sultanas, apricots, cranberries or pineapple)

¾ cup milk (any kind*)

**using dairy-free milk turns this cake vegan.*

Preheat the oven to 180°C (350°F). Combine the dry ingredients in a mixing bowl and gradually stir in the milk. Pour into a well-greased cake tin (I use a ring pan because it cooks so well), and bake for 40 to 45 minutes.

Sticky Date Pudding

with butterscotch sauce

Feeds 4-6 · Prep 25 mins · Cook 45-50 mins

2 tbsp ground coffee beans

1 ¼ cup boiling water

250g (9oz) dates, pitted and chopped

1 tbsp cacao (or cocoa) powder

1 tbsp rice malt (or golden) syrup

1 tsp bicarbonate of soda (baking soda)

100g (3.5oz) butter, softened

⅔ cup caster (superfine) sugar

2 large free-range eggs

1 ½ cups self-raising flour

Serve with whipped or double cream

Butterscotch Sauce

1 ½ cups brown sugar

¾ cup cream

150g (5.5oz) butter

Preheat the oven to 180°C (350°F). Spray or brush a square 20-25cm (8-10in) baking tin with oil and line it with baking paper. Brew yourself a good coffee any way you like. If using a plunger, add 2 tablespoons of ground coffee beans and 1 ¼ cups of boiling water, leave for 1 minute, plunge and pour into a medium saucepan. Add the chopped dates, cacao or cocoa powder and rice malt (or golden) syrup, and bring the mixture to the boil. Boil for 1 minute, take off the heat, stir in the bicarbonate of soda and set aside to cool.

In a mixing bowl, cream the softened butter and sugar until pale. Add the eggs, one at a time, beating well, and gently fold in the sifted flour and the date mixture. Don't over-mix.

Pour the batter into the prepared baking tin and bake for 45-50 minutes, until a skewer inserted into the centre comes away clean. Leave the pudding in the tin for 10 minutes, then carefully lift it out and cut it into squares.

For the butterscotch sauce, combine all ingredients in a saucepan over medium heat and stir until the sugar dissolves and the butter melts. Bring to the boil, reduce the heat and simmer for 2 minutes, stirring. Serve the pudding with a generous drizzle of butterscotch sauce and whipped or double cream.

Almond & Cherry Panforte

Feeds 12 · Prep 20 mins · Cook 30-35 mins

Just 40g of dark chocolate contains as many antioxidants as a glass of red wine, so imagine the health benefits of consuming them together! Eating dark chocolate regularly has been linked to a reduced risk of heart disease, so not eating the stuff seems like a terrible idea (plus panforte is delicious and just a little bit festive too).

¾ cup (100g) almonds

¾ cup (100g) hazelnuts

1 cup (200g) glace cherries

½ cup (100g) glace pineapple pieces

⅔ cup (100g) dark chocolate, roughly chopped

2 tbsp of cacao or cocoa powder

¾ cup plain (all-purpose) flour

1 tsp ground cinnamon

⅓ cup caster (superfine) sugar

⅔ cup honey

Preheat the oven to 150°C (300°F). Roast the almonds and hazelnuts on a tray for 10-15 minutes, remove from the oven and turn up the heat to 180°C (350°F). Line a 20cm (8in) springform pan with baking paper. Place the nuts, dried fruit and half the chocolate into a large mixing bowl. Sift in the cacao or cocoa powder, flour and cinnamon and stir thoroughly.

Melt the sugar, honey and remaining chocolate in a small saucepan over low heat, stirring occasionally. When the sugar dissolves, turn up the heat and bring it to the boil, then reduce the heat and simmer for 2 minutes.

Pour the chocolate mixture into the dry ingredients, stir thoroughly with a wooden spoon, working quickly, and then pour immediately into the prepared tin. Use the back of a spoon to smooth the surface. Bake for 30-35 minutes or until firm. Stand on a wire rack to cool. When cold, dust with icing sugar and slice into thin wedges.

Dairy-free Cherry Cakes

Makes 8 • Prep 10 mins • Cook 30-35 mins • V

Gently shoaling and gloriously protected, Margaret Bay is a favourite Cape York anchorage with a dubious reputation as a beachcombers' nirvana. Take an empty backpack on the wild, muddy wander across Indian Head to reach a south-facing beach that gathers vast amounts of junk. There are fishing buoys, plastic buckets and toothbrushes, and curious treasures, too. We've picked up fishing lures and wetsuits, hand reels and big nautilus shells, a jerry can, a kayak paddle and even a matching pair of snorkelling fins. When Dave's sandal got sucked into the peat marsh and snapped, we hunted for the perfect size of thong to help him limp back home. But the strangest thing we ever picked up was a packet of Arnott's Assorted Creams. Because we travel with a wildly curious small person, and because we were hungry, everyone was dared to nibble a Monte Carlo and see if they were stale. They were, so we left them for the pigs and went home to devour these tasty cakes instead. What I love about these moist, little fruit cakes is that you can make them when you are really faraway. All you need is flour, dried fruits, tinned juice and mashed pumpkin.

⅔ cup whole glace cherries
2 cups mixed dried fruit
⅔ cup chopped pitted dates
1 cup apricot nectar or apple juice
1 cup mashed pumpkin
1 ½ cups self-raising flour
1 tsp ground mixed spice
1 tsp bicarbonate of soda (baking soda)

Preheat the oven to 170°C (340°F). Grease or spray an 8-hole muffin tray well. In a small saucepan, combine a 1/2 cup of glace cherries, the mixed fruit, dates and nectar or juice, and bring to the boil. Turn down the heat and simmer for 3 minutes. Pour into a mixing bowl and leave to cool.

Sift together the self-raising flour, mixed spice and bicarbonate of soda, and add to your bowl together with the pumpkin mash. Combine well, then spoon into the prepared muffin pan. Pop extra glace cherries on top and bake for 30-35 minutes. They're ready when a bamboo skewer poked into the top comes out clean. Remove the tray from the oven and cool on a wire rack.

Nectarine & Yoghurt Squares

Makes 12 • Prep 20 mins • Cook 40-45 mins

The creamy custard filling, sandwiched between a lemon-scented biscuit base and plump nectarine slices, makes this dessert really sing. It's surprisingly quick and easy to make (no whisking or blending required), and you can use any ripe stone fruit you can get your hands on – juicy plums and peaches work just as well.

zest of 1 lemon
⅔ cup sugar
1 cup plain (all-purpose) flour
1 cup rolled oats
½ tsp baking powder
¼ tsp salt
½ cup (115g) unsalted butter, softened
1 tsp vanilla extract

Topping

450g (16oz) Greek yoghurt
1 tbsp sugar
2 tbsp cornflour (cornstarch)
2-3 fresh nectarines, sliced

Preheat the oven to 180°C (350°F), and line a square 20cm (8in) pan with baking paper. In a mixing bowl, rub the lemon zest through the sugar with your fingertips until it's aromatic. Add the flour, oats, baking powder and salt. Rub in the butter and vanilla extract until the mixture resembles breadcrumbs. Reserve 2/3 cup of the crumb mixture for the topping, and firmly press the rest into the lined baking pan.

In a separate bowl, combine the yoghurt, sugar and cornflour for the topping. Spread this over the base, top with nectarine slices, sprinkle the reserved crumb mixture on top, and bake for 40-45 minutes or until golden. Set the slice aside to cool completely, then refrigerate for 2 hours or more before slicing and serving.

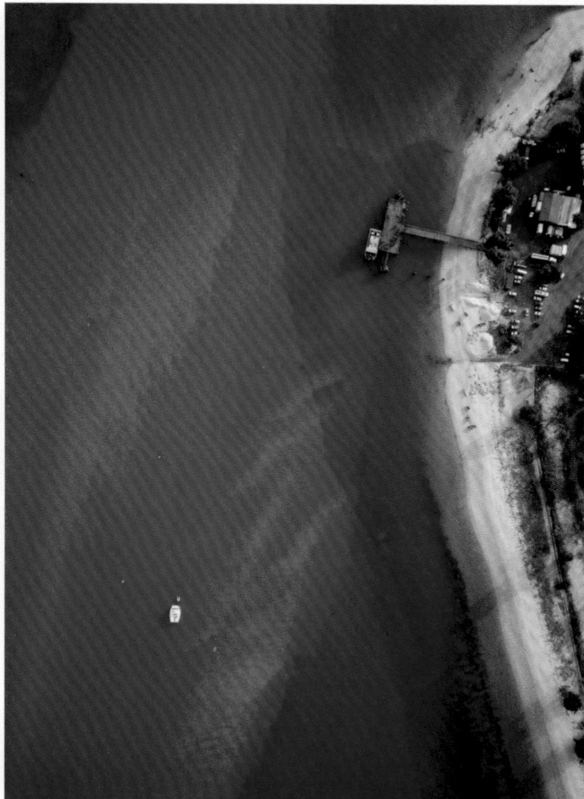

FINNA

INDEX

The Hunter & The Gatherer was first published in April 2023 by Exploring Eden Media.

ISBN: 978-0-6455226-3-1

All enquiries should be made to:

Exploring Eden Media Pty Ltd
250 Princes Highway, Bulli, NSW, 2516
publications@exploringedenmedia.com

A catalogue record for this book is available from the National Library of Australia

Author: Catherine Lawson (@wildtravelwoman) and David Bristow (@wildtravelstory)
Publisher: Melissa Connell
Editor: Brendan Batty
Design and illustration: Casey Schuurman
Photography: David Bristow, Catherine Lawson and Maya Bristow

Printed in China by C & C Offset Printing Co.

One book, one tree. This book's carbon footprint is approximately 2.5kg (5lb). But when you bought it, we planted a tree on your behalf as part of our commitment to make sure our books plant forests. Find out more about how we're making sure our books do more good than harm at **exploringedenbooks.com**.

The paper used in this book was sourced from sustainable forests certified by Forest Stewardship Council™ as part of our commitment to environmental responsibility. Find out more at fsc.org.